THE THIRD
Garfield
TREASURY!

THE THIRD

Garfield

TREASURY!

BY: JIM DAVIS

BALLANTINE BOOKS • NEW YORK

The Sunday strips appearing here in color were previously included in black and white in *GARFIELD Tips the Scales, GARFIELD Loses His Feet, GARFIELD Makes It Big,* and *GARFIELD Rolls On.*

 Published in the United States by Ballantine Books, a division of Random House, Inc., New York, and simultaneously in Canada by Random House of Canada Limited, Toronto.

Library of Congress Catalog Card Number: 85-90577

ISBN: 0-345-32635-0

Manufactured in the United States of America

Designed by Gene Siegel

First Edition: November 1985

10 9 8 7 6 5 4 3 2 1

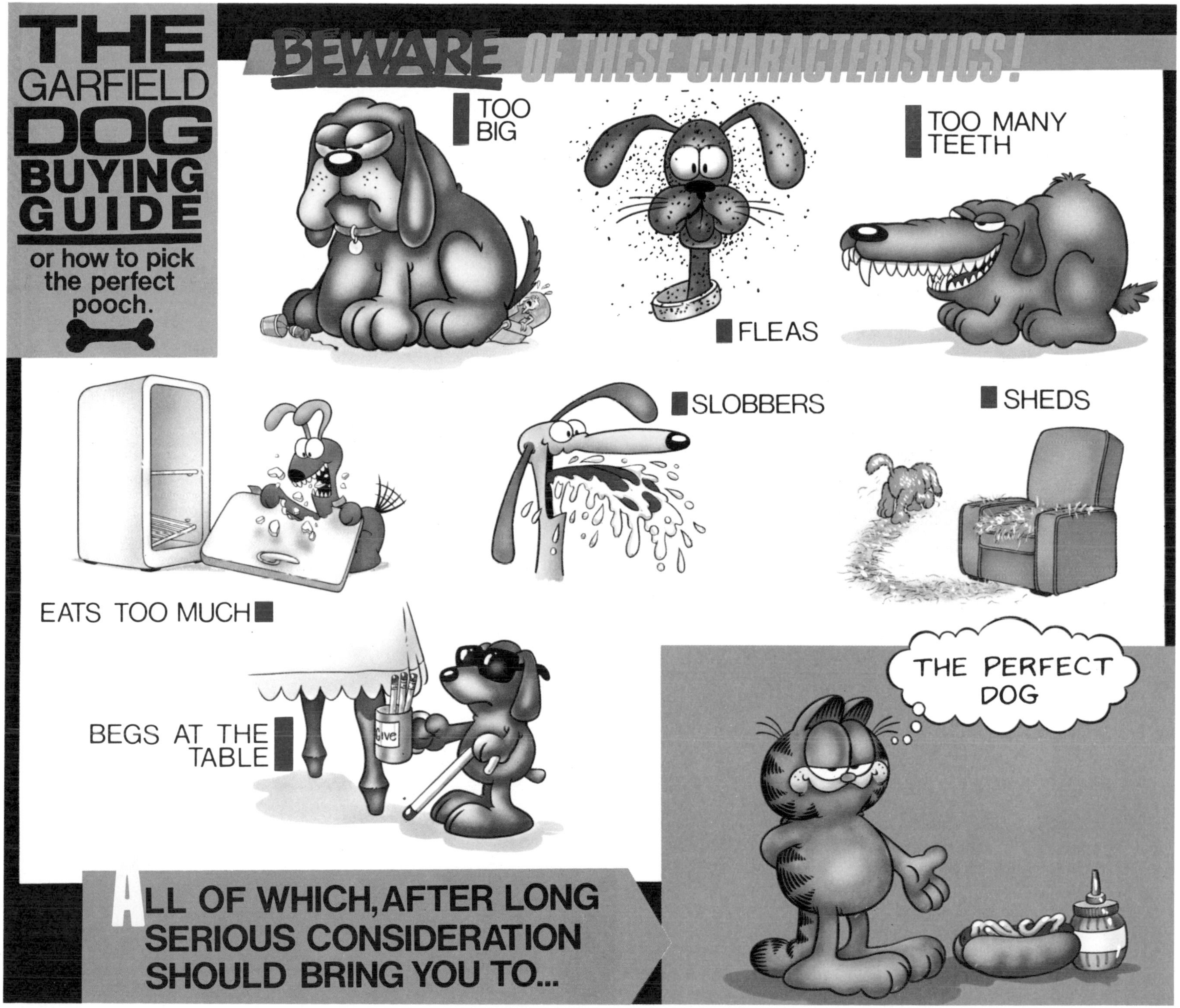
THE GARFIELD DOG BUYING GUIDE
or how to pick the perfect pooch.
BEWARE OF THESE CHARACTERISTICS!
TOO BIG
FLEAS
TOO MANY TEETH
EATS TOO MUCH
SLOBBERS
SHEDS
BEGS AT THE TABLE
Give
ALL OF WHICH, AFTER LONG SERIOUS CONSIDERATION SHOULD BRING YOU TO...
THE PERFECT DOG

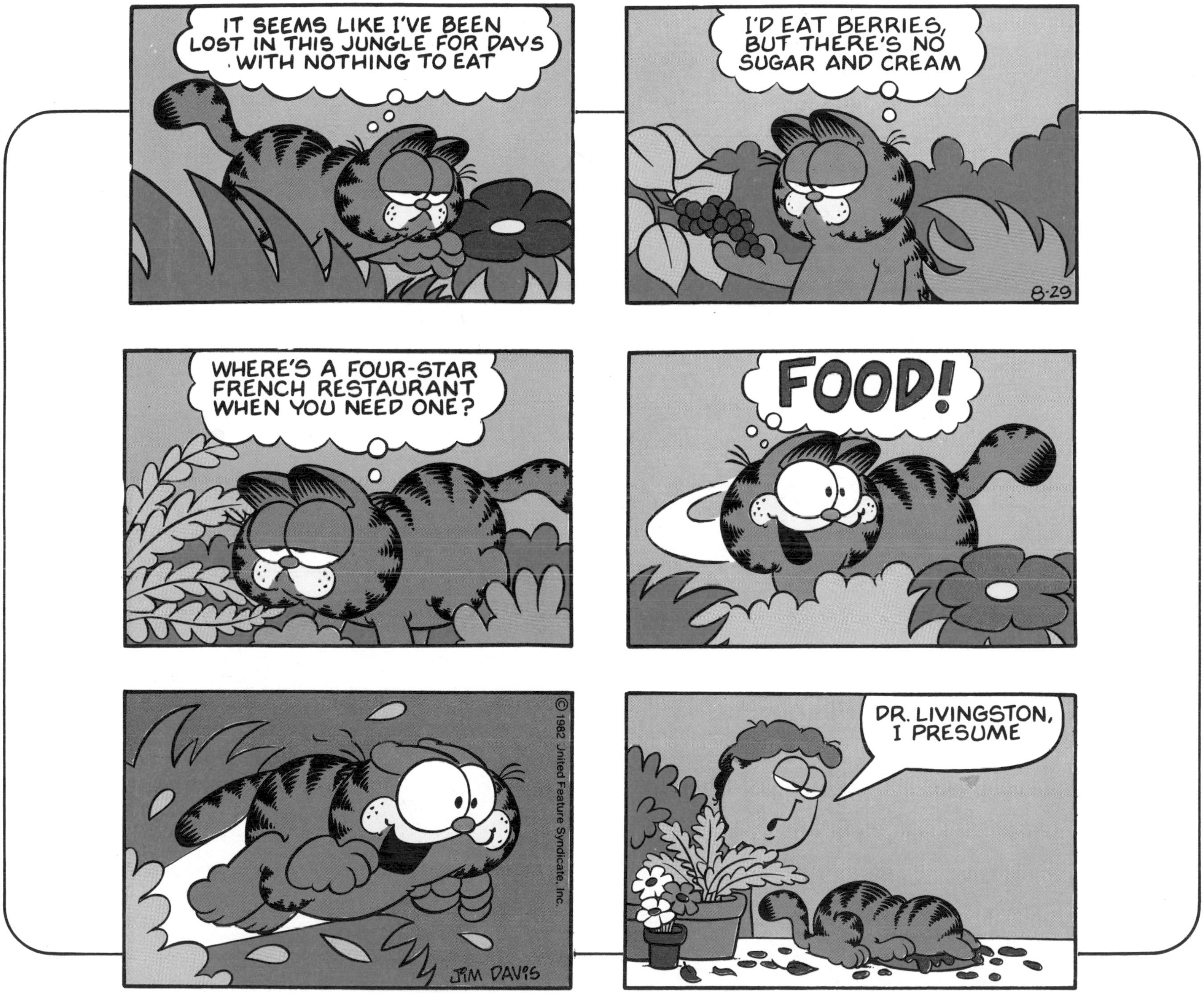
IT SEEMS LIKE I'VE BEEN LOST IN THIS JUNGLE FOR DAYS WITH NOTHING TO EAT
I'D EAT BERRIES, BUT THERE'S NO SUGAR AND CREAM
8-29
WHERE'S A FOUR-STAR FRENCH RESTAURANT WHEN YOU NEED ONE?
FOOD!
© 1982 United Feature Syndicate, Inc.
JIM DAVIS
DR. LIVINGSTON, I PRESUME

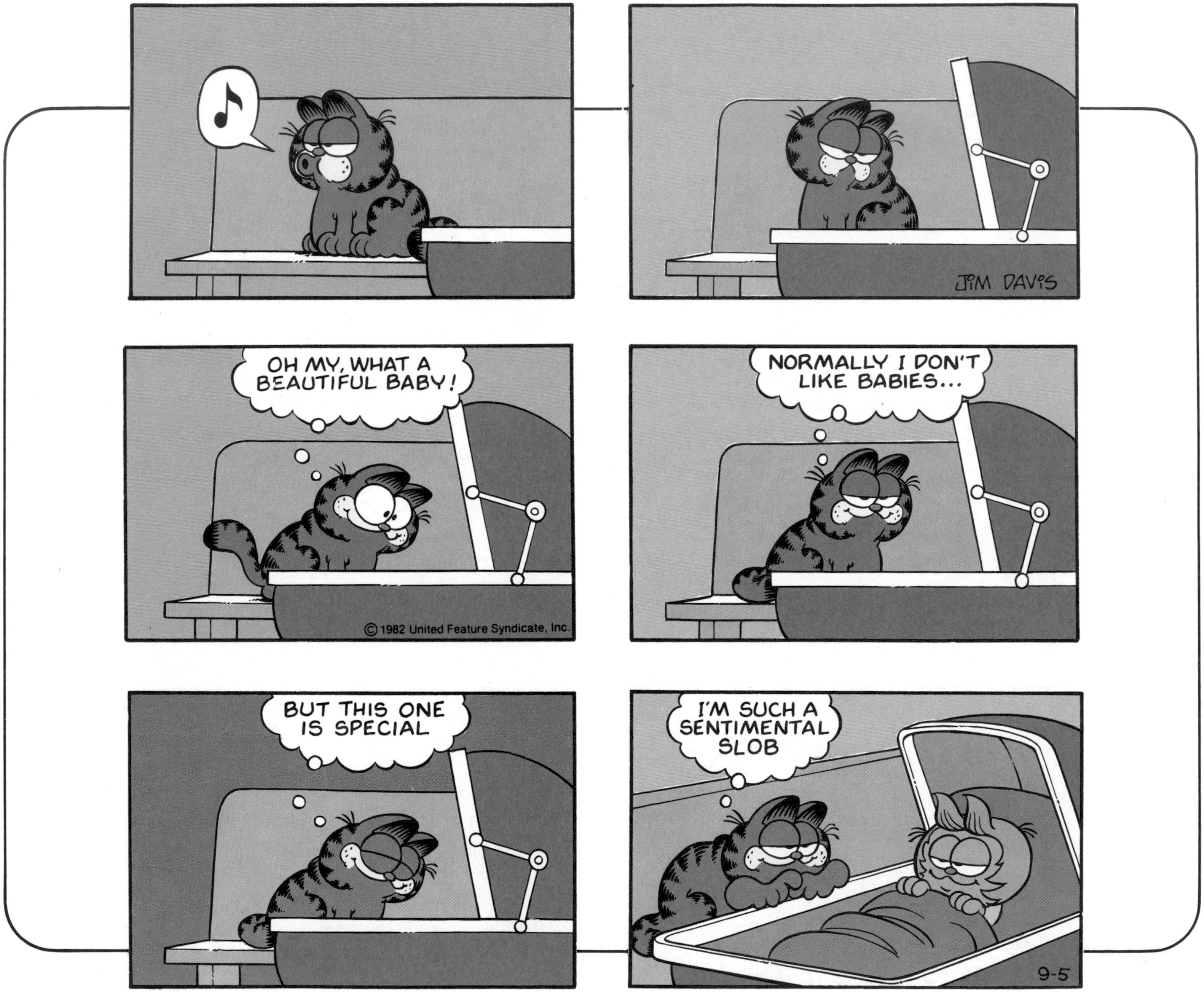
♪
JIM DAVIS
OH MY, WHAT A BEAUTIFUL BABY!
NORMALLY I DON'T LIKE BABIES...
BUT THIS ONE IS SPECIAL
I'M SUCH A SENTIMENTAL SLOB
© 1982 United Feature Syndicate, Inc.
9-5

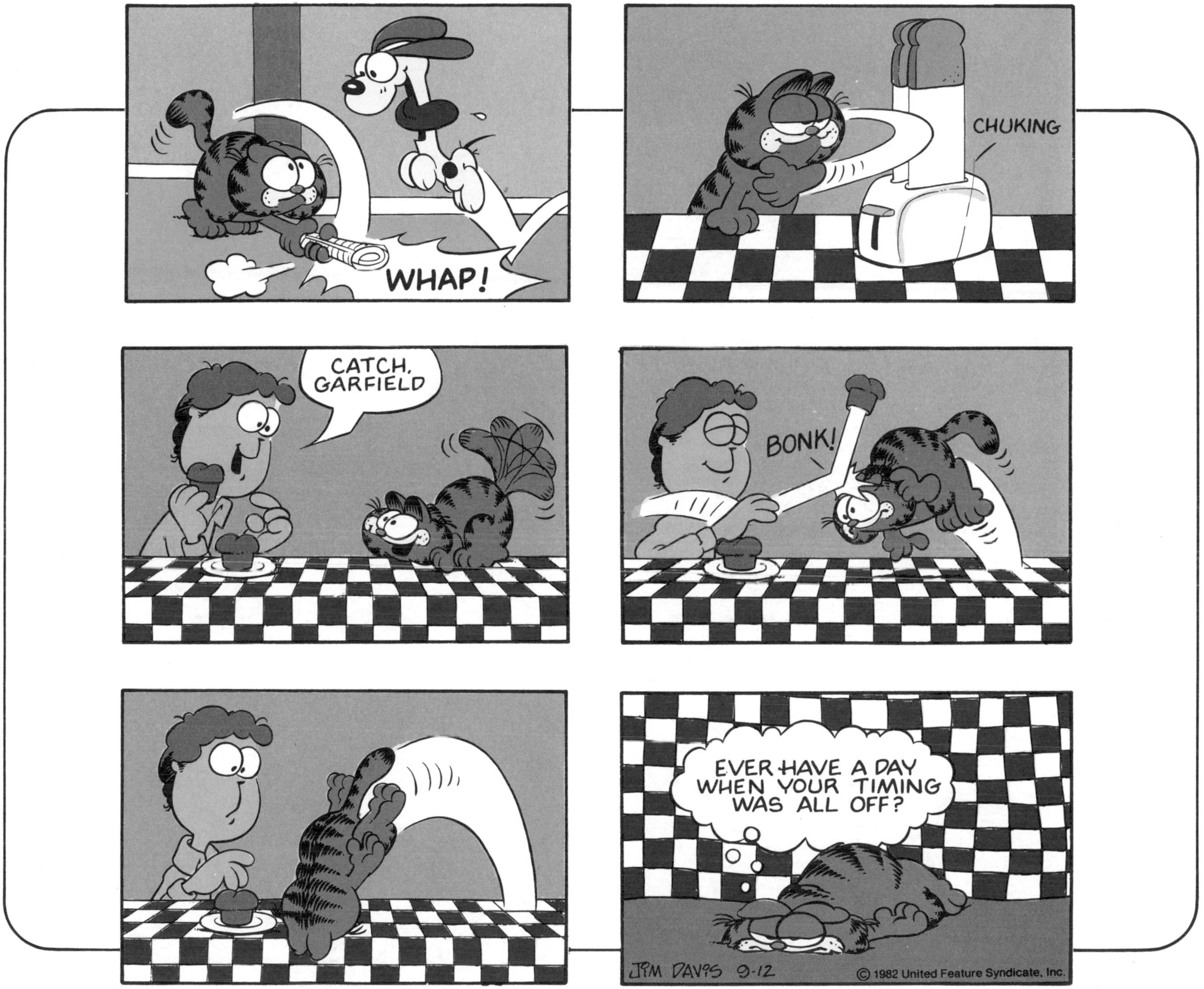
WHAP!
CHUKING
CATCH, GARFIELD
BONK!
EVER HAVE A DAY WHEN YOUR TIMING WAS ALL OFF?
JIM DAVIS 9-12
© 1982 United Feature Syndicate, Inc.

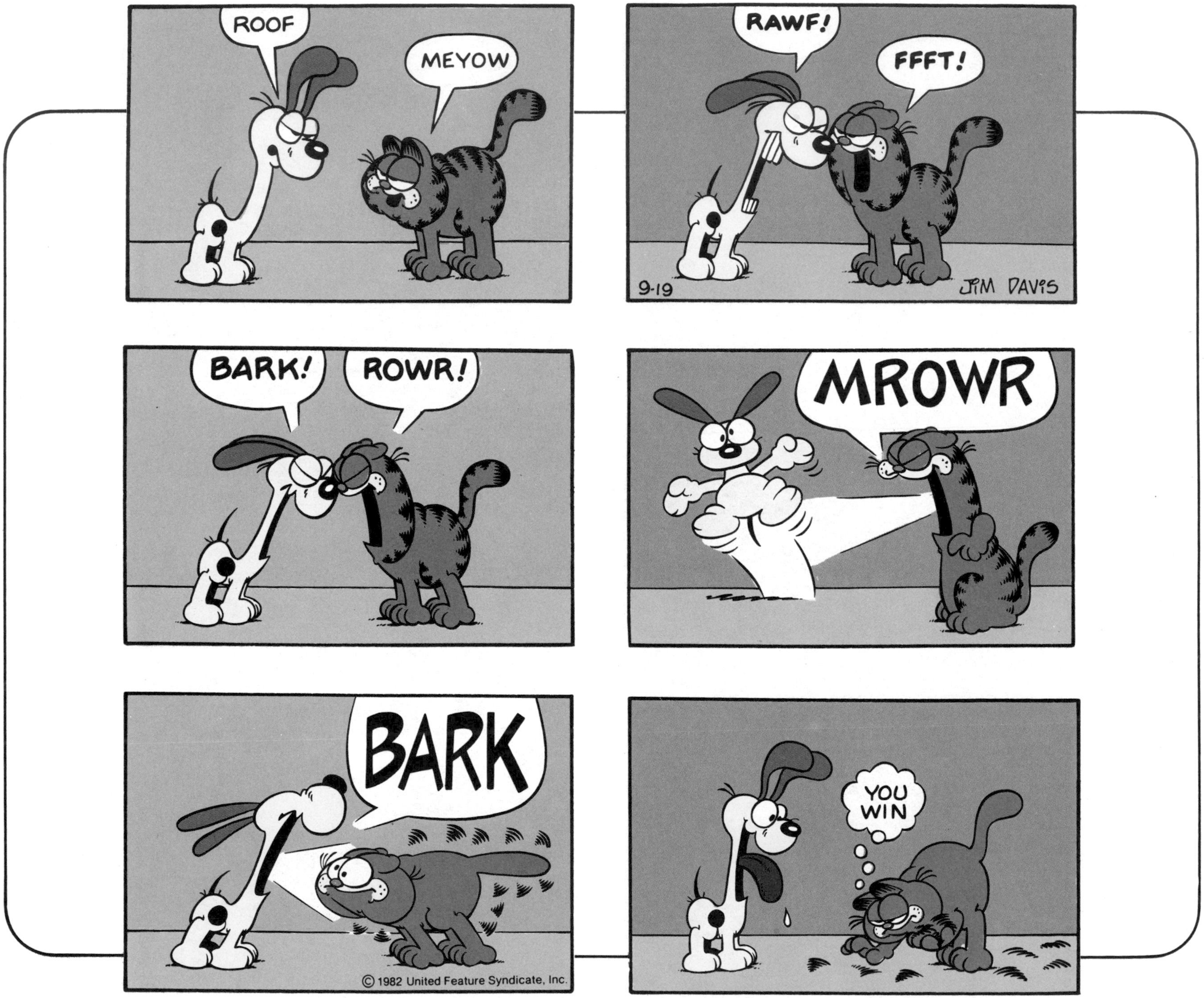
ROOF
MEYOW
RAWF!
FFFT!
9-19
JIM DAVIS
BARK!
ROWR!
MROWR
BARK
© 1982 United Feature Syndicate, Inc.
YOU WIN

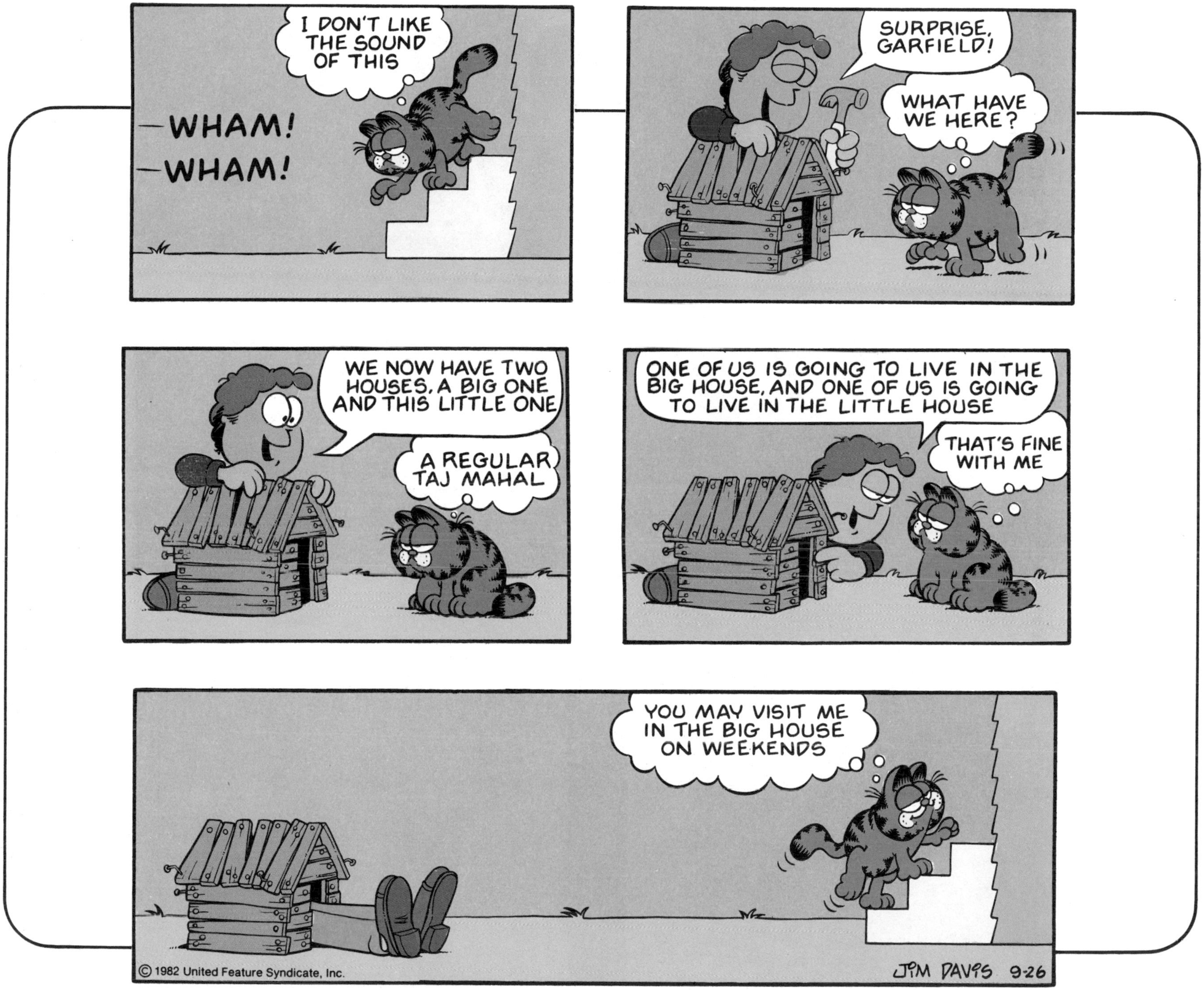

WHAM!
WHAM!
I DON'T LIKE THE SOUND OF THIS
SURPRISE, GARFIELD!
WHAT HAVE WE HERE?
WE NOW HAVE TWO HOUSES, A BIG ONE AND THIS LITTLE ONE
A REGULAR TAJ MAHAL
ONE OF US IS GOING TO LIVE IN THE BIG HOUSE, AND ONE OF US IS GOING TO LIVE IN THE LITTLE HOUSE
THAT'S FINE WITH ME
YOU MAY VISIT ME IN THE BIG HOUSE ON WEEKENDS
© 1982 United Feature Syndicate, Inc.
JIM DAVIS 9-26

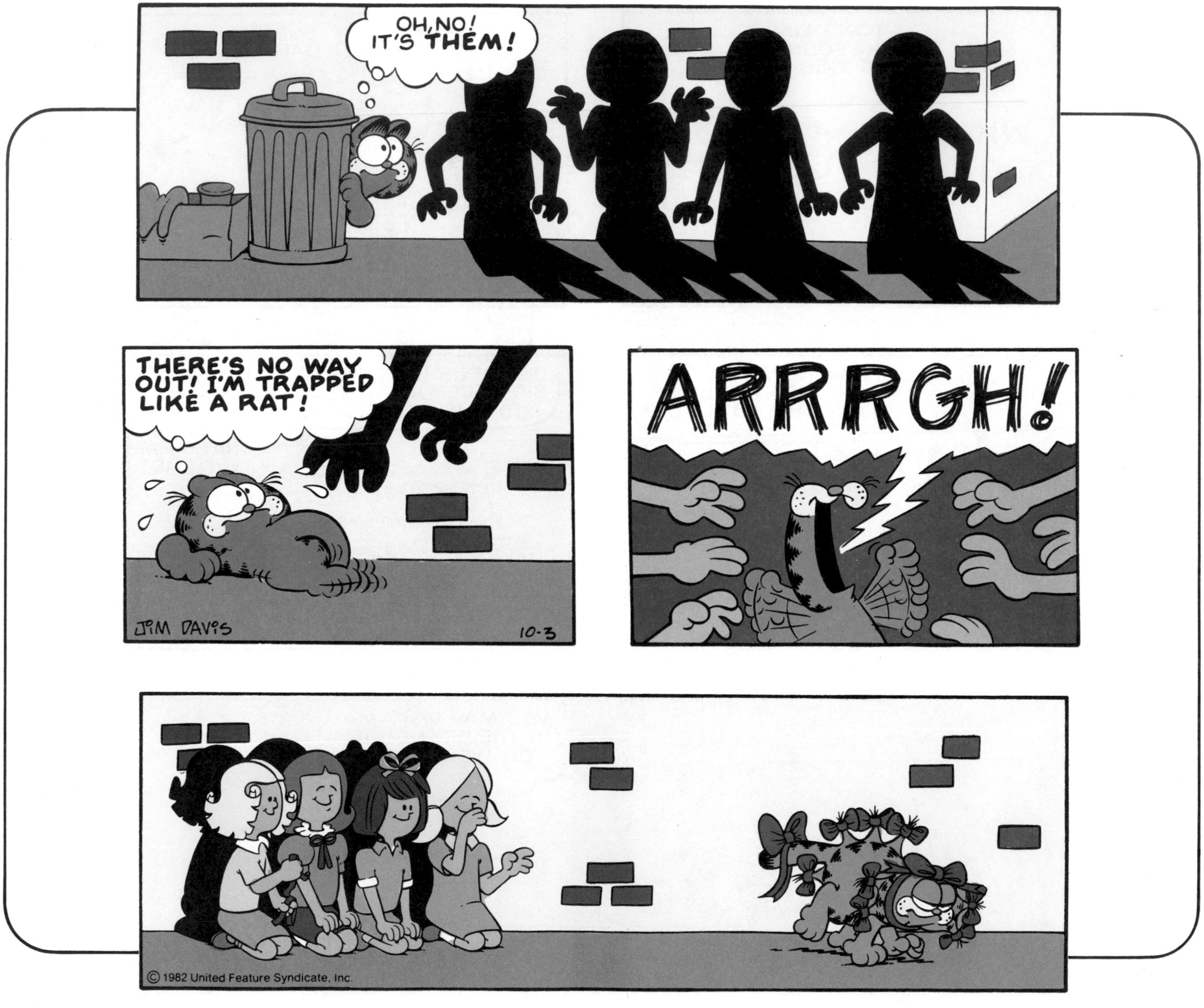
OH, NO! IT'S THEM!
THERE'S NO WAY OUT! I'M TRAPPED LIKE A RAT!
JIM DAVIS
10-3
ARRRRGH!
© 1982 United Feature Syndicate, Inc.

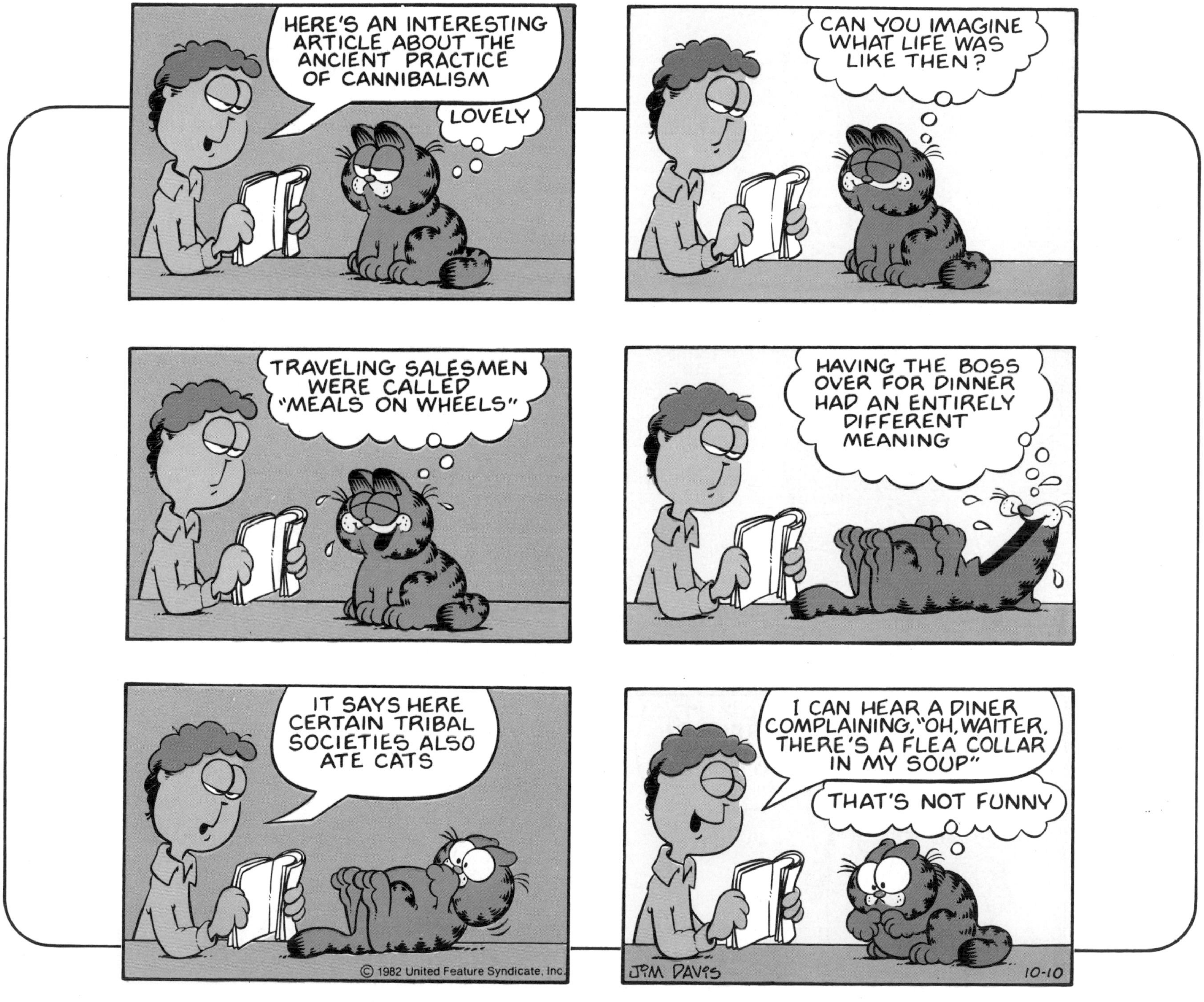
HERE'S AN INTERESTING ARTICLE ABOUT THE ANCIENT PRACTICE OF CANNIBALISM
LOVELY
CAN YOU IMAGINE WHAT LIFE WAS LIKE THEN?
TRAVELING SALESMEN WERE CALLED "MEALS ON WHEELS"
HAVING THE BOSS OVER FOR DINNER HAD AN ENTIRELY DIFFERENT MEANING
IT SAYS HERE CERTAIN TRIBAL SOCIETIES ALSO ATE CATS
I CAN HEAR A DINER COMPLAINING, "OH, WAITER, THERE'S A FLEA COLLAR IN MY SOUP"
THAT'S NOT FUNNY
© 1982 United Feature Syndicate, Inc.
JIM DAVIS
10-10

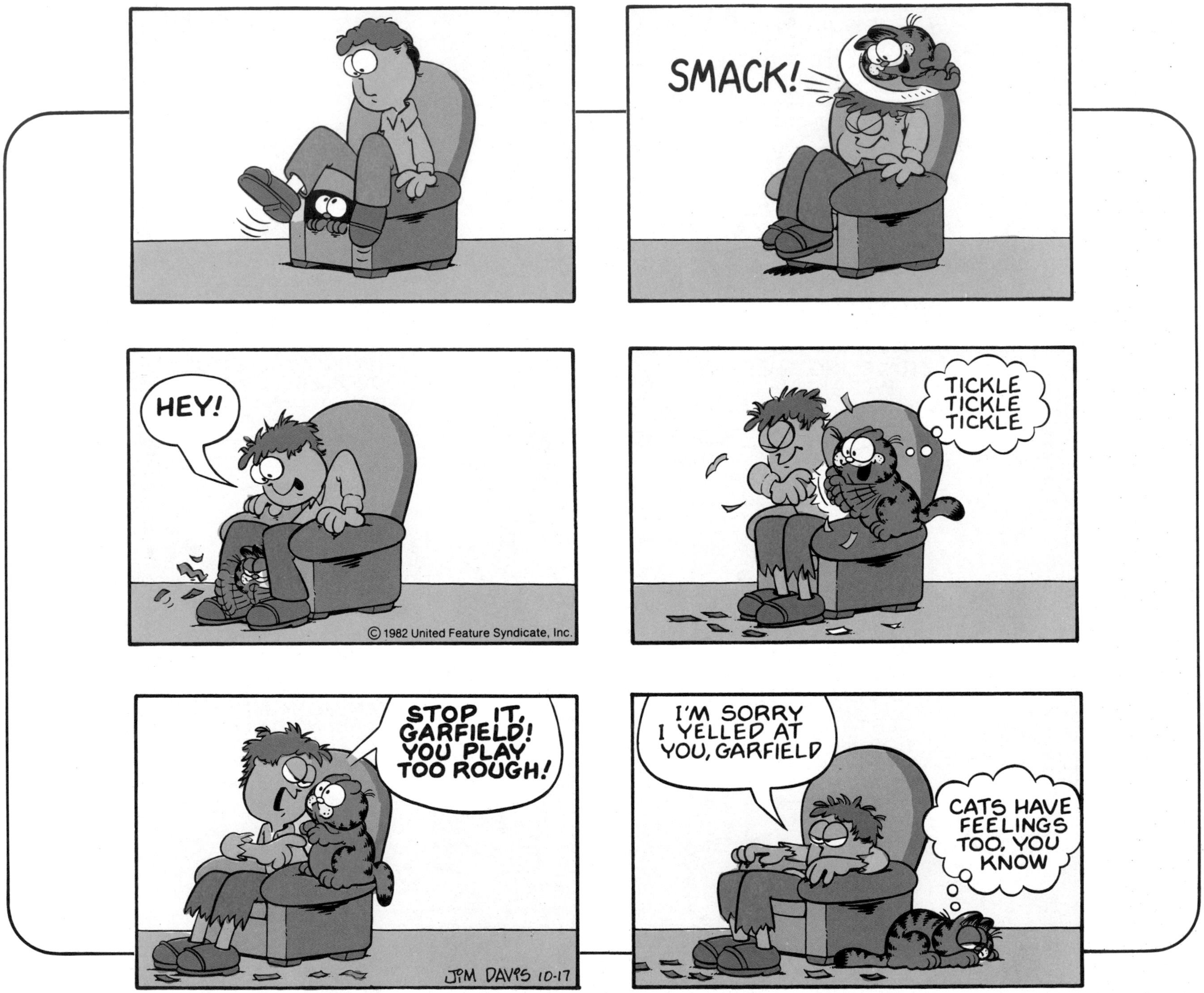
SMACK!
HEY!
© 1982 United Feature Syndicate, Inc.
TICKLE TICKLE TICKLE
STOP IT, GARFIELD! YOU PLAY TOO ROUGH!
JIM DAVIS 10-17
I'M SORRY I YELLED AT YOU, GARFIELD
CATS HAVE FEELINGS TOO, YOU KNOW

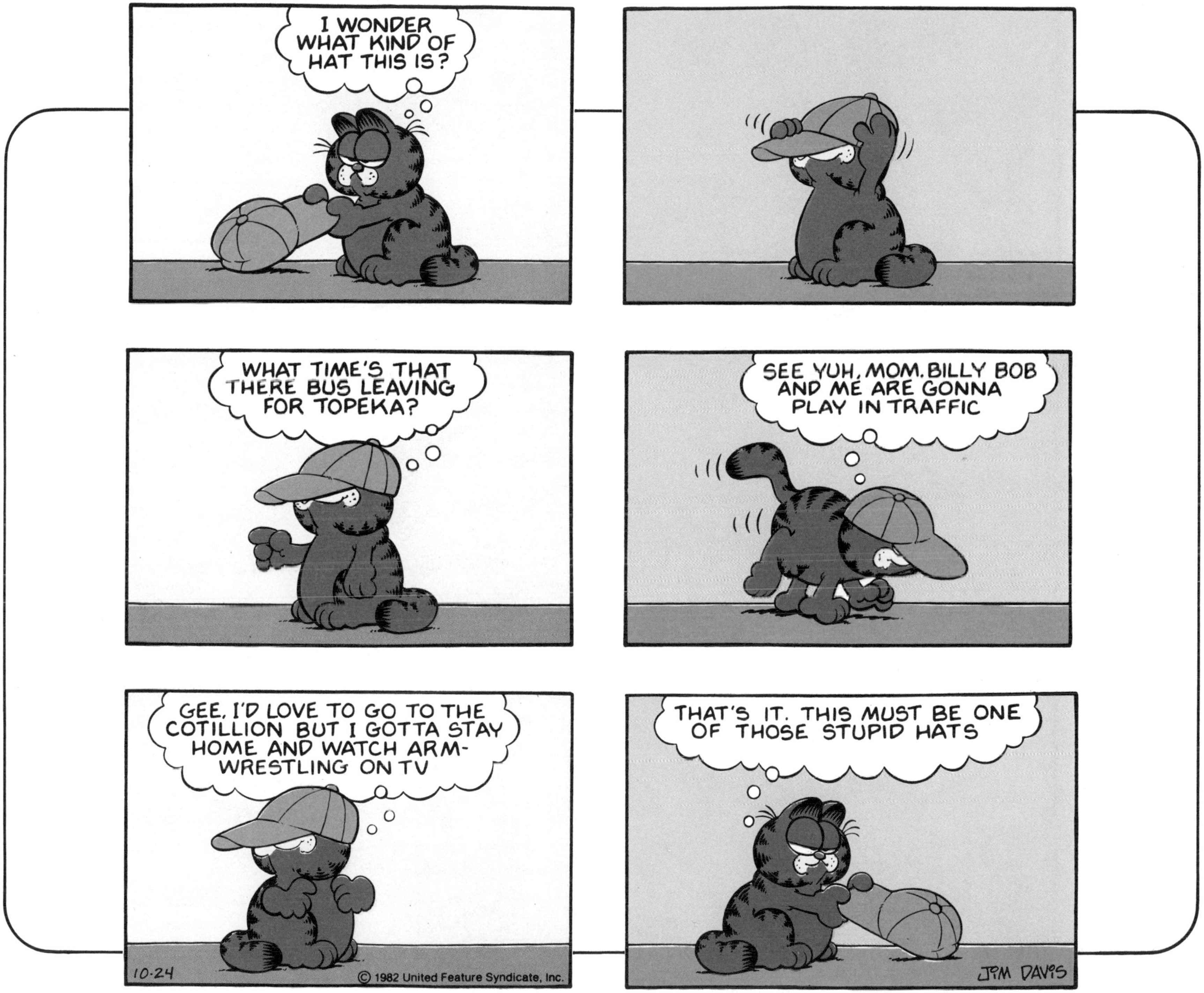
I WONDER WHAT KIND OF HAT THIS IS?
WHAT TIME'S THAT THERE BUS LEAVING FOR TOPEKA?
SEE YUH, MOM. BILLY BOB AND ME ARE GONNA PLAY IN TRAFFIC
GEE, I'D LOVE TO GO TO THE COTILLION BUT I GOTTA STAY HOME AND WATCH ARM-WRESTLING ON TV
THAT'S IT. THIS MUST BE ONE OF THOSE STUPID HATS
10-24
© 1982 United Feature Syndicate, Inc.
JIM DAVIS

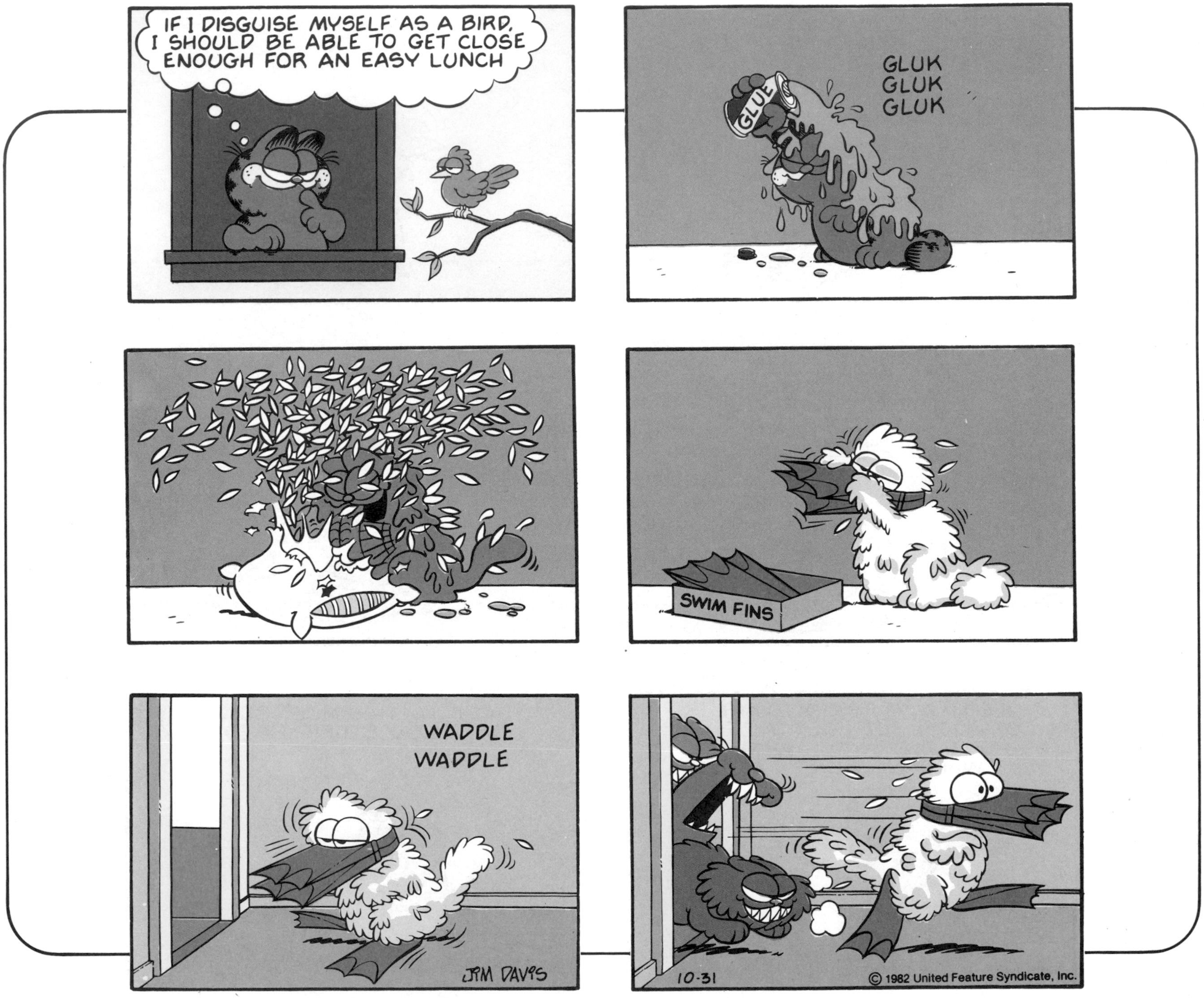
IF I DISGUISE MYSELF AS A BIRD, I SHOULD BE ABLE TO GET CLOSE ENOUGH FOR AN EASY LUNCH
GLUE
GLUK GLUK GLUK
SWIM FINS
WADDLE WADDLE
JIM DAVIS
10-31
© 1982 United Feature Syndicate, Inc.

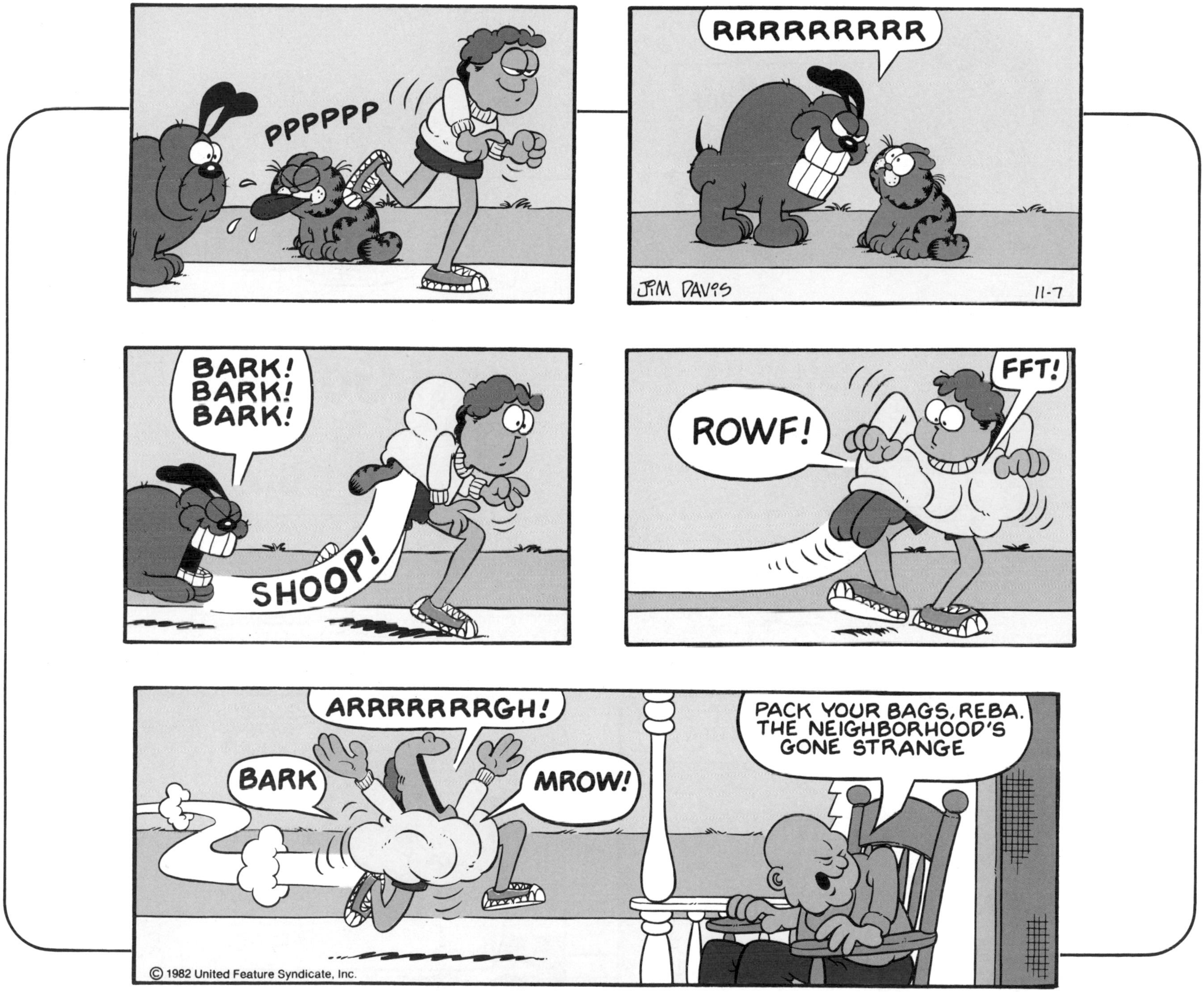
PPPPPP
RRRRRRRRR
JIM DAVIS
11-7
BARK! BARK! BARK!
SHOOP!
ROWF!
FFT!
ARRRRRRRGH!
BARK
MROW!
PACK YOUR BAGS, REBA. THE NEIGHBORHOOD'S GONE STRANGE
© 1982 United Feature Syndicate, Inc.

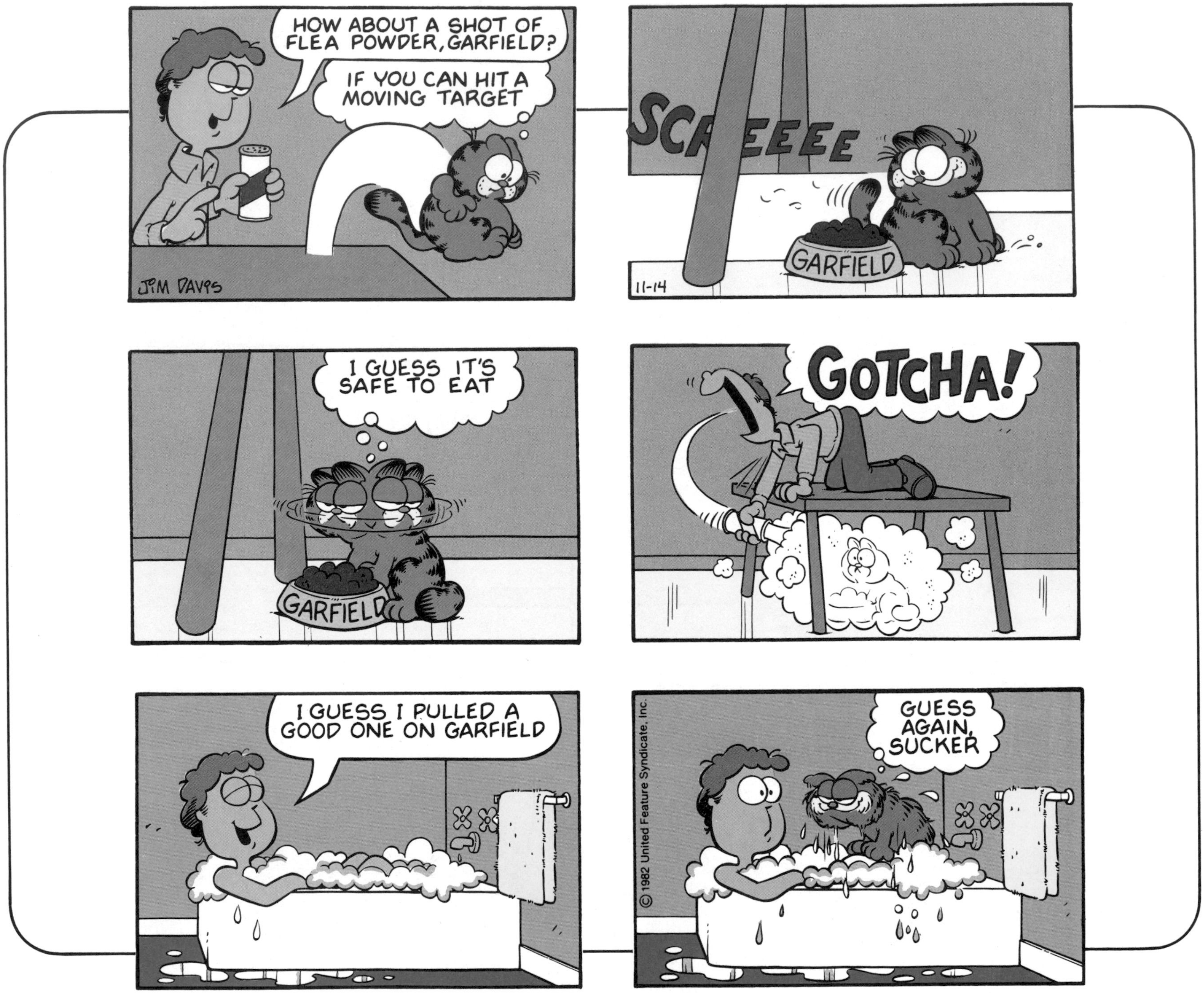
HOW ABOUT A SHOT OF FLEA POWDER, GARFIELD?
IF YOU CAN HIT A MOVING TARGET
JIM DAVIS
SCREEEEE
GARFIELD
11-14
I GUESS IT'S SAFE TO EAT
GARFIELD
GOTCHA!
I GUESS I PULLED A GOOD ONE ON GARFIELD
© 1982 United Feature Syndicate, Inc.
GUESS AGAIN, SUCKER

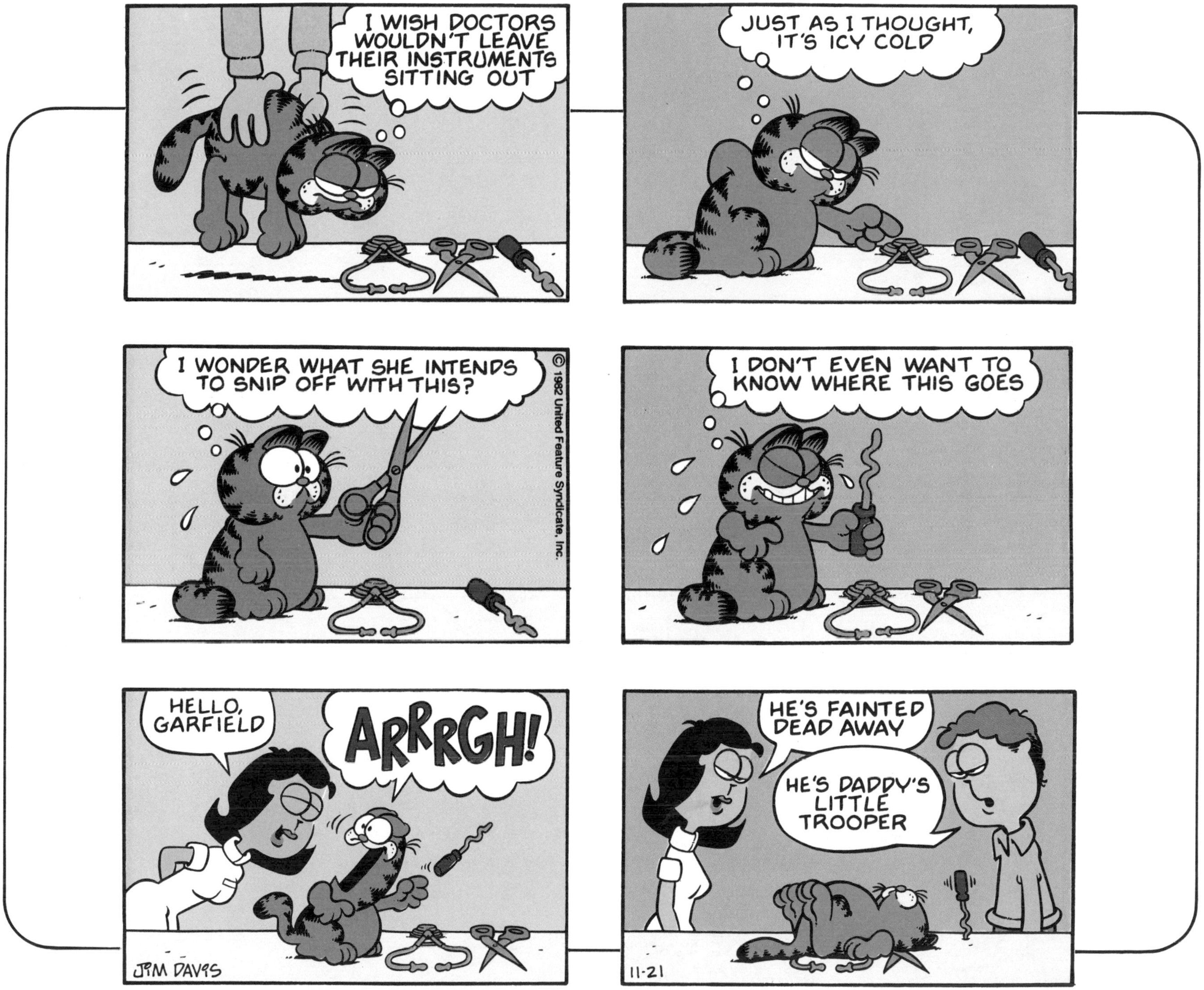
I WISH DOCTORS WOULDN'T LEAVE THEIR INSTRUMENTS SITTING OUT
JUST AS I THOUGHT, IT'S ICY COLD
I WONDER WHAT SHE INTENDS TO SNIP OFF WITH THIS?
© 1982 United Feature Syndicate, Inc.
I DON'T EVEN WANT TO KNOW WHERE THIS GOES
HELLO, GARFIELD
ARRRGH!
HE'S FAINTED DEAD AWAY
HE'S DADDY'S LITTLE TROOPER
JIM DAVIS
11-21

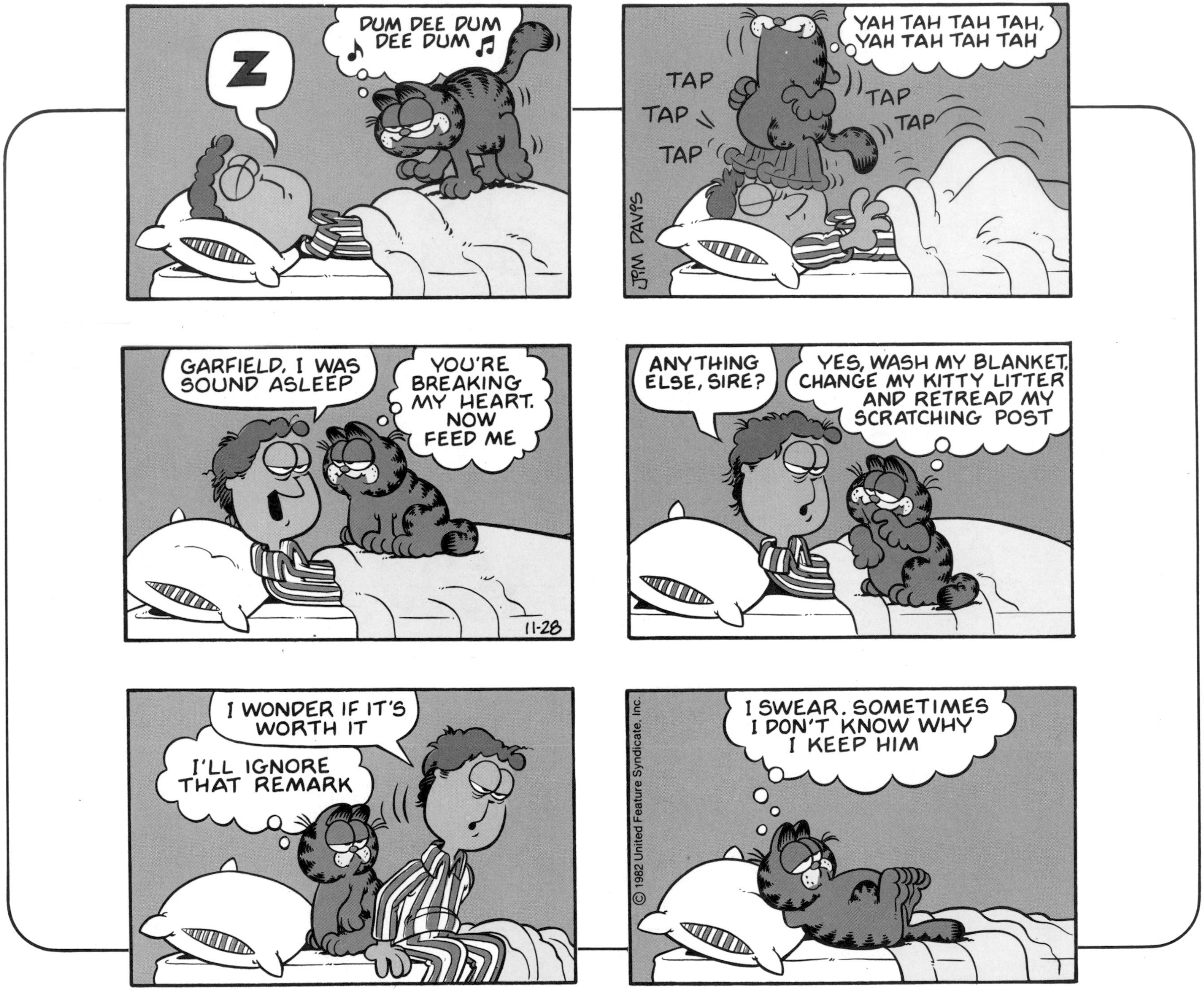
Z
DUM DEE DUM DEE DUM
YAH TAH TAH TAH, YAH TAH TAH TAH
TAP TAP TAP TAP TAP
JIM DAVIS
GARFIELD, I WAS SOUND ASLEEP
YOU'RE BREAKING MY HEART. NOW FEED ME
11-28
ANYTHING ELSE, SIRE?
YES, WASH MY BLANKET, CHANGE MY KITTY LITTER AND RETREAD MY SCRATCHING POST
I WONDER IF IT'S WORTH IT
I'LL IGNORE THAT REMARK
© 1982 United Feature Syndicate, Inc.
I SWEAR. SOMETIMES I DON'T KNOW WHY I KEEP HIM

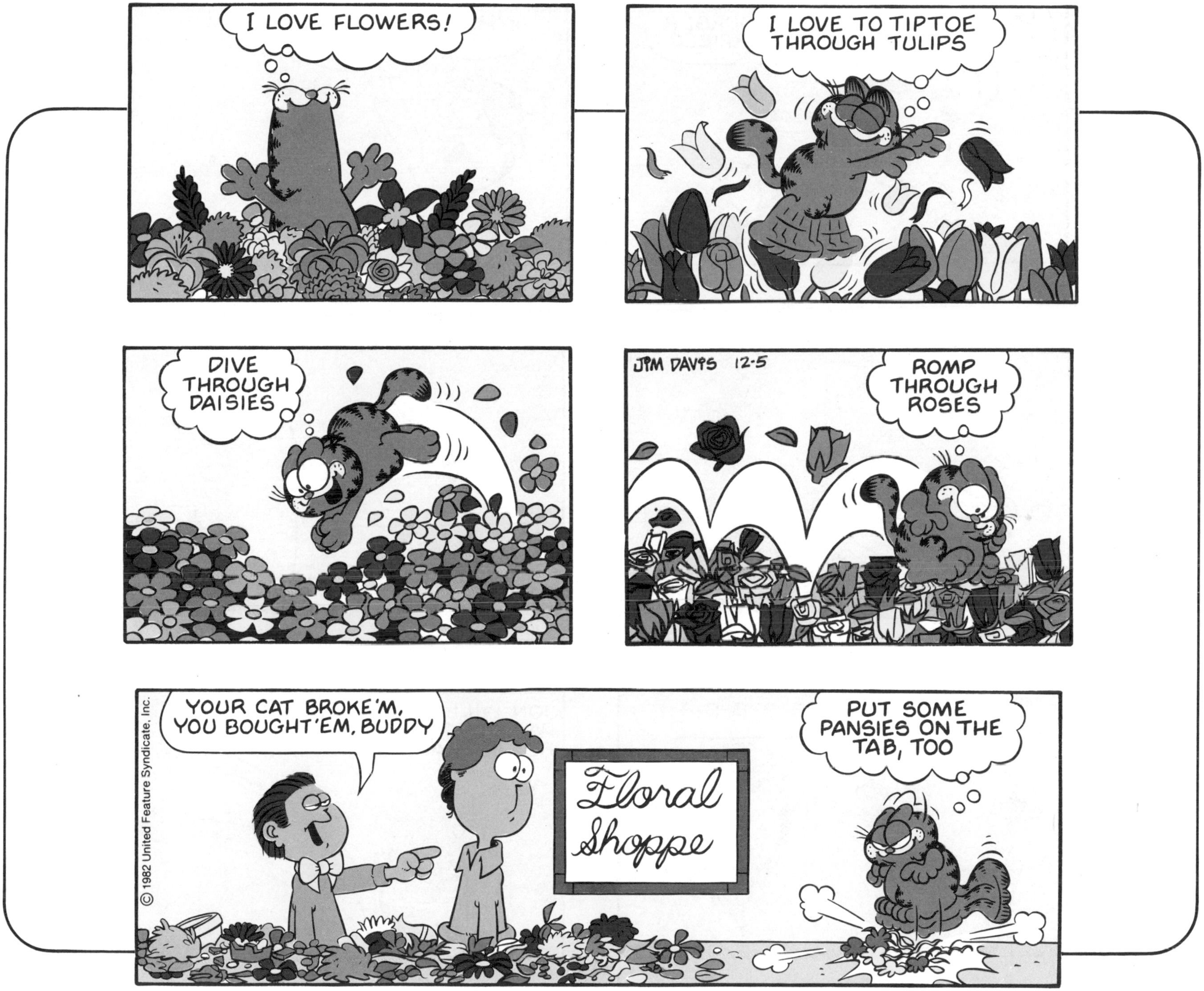
I LOVE FLOWERS!
I LOVE TO TIPTOE THROUGH TULIPS
DIVE THROUGH DAISIES
JIM DAVIS 12-5
ROMP THROUGH ROSES
© 1982 United Feature Syndicate, Inc.
YOUR CAT BROKE'M, YOU BOUGHT'EM, BUDDY
Floral Shoppe
PUT SOME PANSIES ON THE TAB, TOO

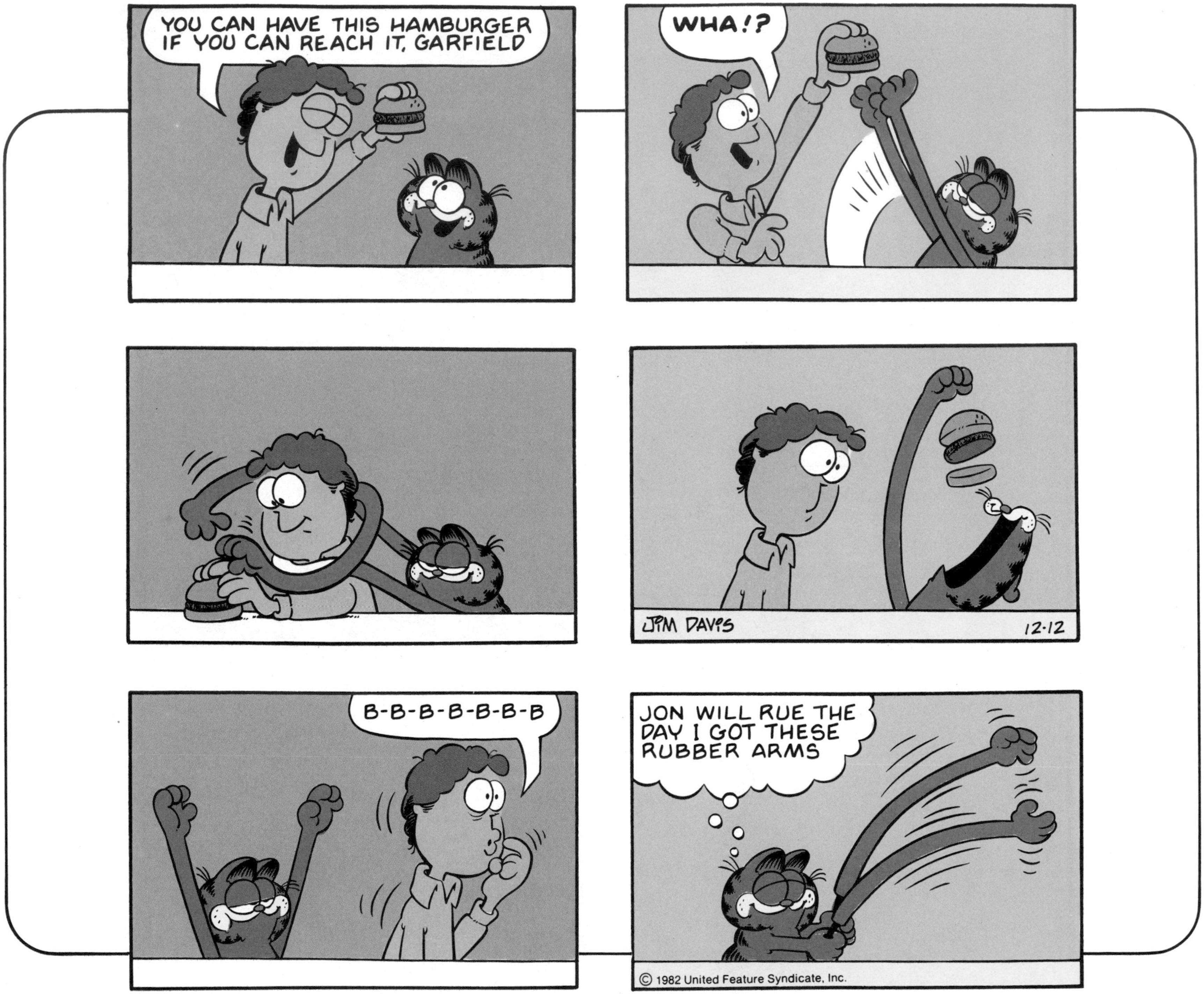
YOU CAN HAVE THIS HAMBURGER IF YOU CAN REACH IT, GARFIELD
WHA!?
JIM DAVIS
12-12
B-B-B-B-B-B-B
JON WILL RUE THE DAY I GOT THESE RUBBER ARMS
© 1982 United Feature Syndicate, Inc.

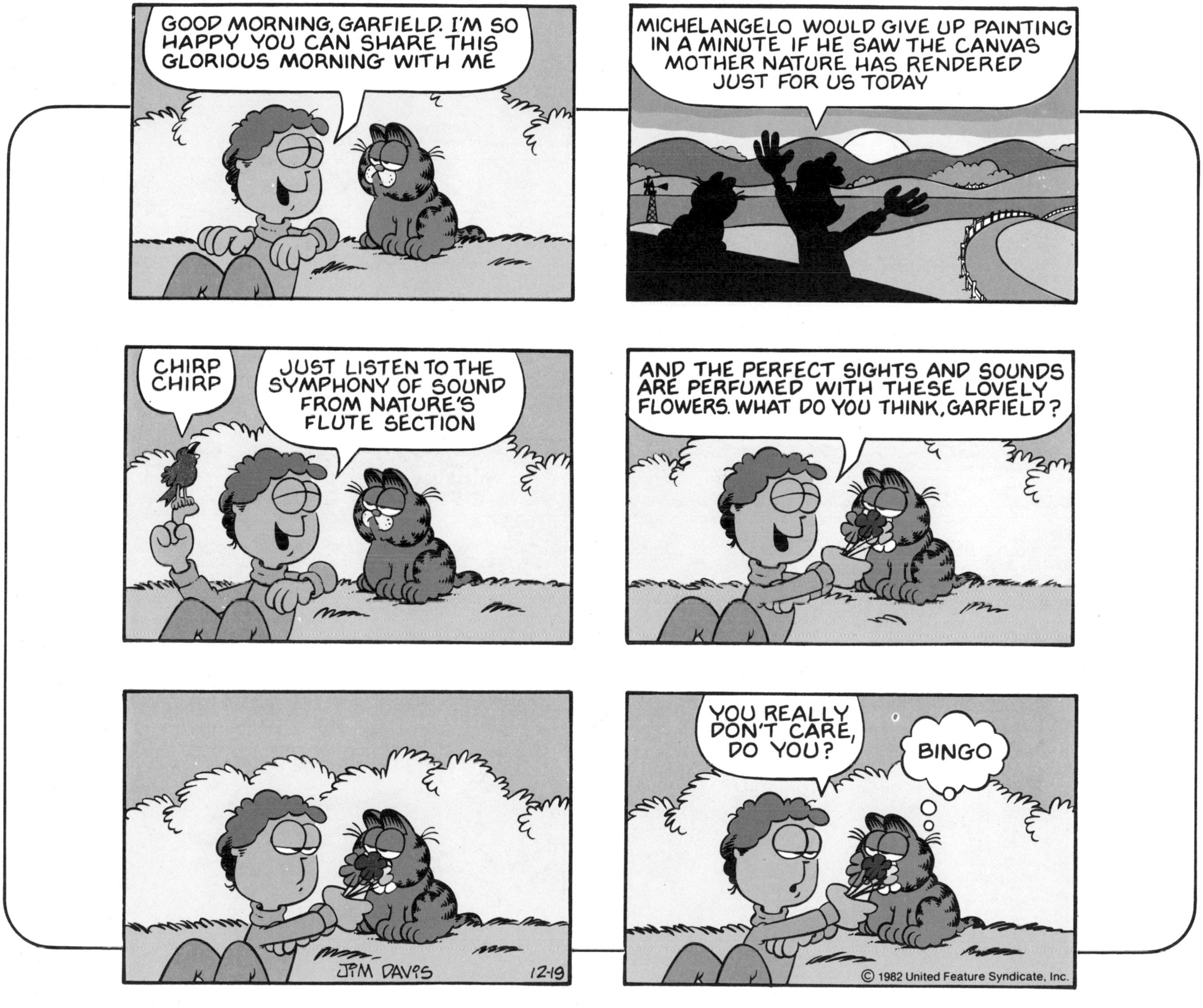
GOOD MORNING, GARFIELD. I'M SO HAPPY YOU CAN SHARE THIS GLORIOUS MORNING WITH ME
MICHELANGELO WOULD GIVE UP PAINTING IN A MINUTE IF HE SAW THE CANVAS MOTHER NATURE HAS RENDERED JUST FOR US TODAY
CHIRP CHIRP
JUST LISTEN TO THE SYMPHONY OF SOUND FROM NATURE'S FLUTE SECTION
AND THE PERFECT SIGHTS AND SOUNDS ARE PERFUMED WITH THESE LOVELY FLOWERS. WHAT DO YOU THINK, GARFIELD?
YOU REALLY DON'T CARE, DO YOU?
BINGO
JIM DAVIS
12-19
© 1982 United Feature Syndicate, Inc.

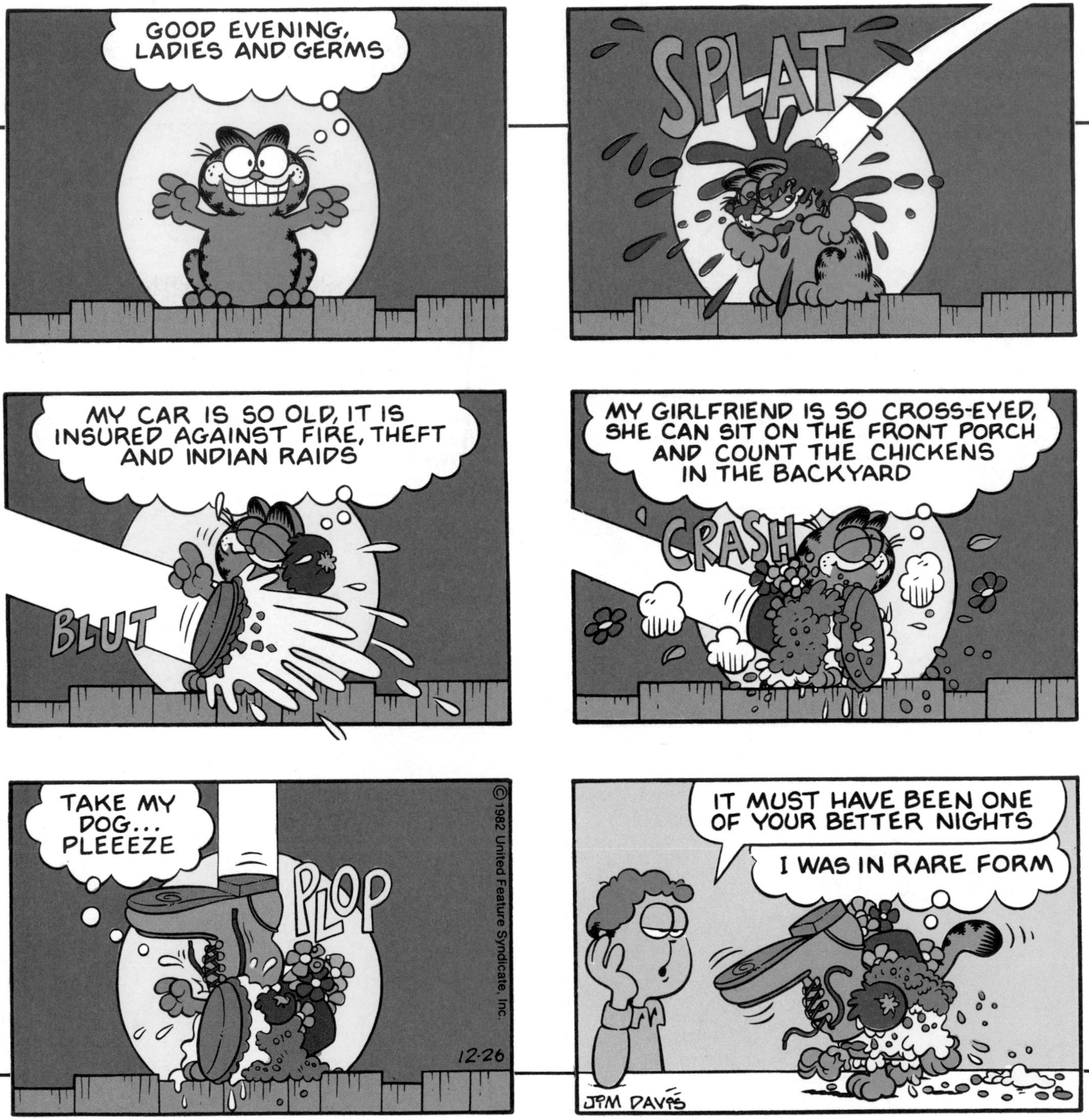
GOOD EVENING, LADIES AND GERMS
SPLAT
MY CAR IS SO OLD, IT IS INSURED AGAINST FIRE, THEFT AND INDIAN RAIDS
BLUT
MY GIRLFRIEND IS SO CROSS-EYED, SHE CAN SIT ON THE FRONT PORCH AND COUNT THE CHICKENS IN THE BACKYARD
CRASH
TAKE MY DOG... PLEEEZE
PLOP
© 1982 United Feature Syndicate, Inc.
12-26
IT MUST HAVE BEEN ONE OF YOUR BETTER NIGHTS
I WAS IN RARE FORM
JIM DAVIS

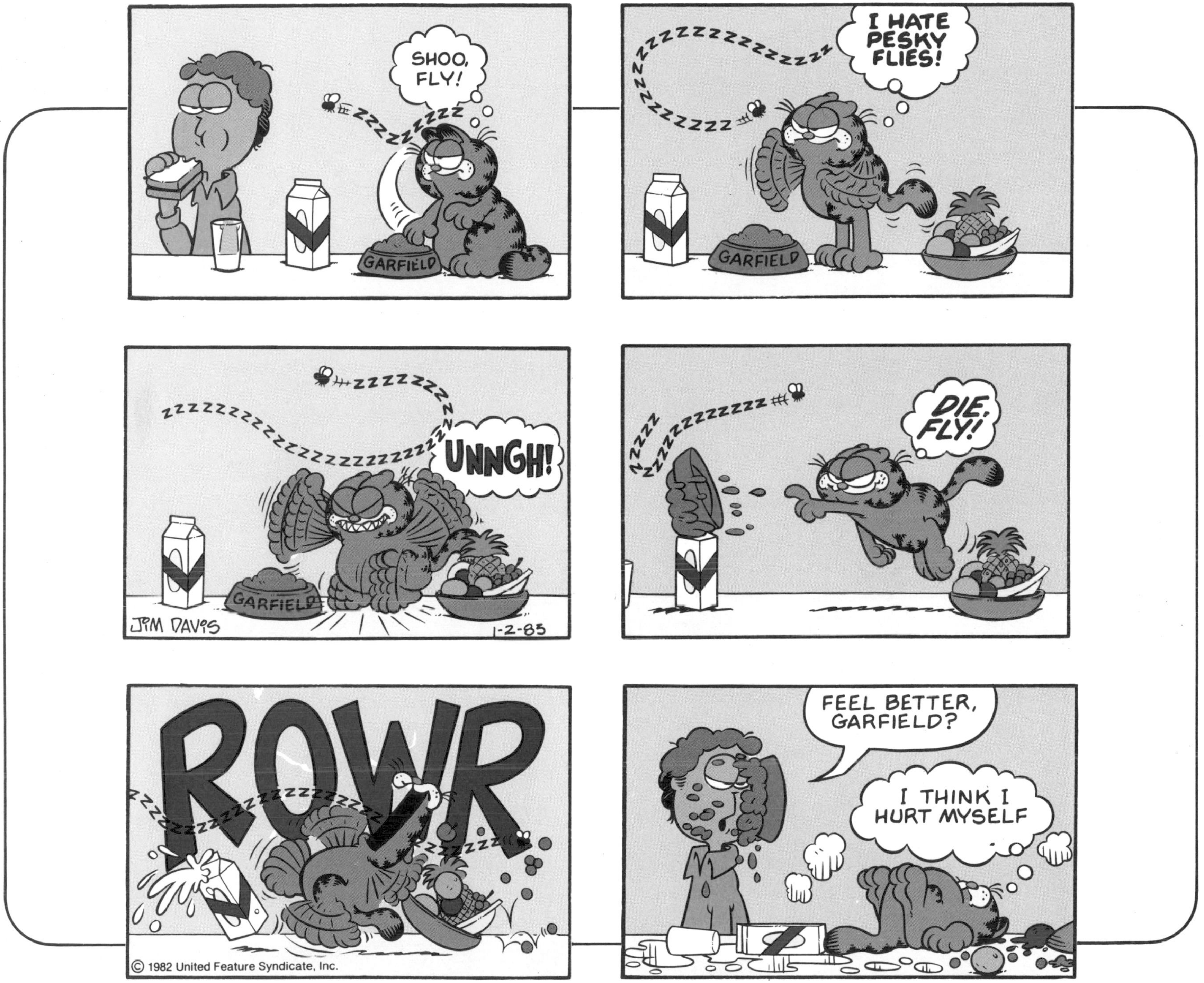
SHOO, FLY!
I HATE PESKY FLIES!
UNNGH!
DIE, FLY!
ROWR
FEEL BETTER, GARFIELD?
I THINK I HURT MYSELF
JIM DAVIS 1-2-83
© 1982 United Feature Syndicate, Inc.

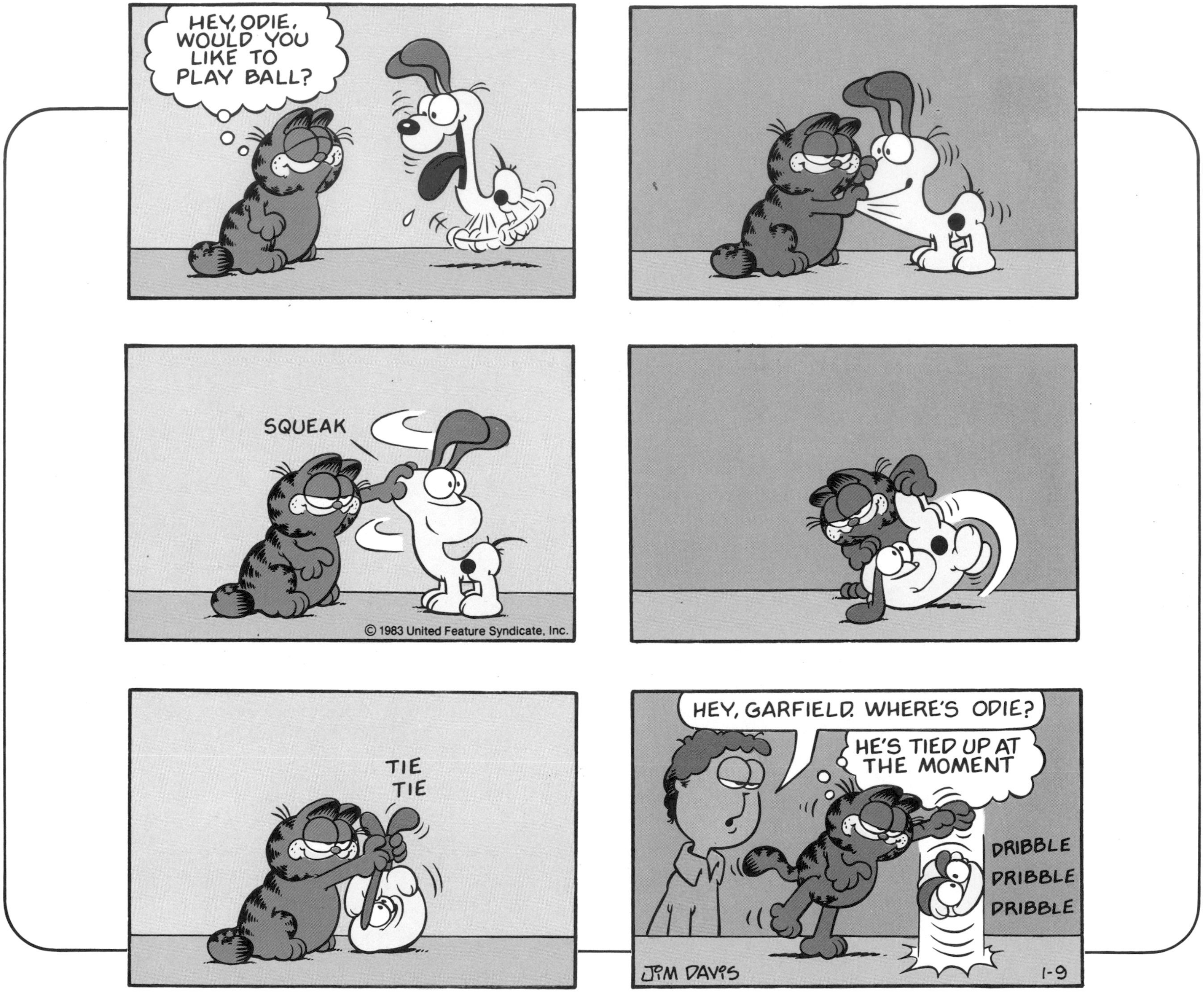
HEY, ODIE, WOULD YOU LIKE TO PLAY BALL?
SQUEAK
© 1983 United Feature Syndicate, Inc.
TIE
TIE
HEY, GARFIELD. WHERE'S ODIE?
HE'S TIED UP AT THE MOMENT
DRIBBLE
DRIBBLE
DRIBBLE
JIM DAVIS
1-9

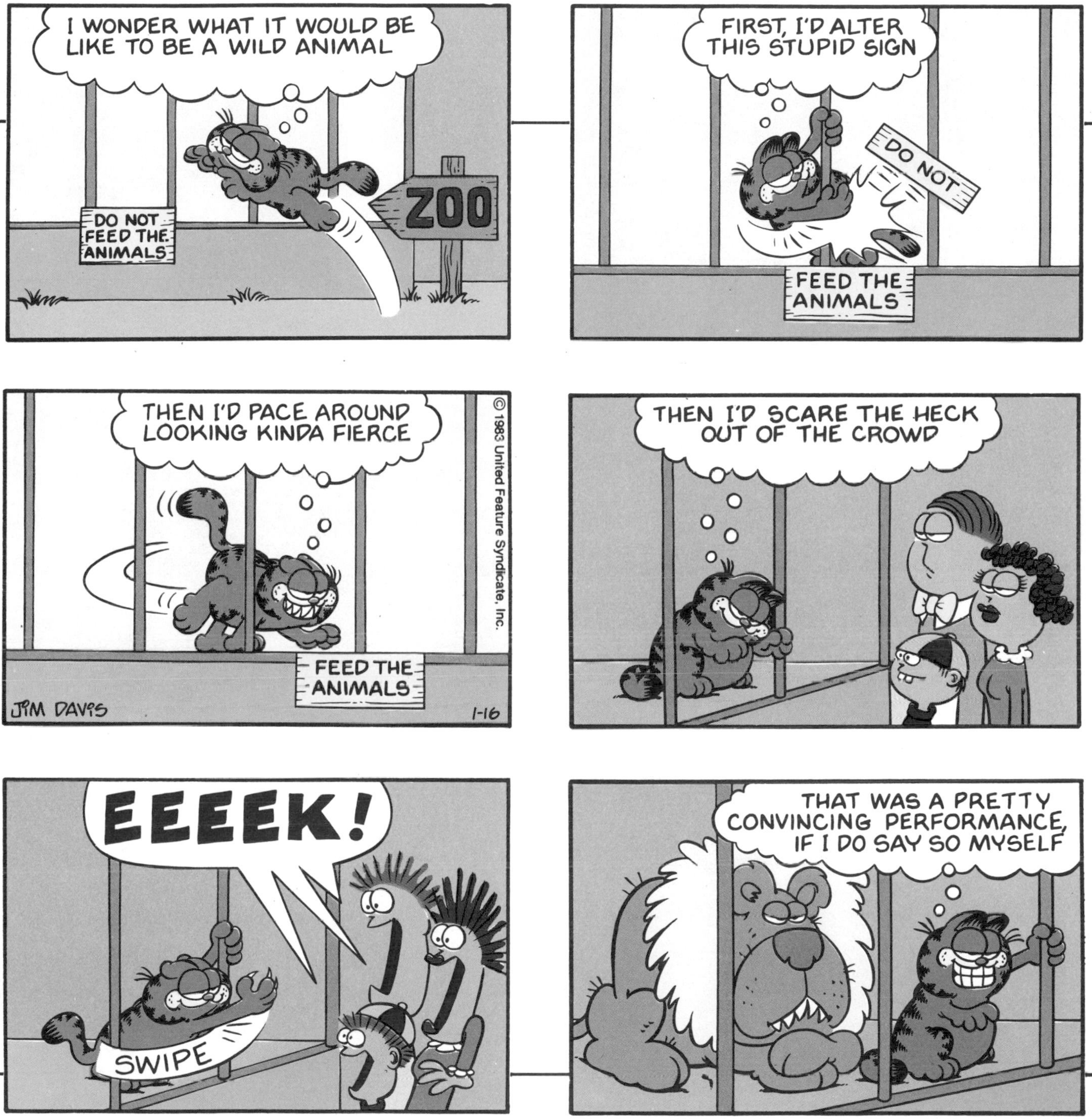
I WONDER WHAT IT WOULD BE LIKE TO BE A WILD ANIMAL
DO NOT FEED THE ANIMALS
ZOO
FIRST, I'D ALTER THIS STUPID SIGN
DO NOT
FEED THE ANIMALS
THEN I'D PACE AROUND LOOKING KINDA FIERCE
FEED THE ANIMALS
© 1983 United Feature Syndicate, Inc.
JIM DAVIS
1-16
THEN I'D SCARE THE HECK OUT OF THE CROWD
EEEEK!
SWIPE
THAT WAS A PRETTY CONVINCING PERFORMANCE, IF I DO SAY SO MYSELF

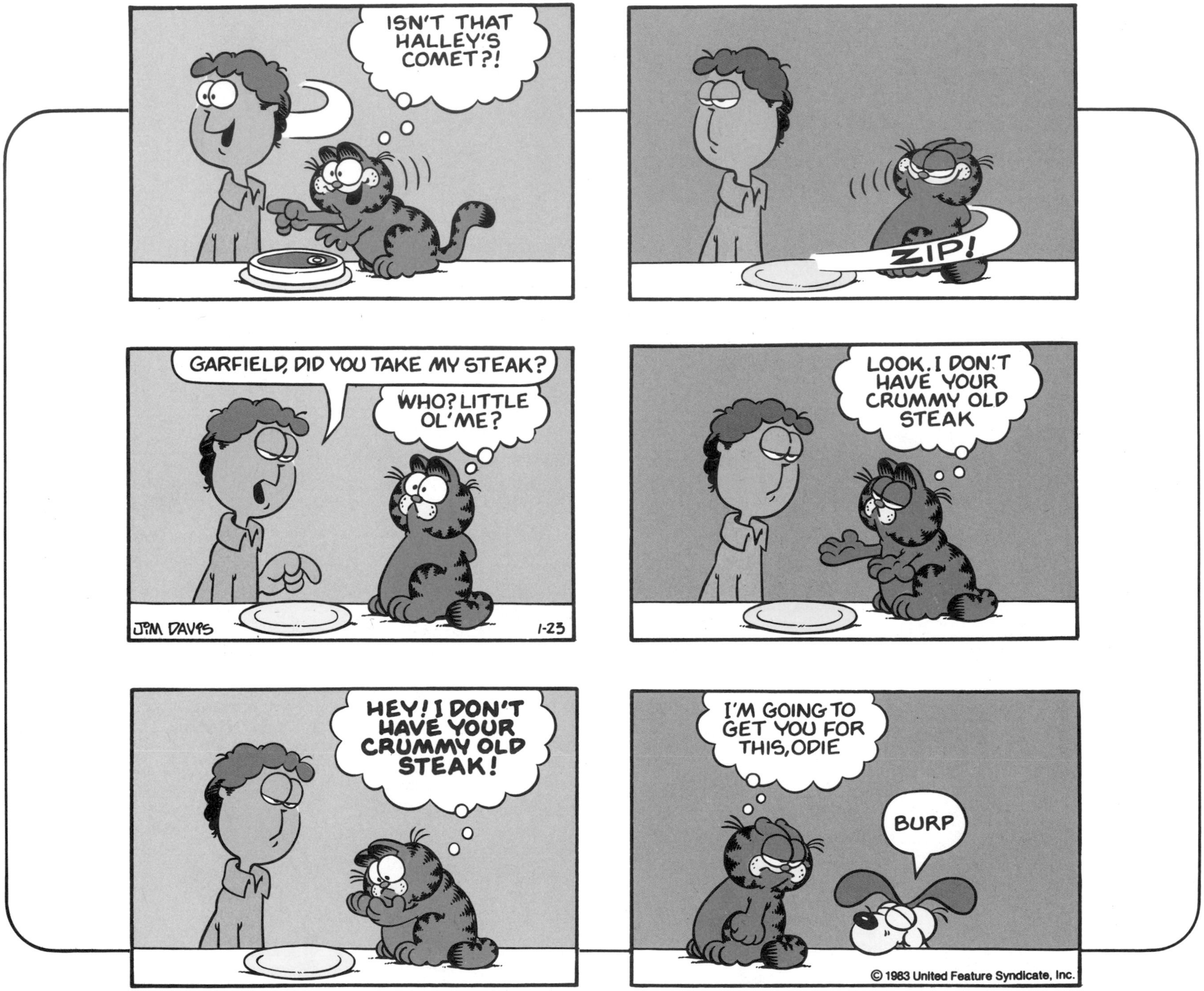
ISN'T THAT HALLEY'S COMET?!
ZIP!
GARFIELD, DID YOU TAKE MY STEAK?
WHO? LITTLE OL' ME?
LOOK. I DON'T HAVE YOUR CRUMMY OLD STEAK
JIM DAVIS
1-23
HEY! I DON'T HAVE YOUR CRUMMY OLD STEAK!
I'M GOING TO GET YOU FOR THIS, ODIE
BURP
© 1983 United Feature Syndicate, Inc.

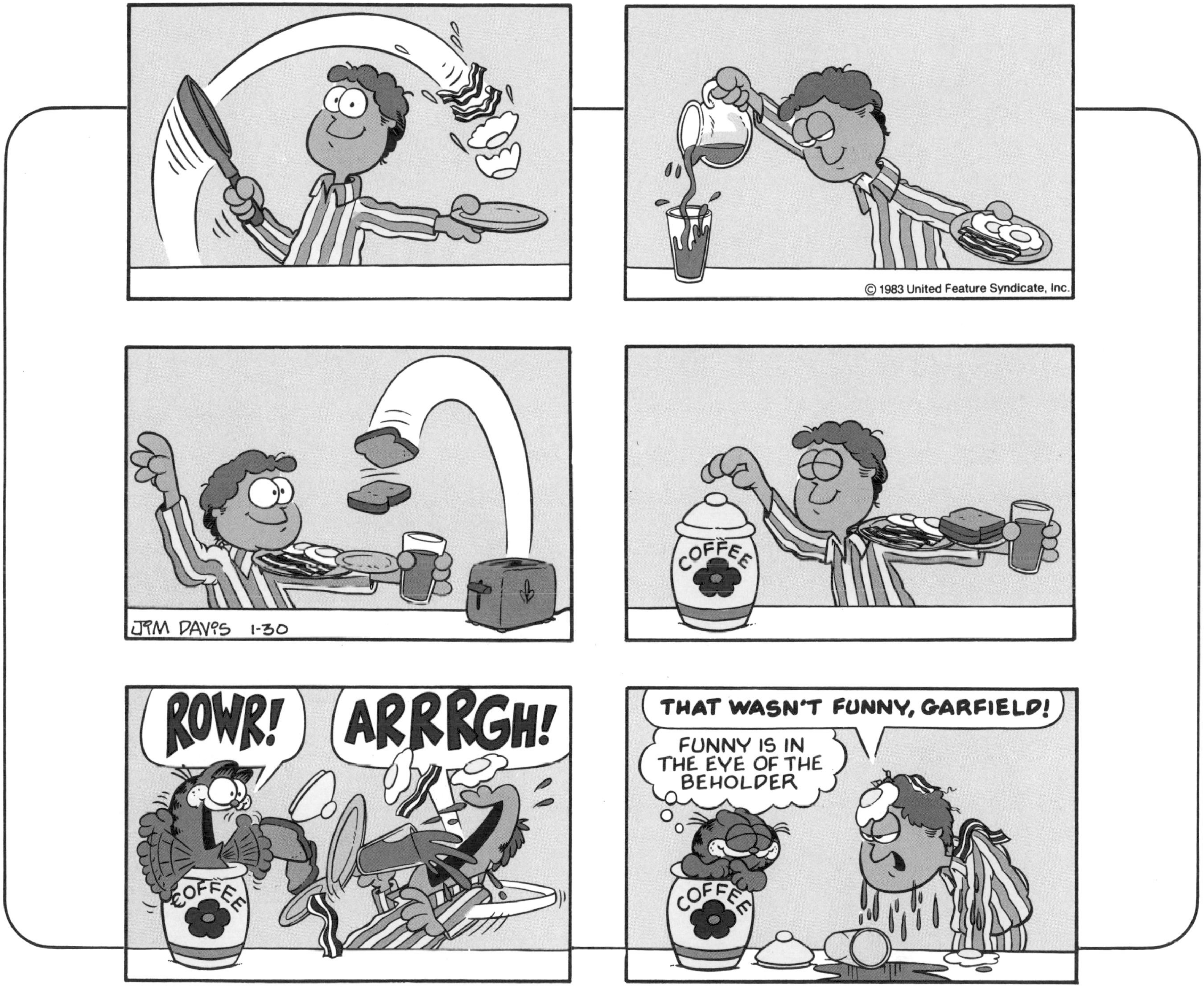
© 1983 United Feature Syndicate, Inc.
JIM DAVIS 1-30
COFFEE
ROWR!
ARRRGH!
COFFEE
THAT WASN'T FUNNY, GARFIELD!
FUNNY IS IN THE EYE OF THE BEHOLDER
COFFEE

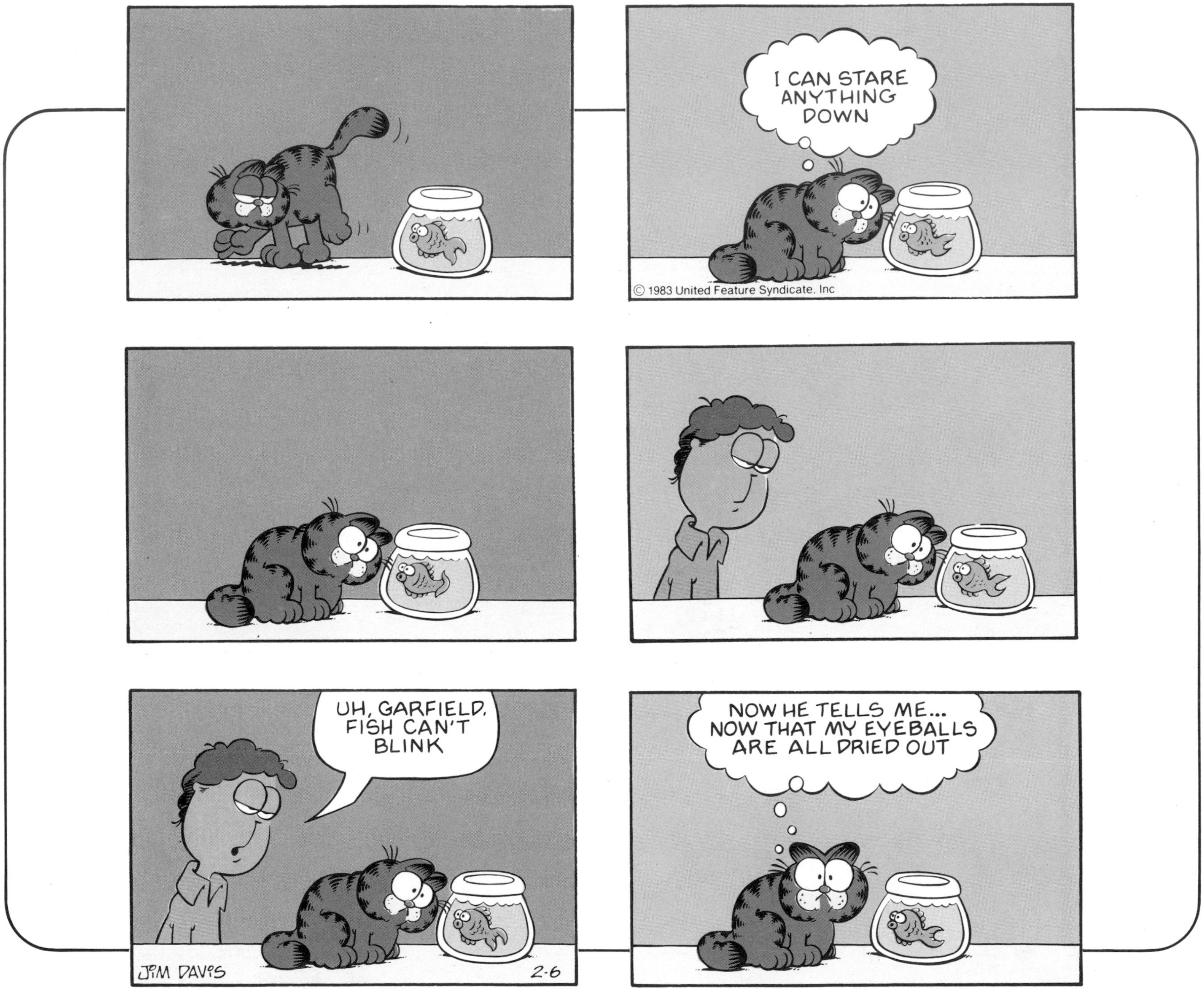
I CAN STARE ANYTHING DOWN
© 1983 United Feature Syndicate, Inc
UH, GARFIELD, FISH CAN'T BLINK
JIM DAVIS
2-6
NOW HE TELLS ME... NOW THAT MY EYEBALLS ARE ALL DRIED OUT

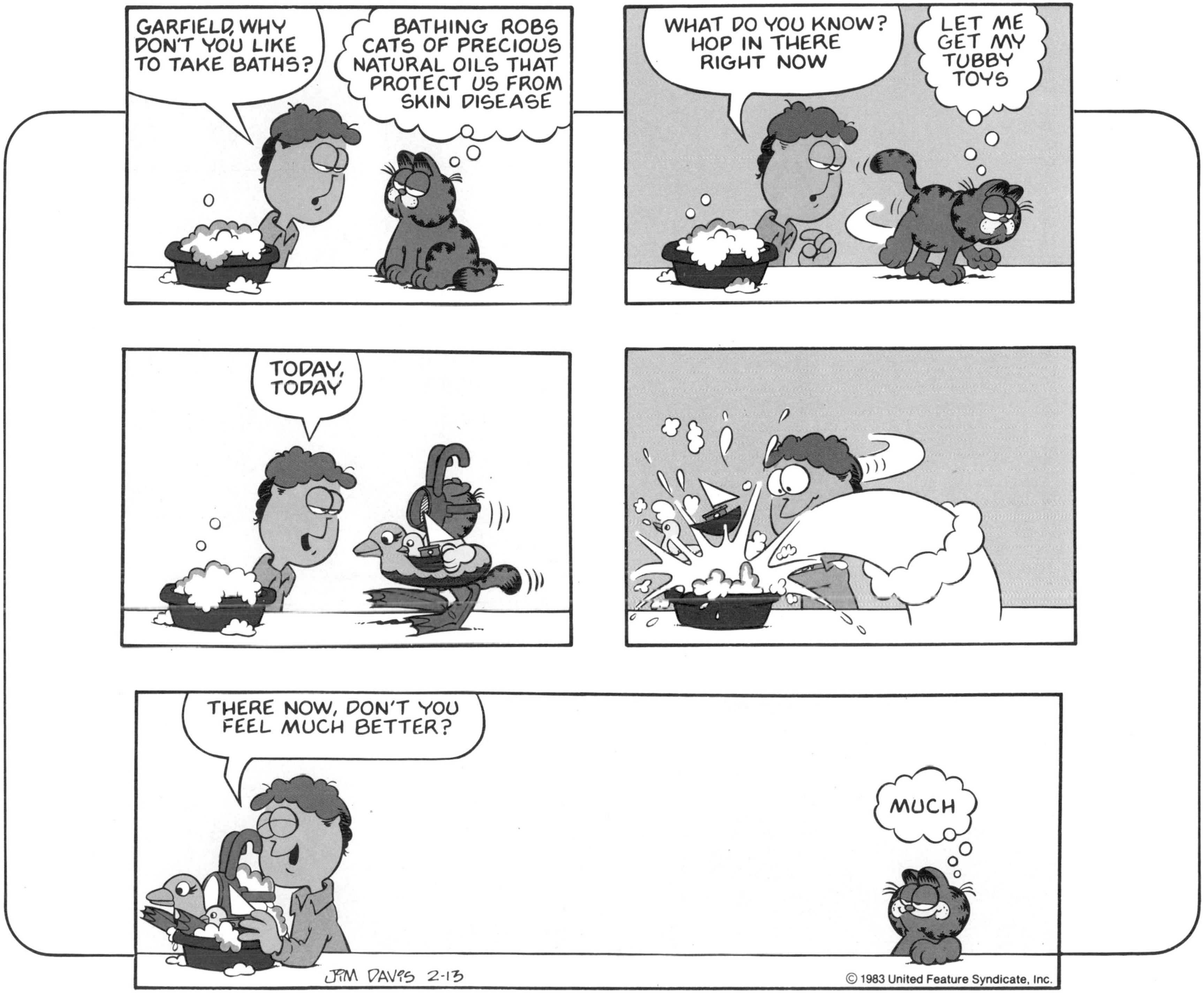
GARFIELD, WHY DON'T YOU LIKE TO TAKE BATHS?
BATHING ROBS CATS OF PRECIOUS NATURAL OILS THAT PROTECT US FROM SKIN DISEASE
WHAT DO YOU KNOW? HOP IN THERE RIGHT NOW
LET ME GET MY TUBBY TOYS
TODAY, TODAY
THERE NOW, DON'T YOU FEEL MUCH BETTER?
MUCH
JIM DAVIS 2-13
© 1983 United Feature Syndicate, Inc.

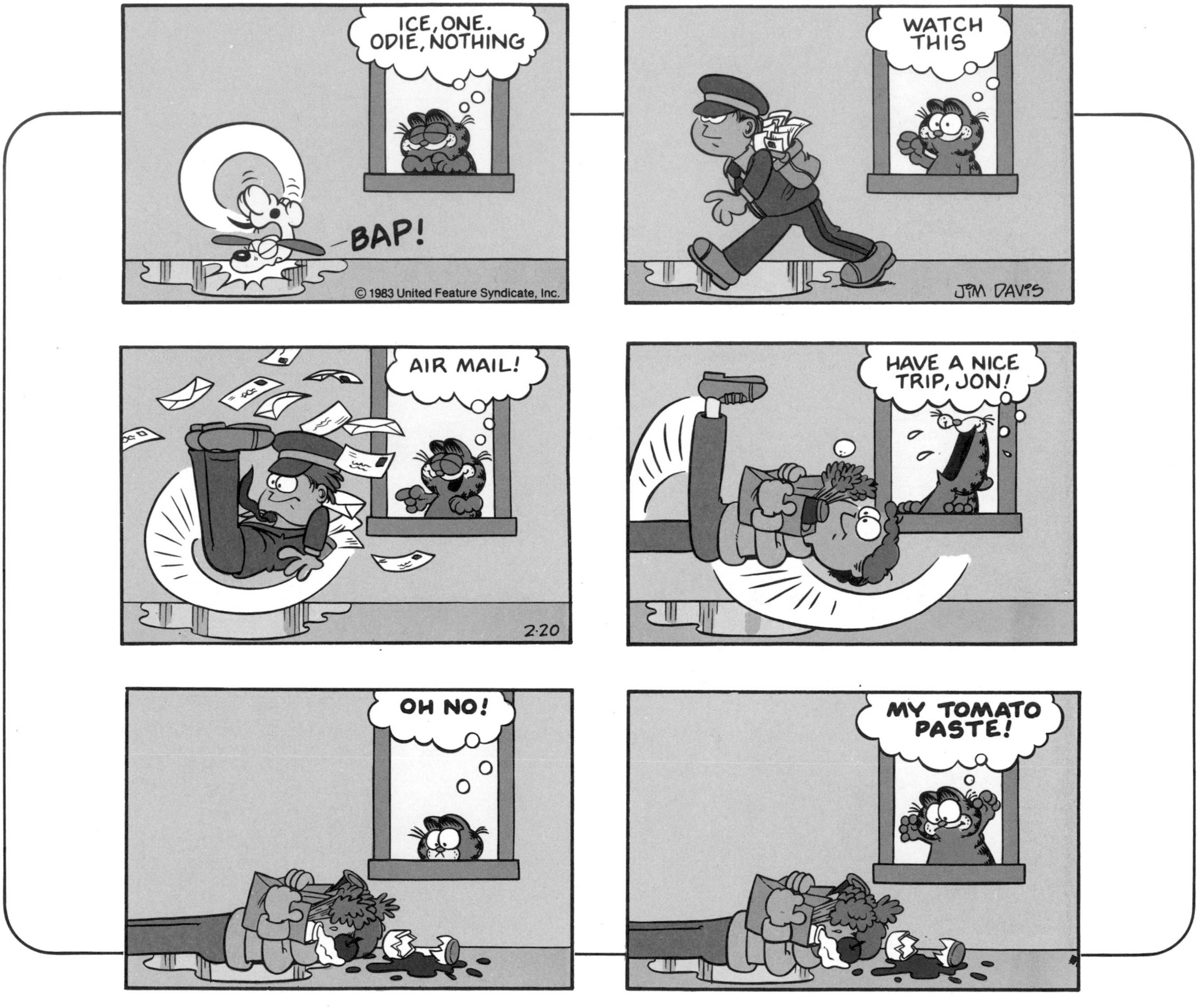
ICE, ONE. ODIE, NOTHING
BAP!
© 1983 United Feature Syndicate, Inc.
WATCH THIS
JIM DAVIS
AIR MAIL!
2·20
HAVE A NICE TRIP, JON!
OH NO!
MY TOMATO PASTE!

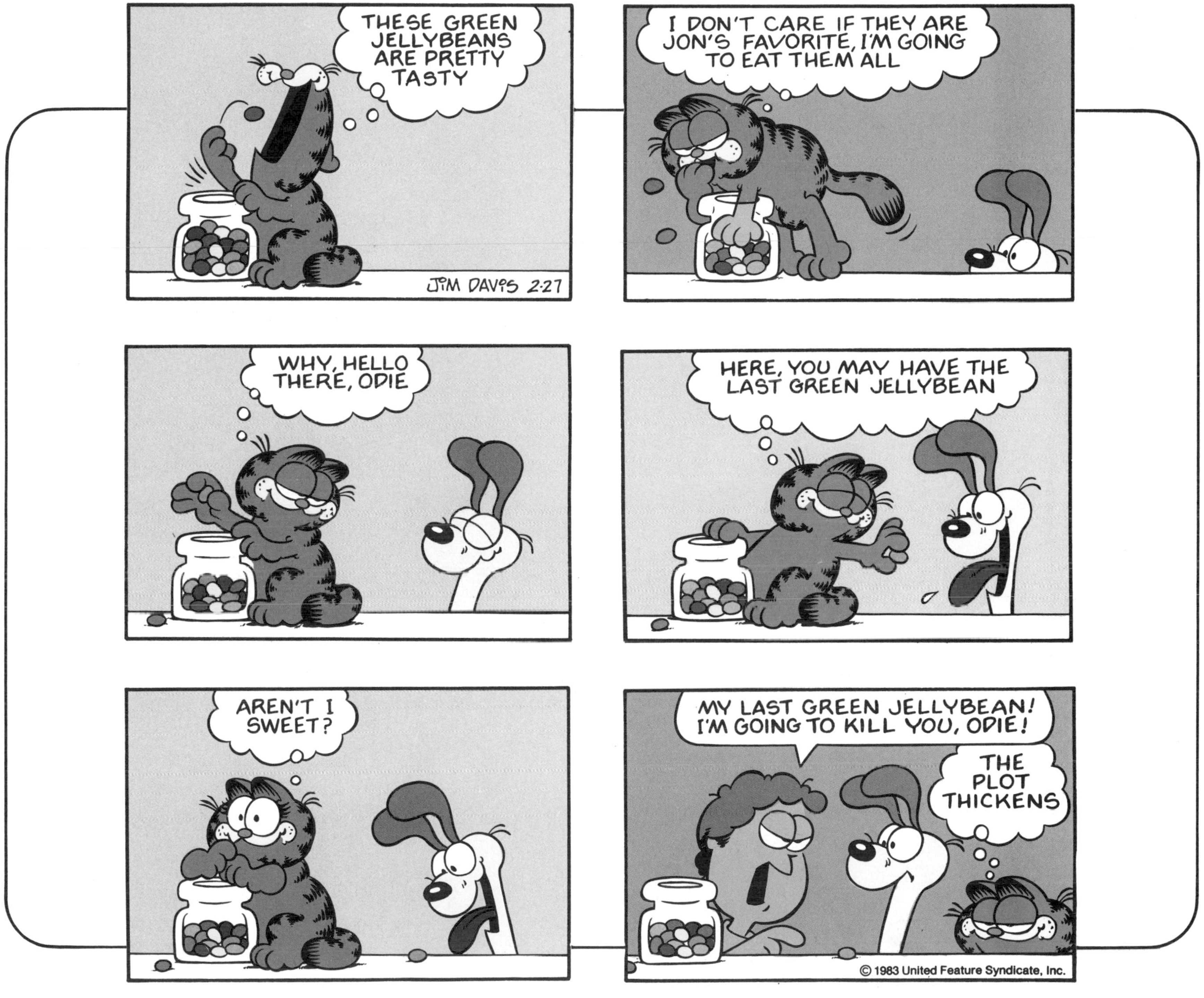
THESE GREEN JELLYBEANS ARE PRETTY TASTY
JIM DAVIS 2·27
I DON'T CARE IF THEY ARE JON'S FAVORITE, I'M GOING TO EAT THEM ALL
WHY, HELLO THERE, ODIE
HERE, YOU MAY HAVE THE LAST GREEN JELLYBEAN
AREN'T I SWEET?
MY LAST GREEN JELLYBEAN! I'M GOING TO KILL YOU, ODIE!
THE PLOT THICKENS
© 1983 United Feature Syndicate, Inc.

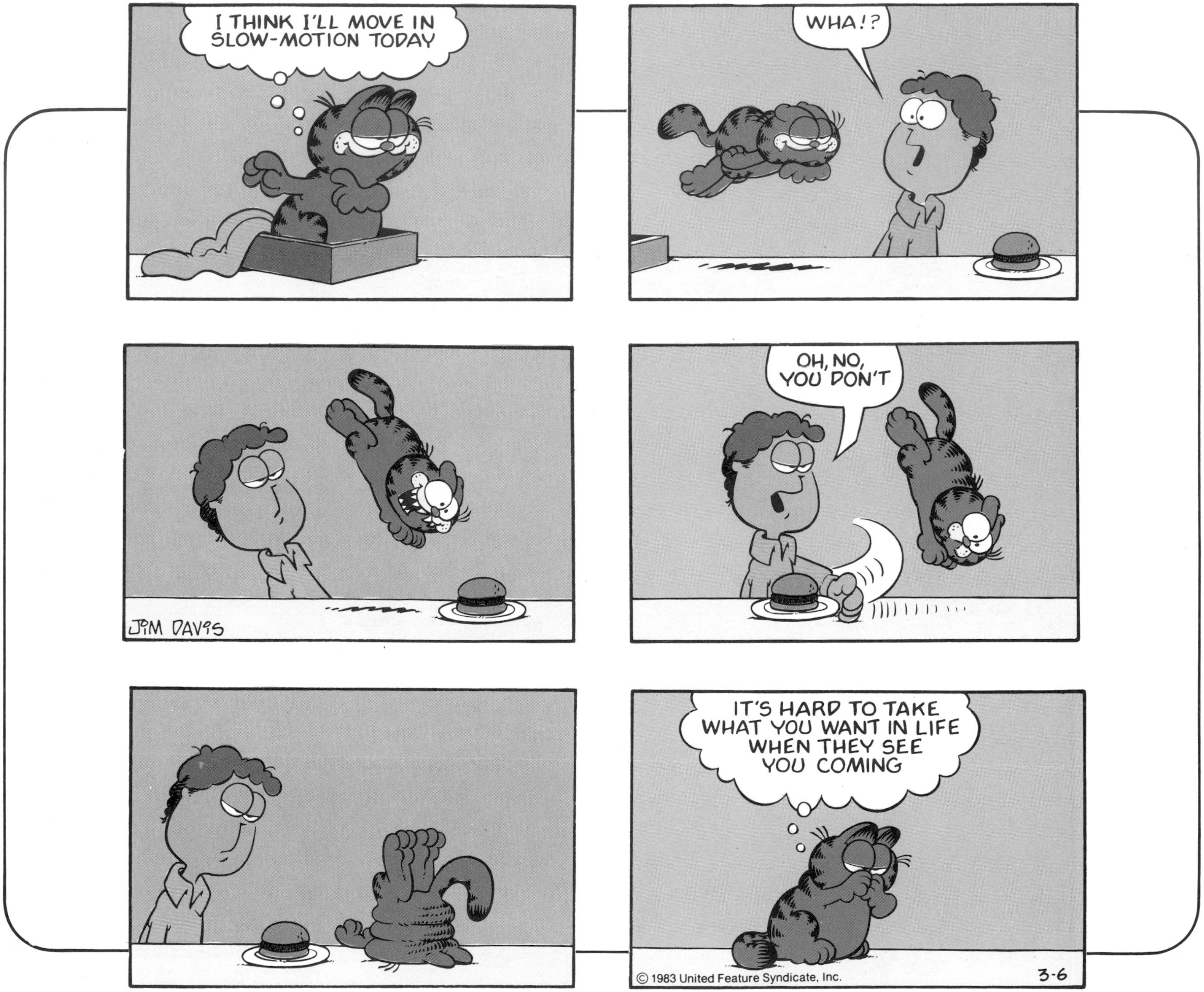
I THINK I'LL MOVE IN SLOW-MOTION TODAY
WHA!?
JIM DAVIS
OH, NO, YOU DON'T
IT'S HARD TO TAKE WHAT YOU WANT IN LIFE WHEN THEY SEE YOU COMING
© 1983 United Feature Syndicate, Inc.
3-6

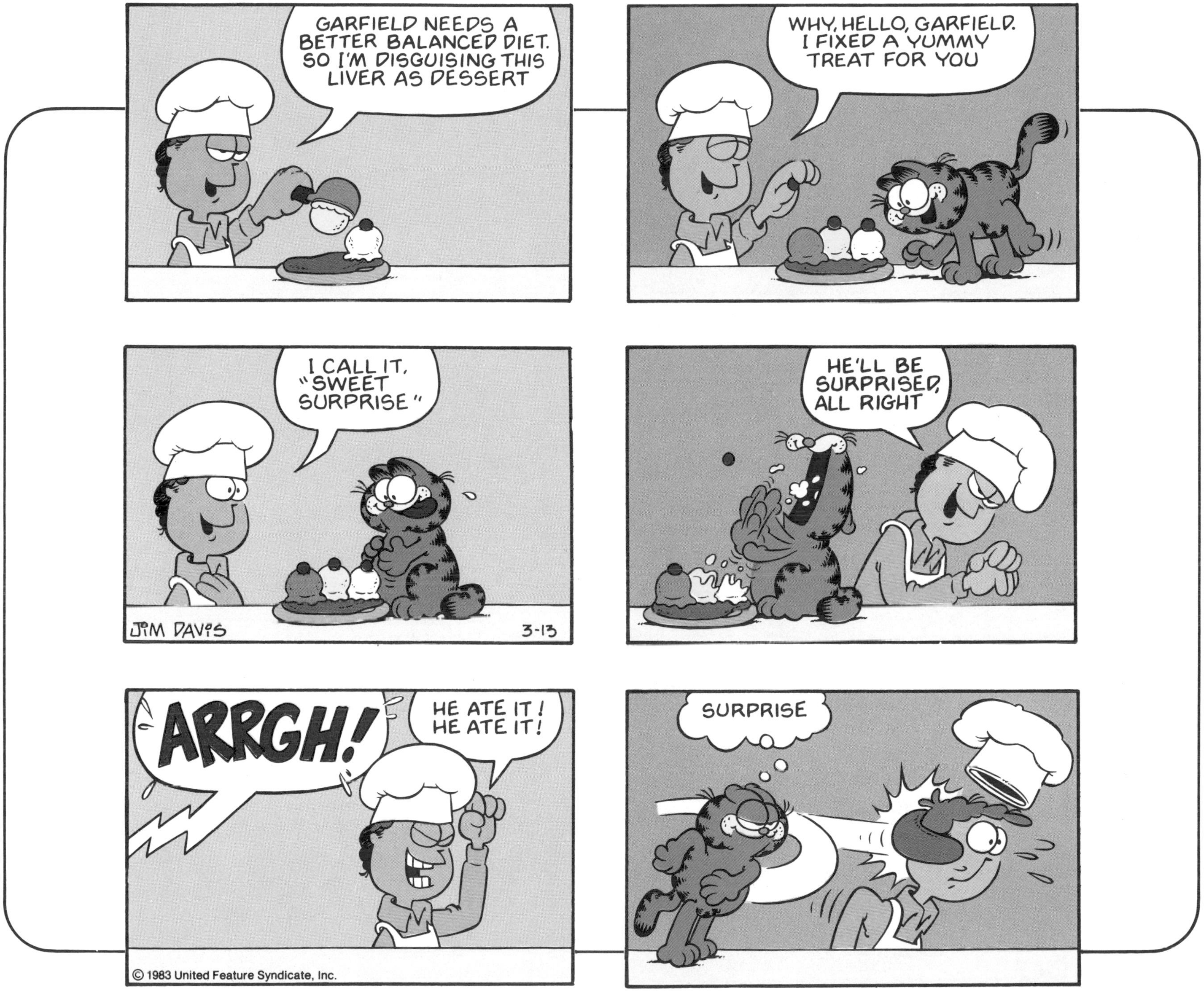
GARFIELD NEEDS A BETTER BALANCED DIET. SO I'M DISGUISING THIS LIVER AS DESSERT
WHY, HELLO, GARFIELD. I FIXED A YUMMY TREAT FOR YOU
I CALL IT, "SWEET SURPRISE"
JIM DAVIS
3-13
HE'LL BE SURPRISED, ALL RIGHT
ARRGH!
HE ATE IT! HE ATE IT!
SURPRISE
© 1983 United Feature Syndicate, Inc.

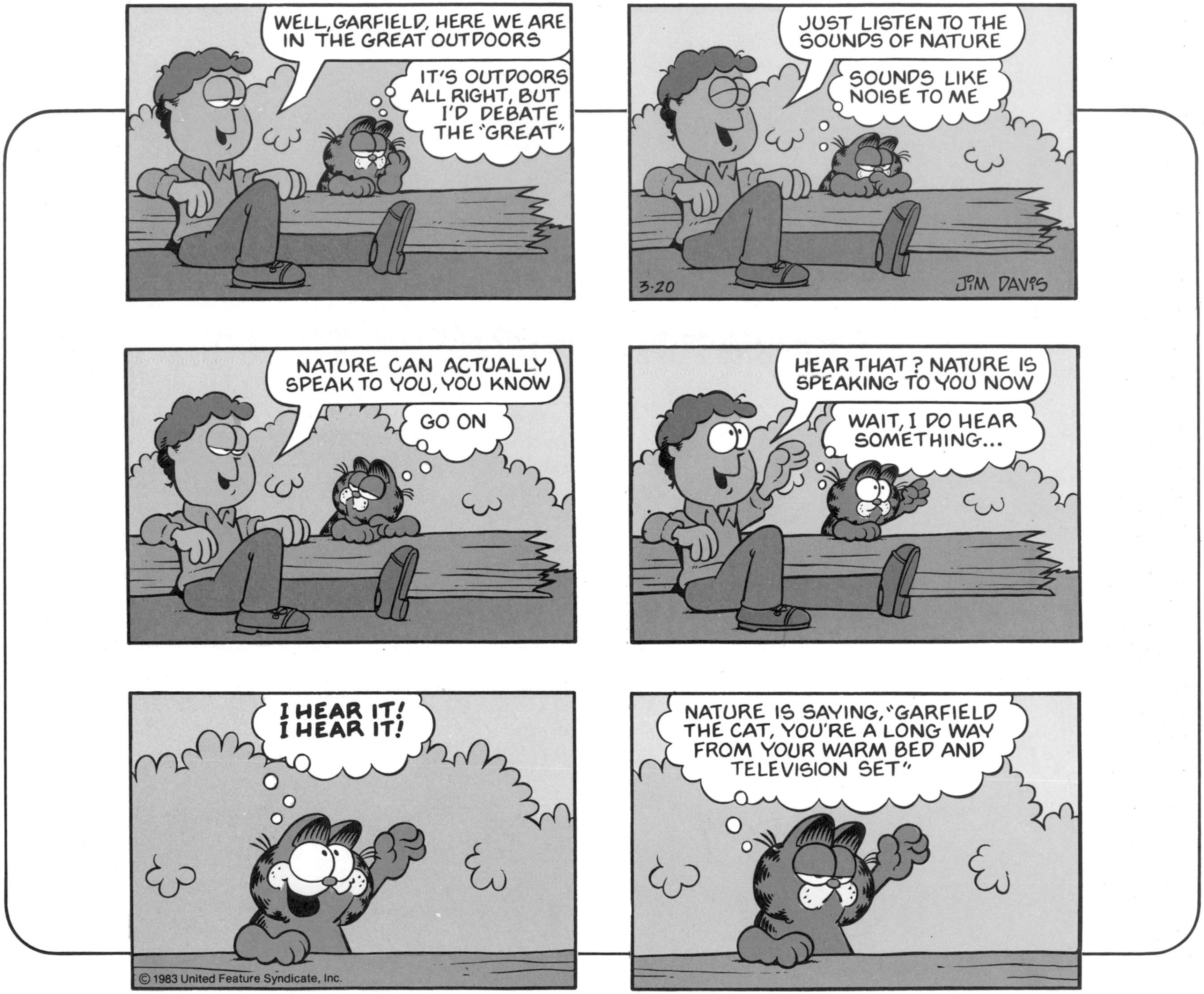
WELL, GARFIELD, HERE WE ARE IN THE GREAT OUTDOORS
IT'S OUTDOORS ALL RIGHT, BUT I'D DEBATE THE "GREAT"
JUST LISTEN TO THE SOUNDS OF NATURE
SOUNDS LIKE NOISE TO ME
3-20
JIM DAVIS
NATURE CAN ACTUALLY SPEAK TO YOU, YOU KNOW
GO ON
HEAR THAT? NATURE IS SPEAKING TO YOU NOW
WAIT, I DO HEAR SOMETHING...
I HEAR IT! I HEAR IT!
NATURE IS SAYING, "GARFIELD THE CAT, YOU'RE A LONG WAY FROM YOUR WARM BED AND TELEVISION SET"
© 1983 United Feature Syndicate, Inc.

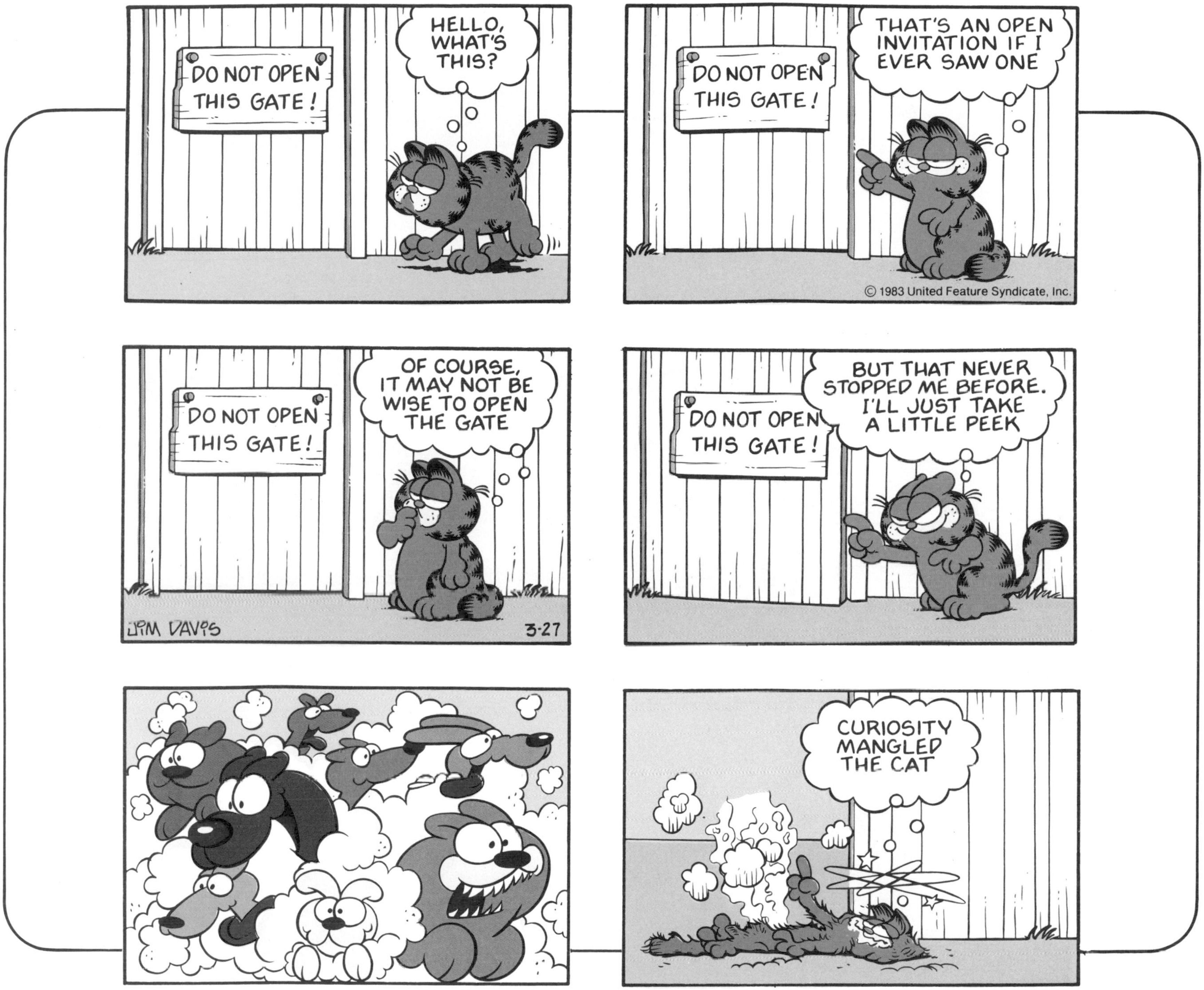

DO NOT OPEN THIS GATE!
HELLO, WHAT'S THIS?
DO NOT OPEN THIS GATE!
THAT'S AN OPEN INVITATION IF I EVER SAW ONE
© 1983 United Feature Syndicate, Inc.
DO NOT OPEN THIS GATE!
OF COURSE, IT MAY NOT BE WISE TO OPEN THE GATE
JIM DAVIS
3-27
DO NOT OPEN THIS GATE!
BUT THAT NEVER STOPPED ME BEFORE. I'LL JUST TAKE A LITTLE PEEK
CURIOSITY MANGLED THE CAT

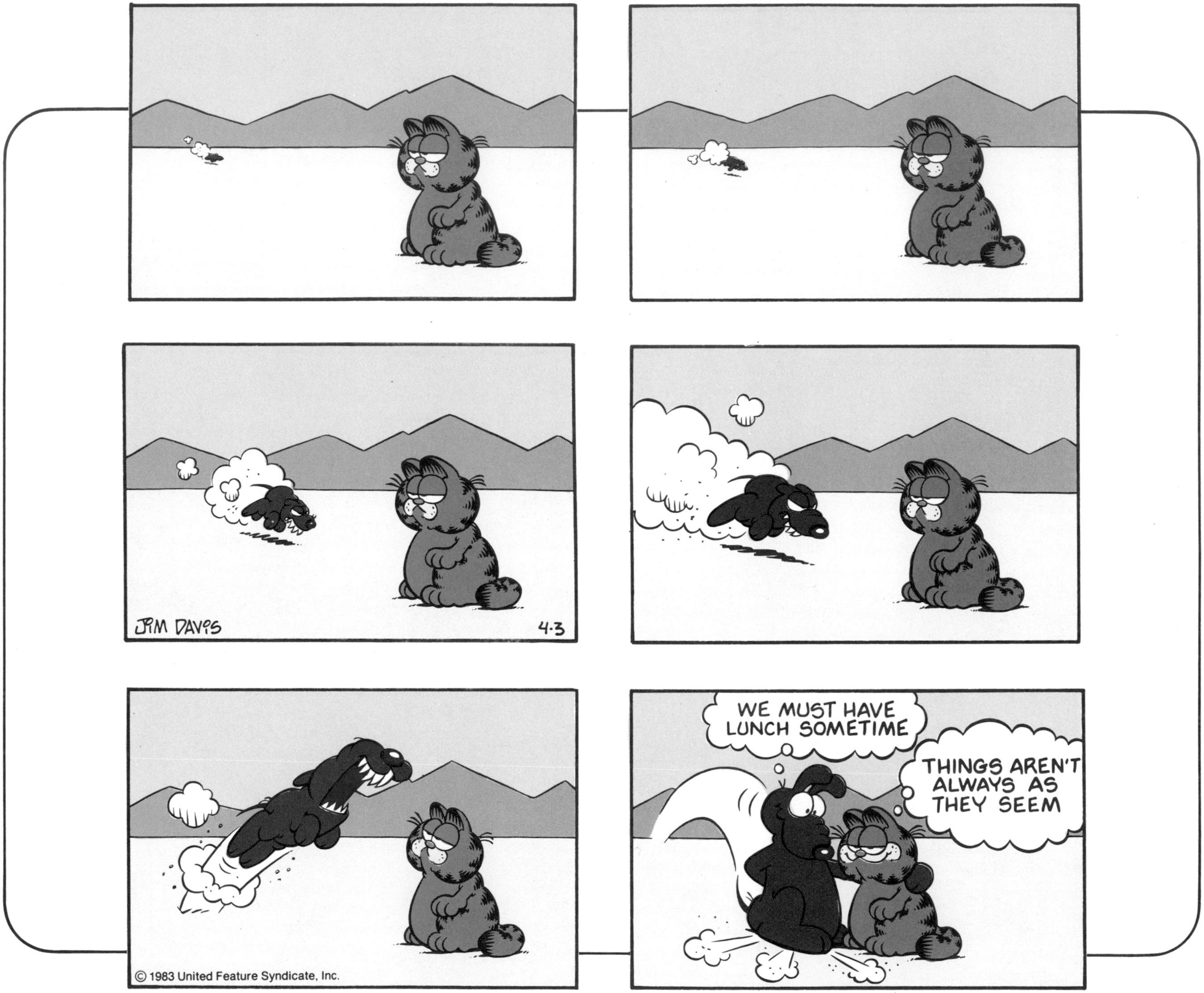
JIM DAVIS
4-3
© 1983 United Feature Syndicate, Inc.
WE MUST HAVE LUNCH SOMETIME
THINGS AREN'T ALWAYS AS THEY SEEM

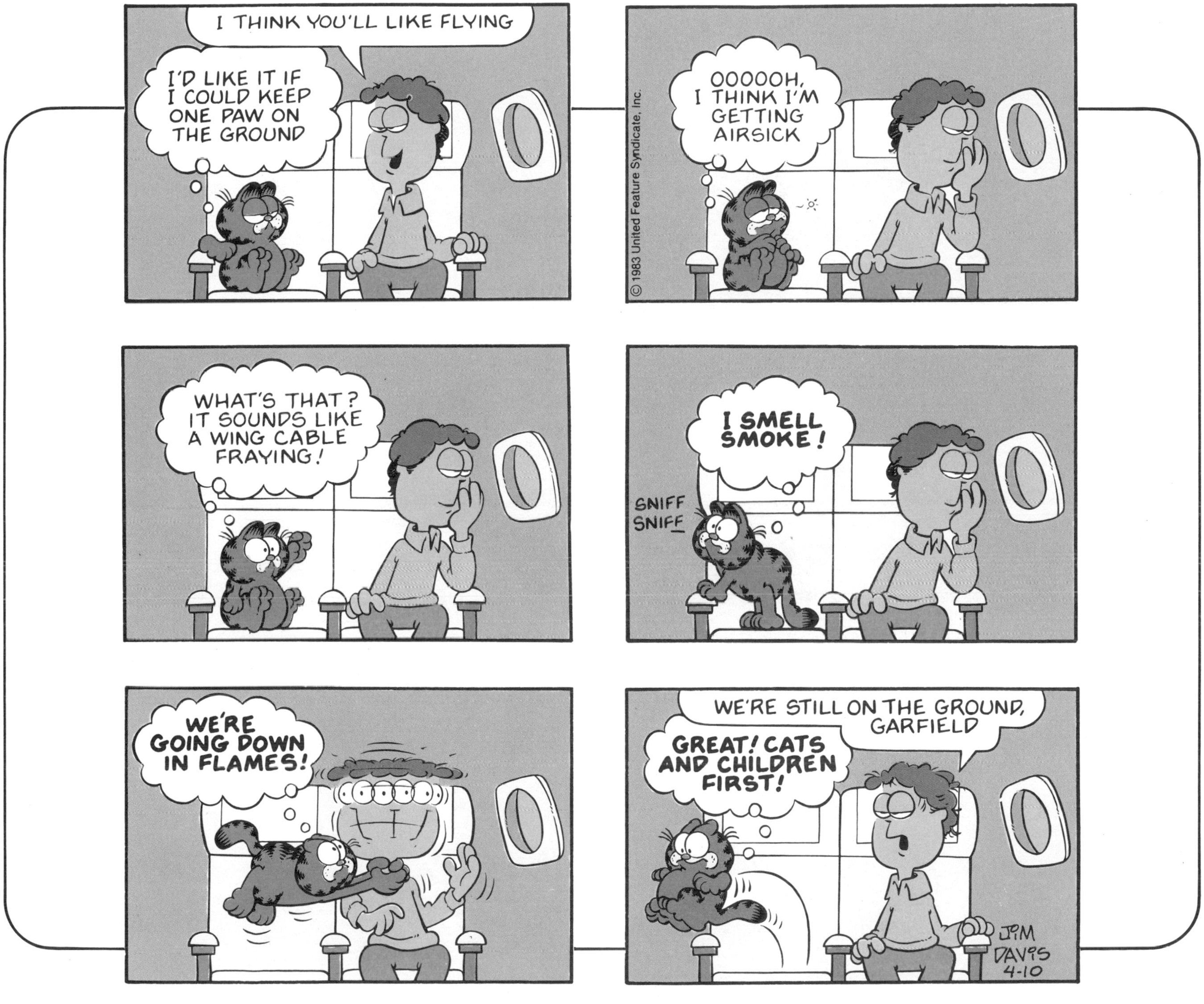
I THINK YOU'LL LIKE FLYING
I'D LIKE IT IF I COULD KEEP ONE PAW ON THE GROUND
OOOOOH, I THINK I'M GETTING AIRSICK
© 1983 United Feature Syndicate, Inc.
WHAT'S THAT? IT SOUNDS LIKE A WING CABLE FRAYING!
SNIFF SNIFF
I SMELL SMOKE!
WE'RE GOING DOWN IN FLAMES!
WE'RE STILL ON THE GROUND, GARFIELD
GREAT! CATS AND CHILDREN FIRST!
JIM DAVIS 4-10

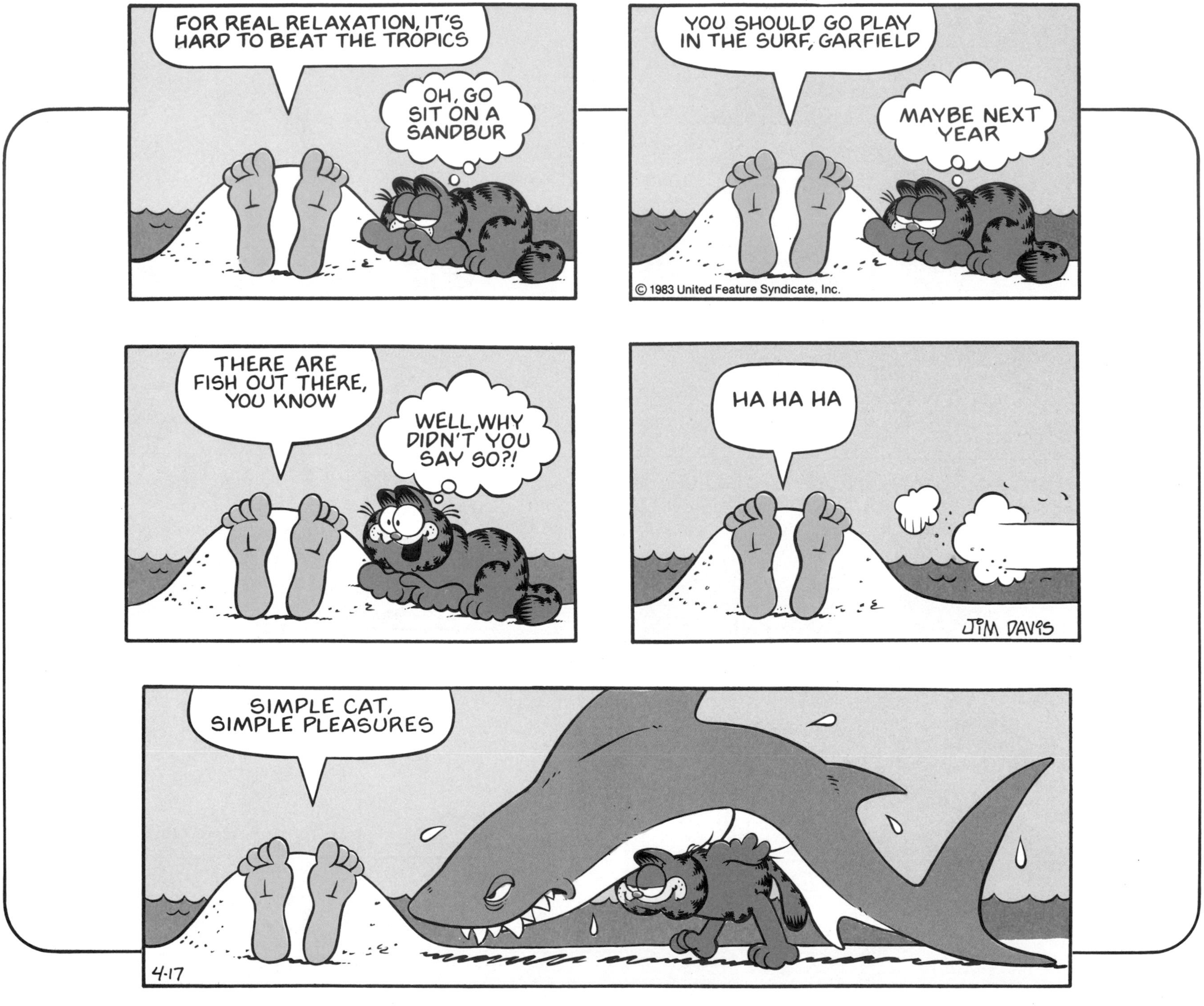
FOR REAL RELAXATION, IT'S HARD TO BEAT THE TROPICS
OH, GO SIT ON A SANDBUR
YOU SHOULD GO PLAY IN THE SURF, GARFIELD
MAYBE NEXT YEAR
© 1983 United Feature Syndicate, Inc.
THERE ARE FISH OUT THERE, YOU KNOW
WELL, WHY DIDN'T YOU SAY SO?!
HA HA HA
JIM DAVIS
SIMPLE CAT, SIMPLE PLEASURES
4·17

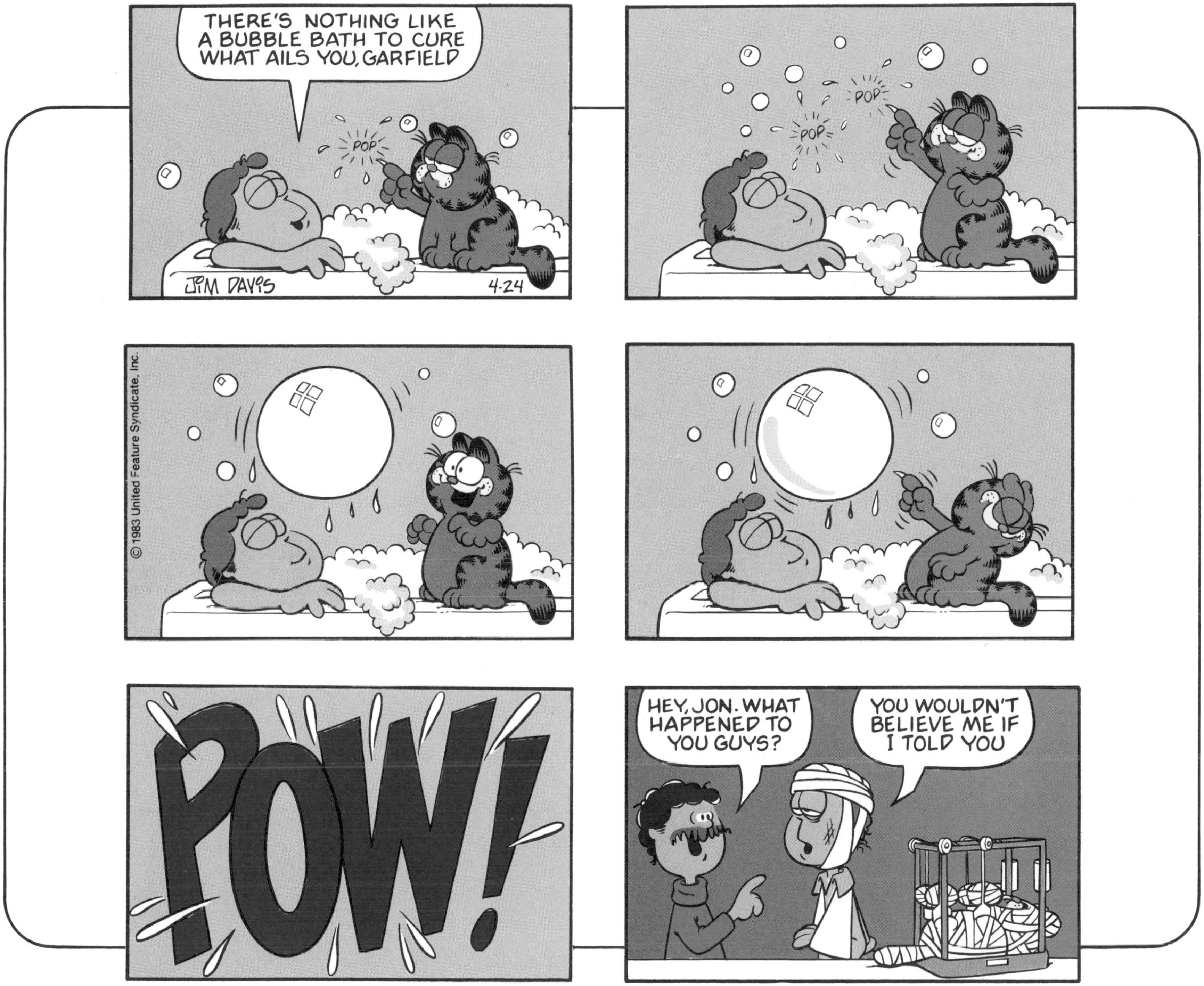
THERE'S NOTHING LIKE A BUBBLE BATH TO CURE WHAT AILS YOU, GARFIELD
POP
JIM DAVIS
4-24
POP
POP
© 1983 United Feature Syndicate, Inc.
POW!
HEY, JON. WHAT HAPPENED TO YOU GUYS?
YOU WOULDN'T BELIEVE ME IF I TOLD YOU

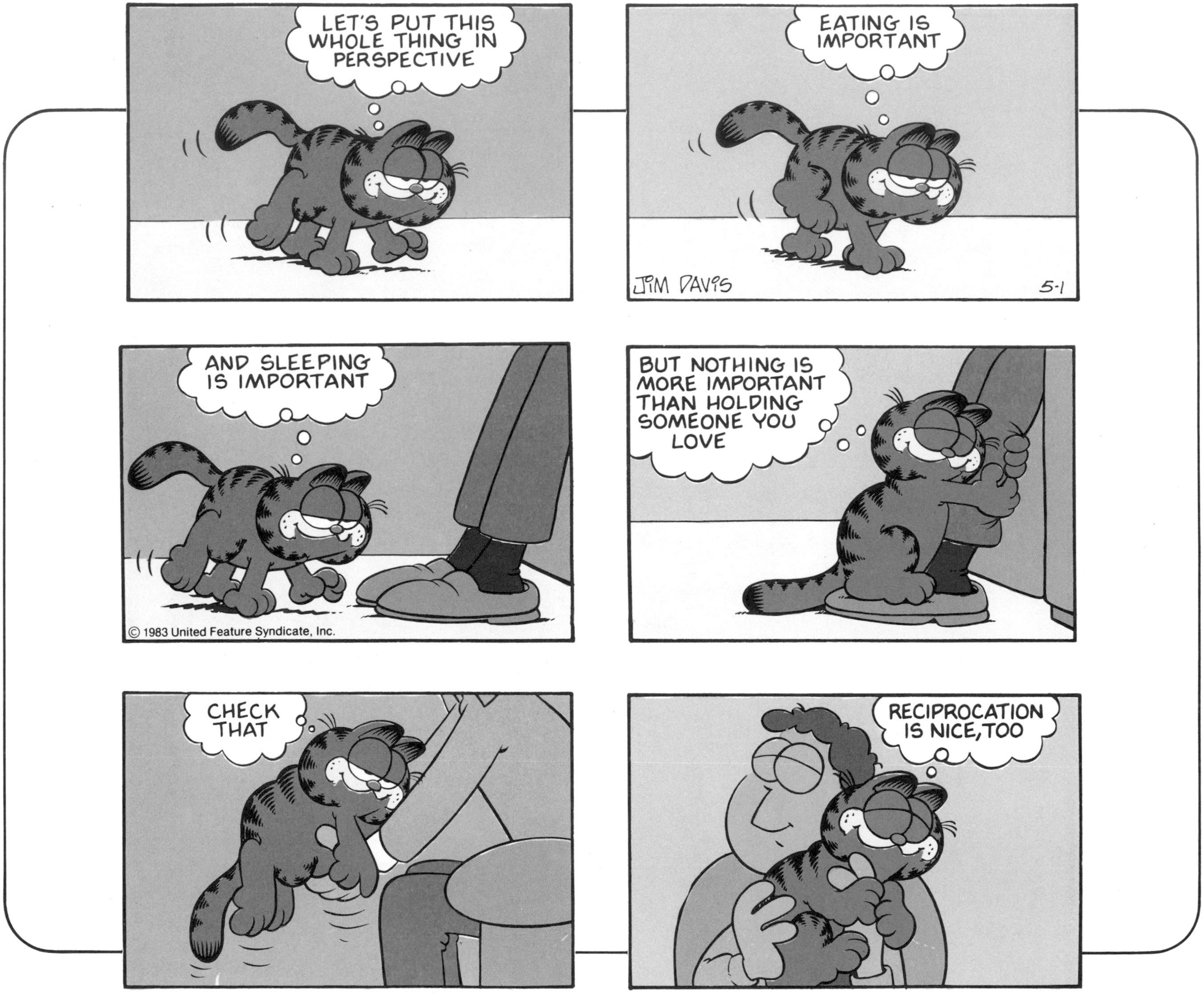
LET'S PUT THIS WHOLE THING IN PERSPECTIVE
EATING IS IMPORTANT
JIM DAVIS
5-1
AND SLEEPING IS IMPORTANT
© 1983 United Feature Syndicate, Inc.
BUT NOTHING IS MORE IMPORTANT THAN HOLDING SOMEONE YOU LOVE
CHECK THAT
RECIPROCATION IS NICE, TOO

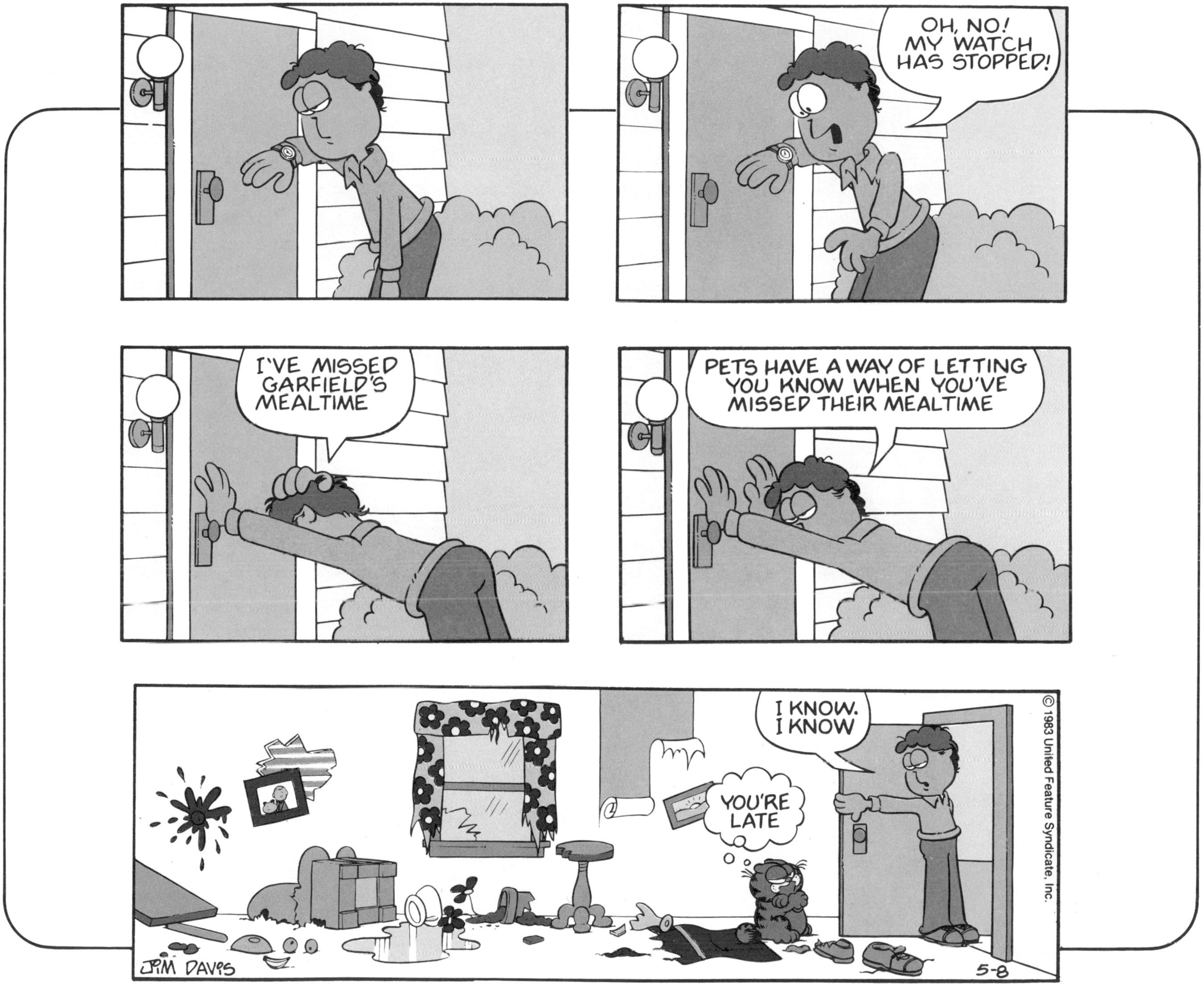
OH, NO! MY WATCH HAS STOPPED!
I'VE MISSED GARFIELD'S MEALTIME
PETS HAVE A WAY OF LETTING YOU KNOW WHEN YOU'VE MISSED THEIR MEALTIME
I KNOW. I KNOW
YOU'RE LATE
JIM DAVIS
5-8
© 1983 United Feature Syndicate, Inc.

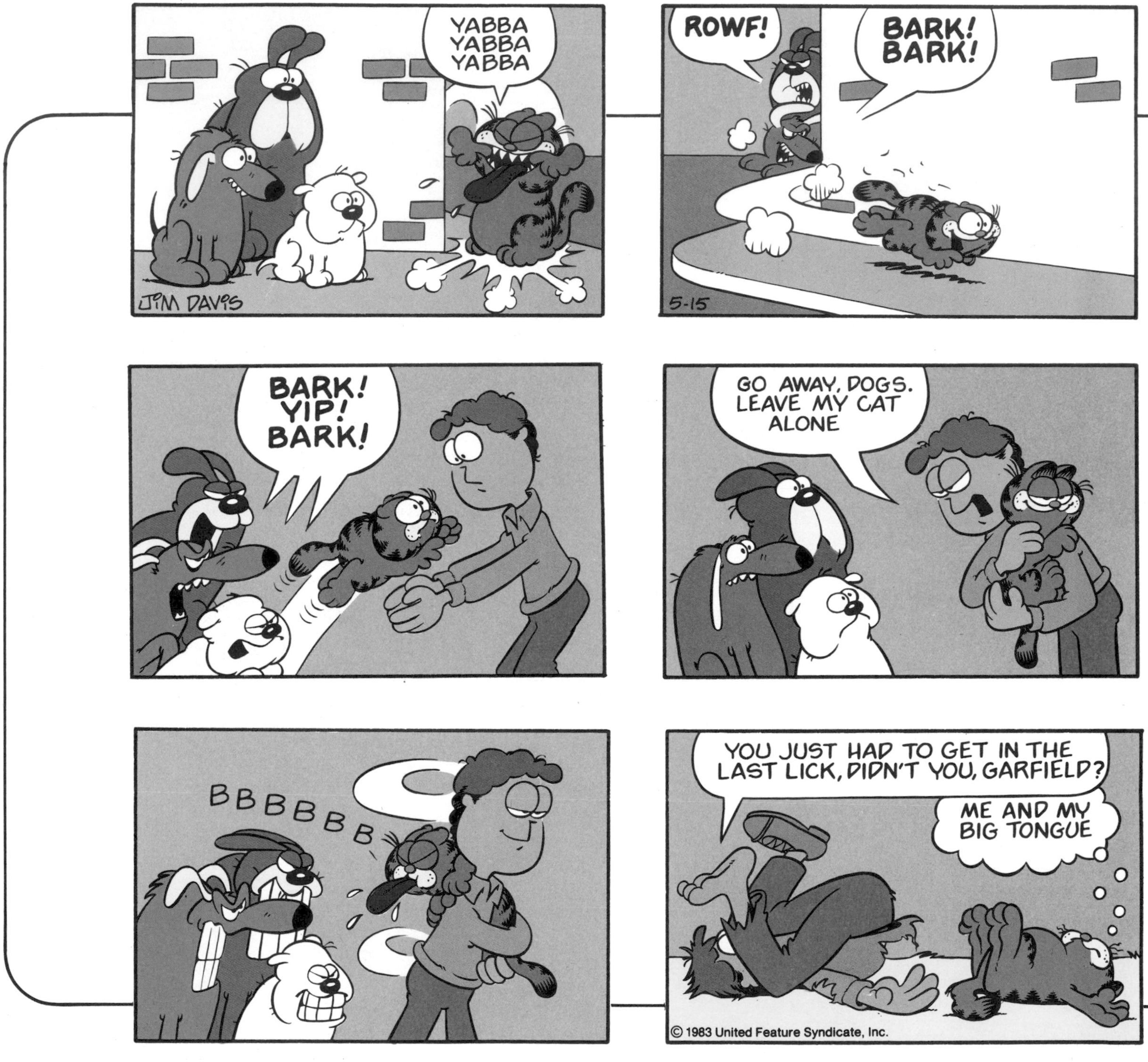
JIM DAVIS
YABBA YABBA YABBA
ROWF!
BARK! BARK!
5-15
BARK! YIP! BARK!
GO AWAY, DOGS. LEAVE MY CAT ALONE
BBBBBBB
YOU JUST HAD TO GET IN THE LAST LICK, DIDN'T YOU, GARFIELD?
ME AND MY BIG TONGUE
© 1983 United Feature Syndicate, Inc.

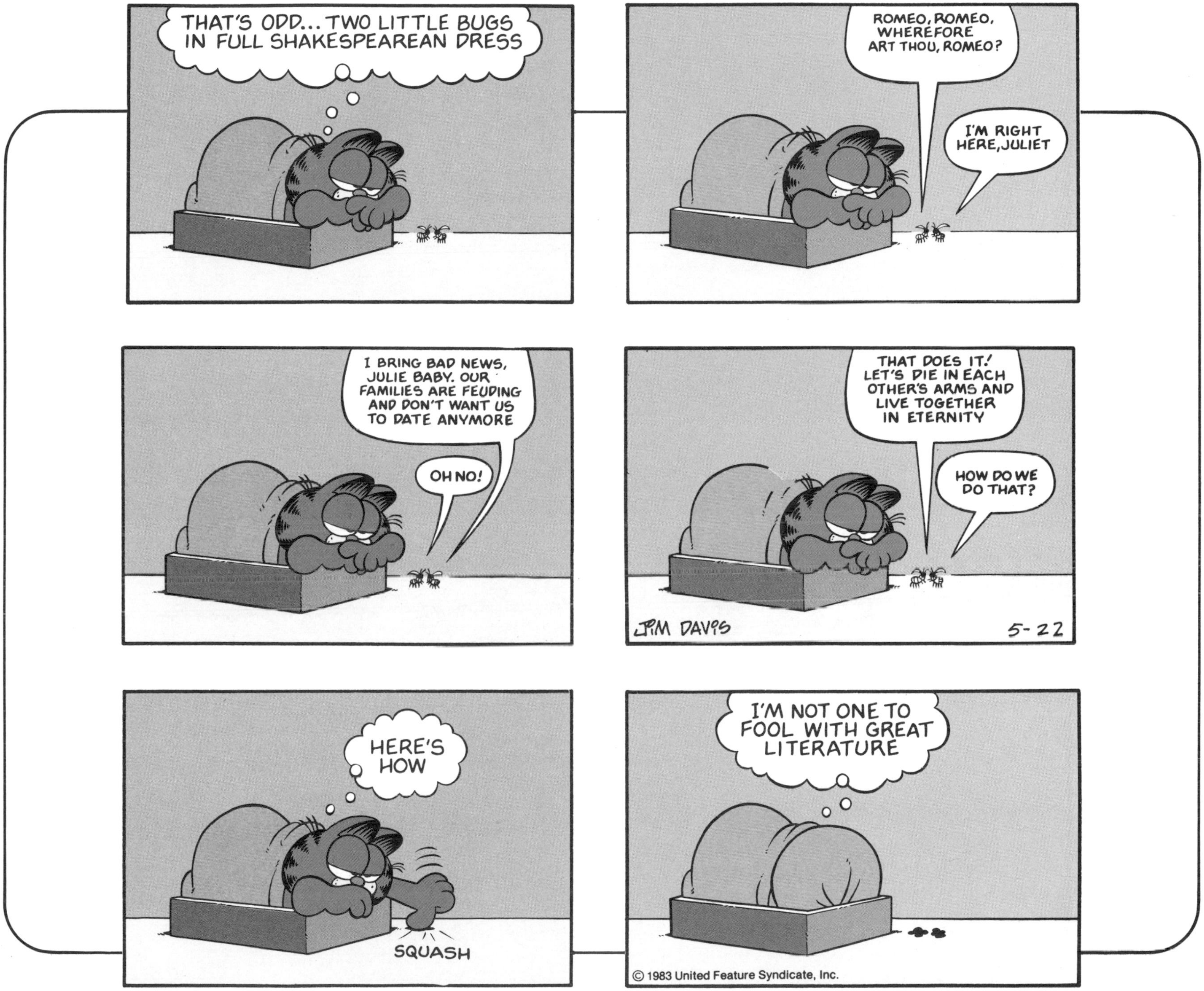
THAT'S ODD... TWO LITTLE BUGS IN FULL SHAKESPEAREAN DRESS
ROMEO, ROMEO, WHEREFORE ART THOU, ROMEO?
I'M RIGHT HERE, JULIET
I BRING BAD NEWS, JULIE BABY. OUR FAMILIES ARE FEUDING AND DON'T WANT US TO DATE ANYMORE
OH NO!
THAT DOES IT! LET'S DIE IN EACH OTHER'S ARMS AND LIVE TOGETHER IN ETERNITY
HOW DO WE DO THAT?
JIM DAVIS
5-22
HERE'S HOW
SQUASH
I'M NOT ONE TO FOOL WITH GREAT LITERATURE
© 1983 United Feature Syndicate, Inc.

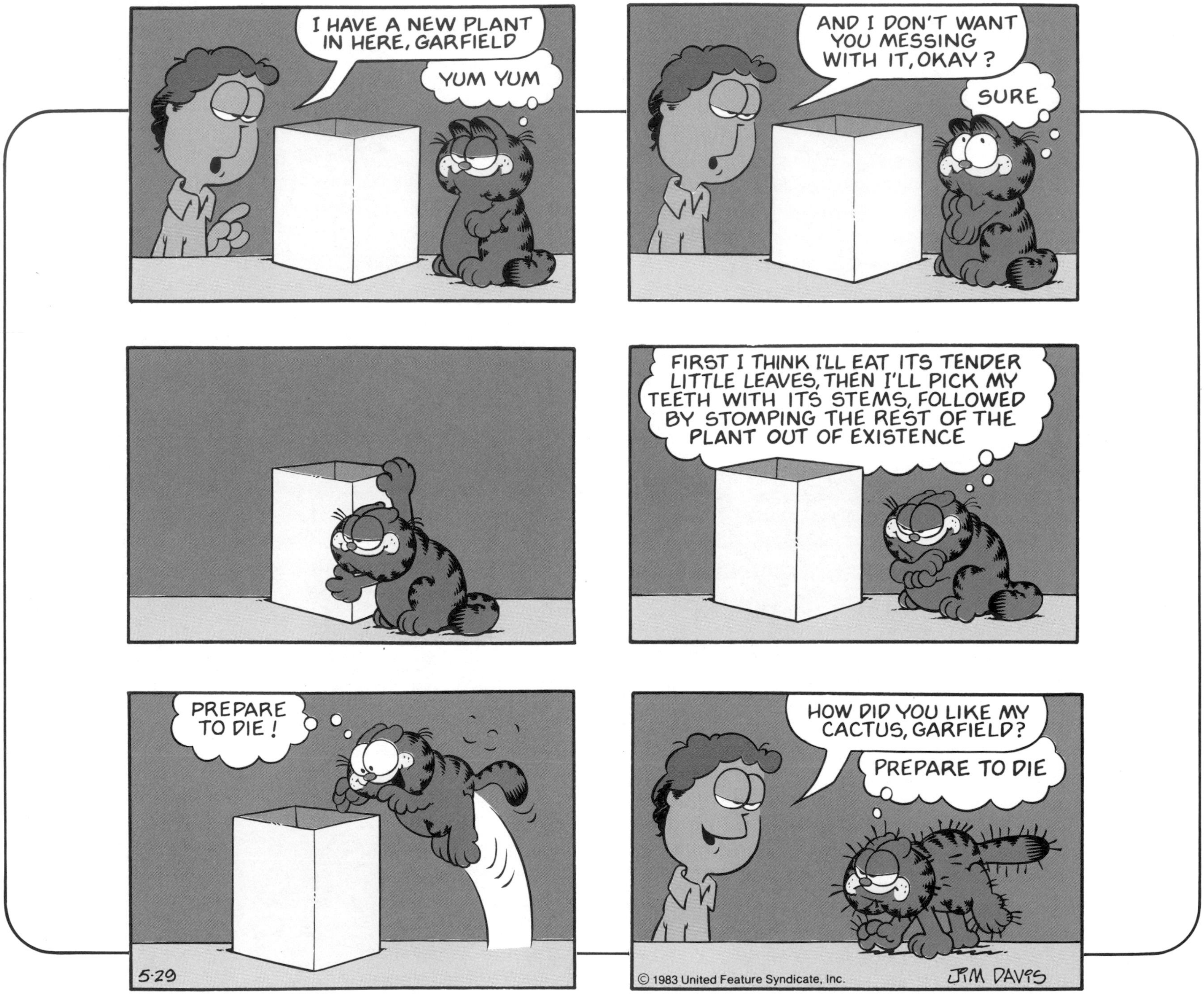
I HAVE A NEW PLANT IN HERE, GARFIELD
YUM YUM
AND I DON'T WANT YOU MESSING WITH IT, OKAY?
SURE
FIRST I THINK I'LL EAT ITS TENDER LITTLE LEAVES, THEN I'LL PICK MY TEETH WITH ITS STEMS, FOLLOWED BY STOMPING THE REST OF THE PLANT OUT OF EXISTENCE
PREPARE TO DIE!
HOW DID YOU LIKE MY CACTUS, GARFIELD?
PREPARE TO DIE
5·29
© 1983 United Feature Syndicate, Inc.
JIM DAVIS

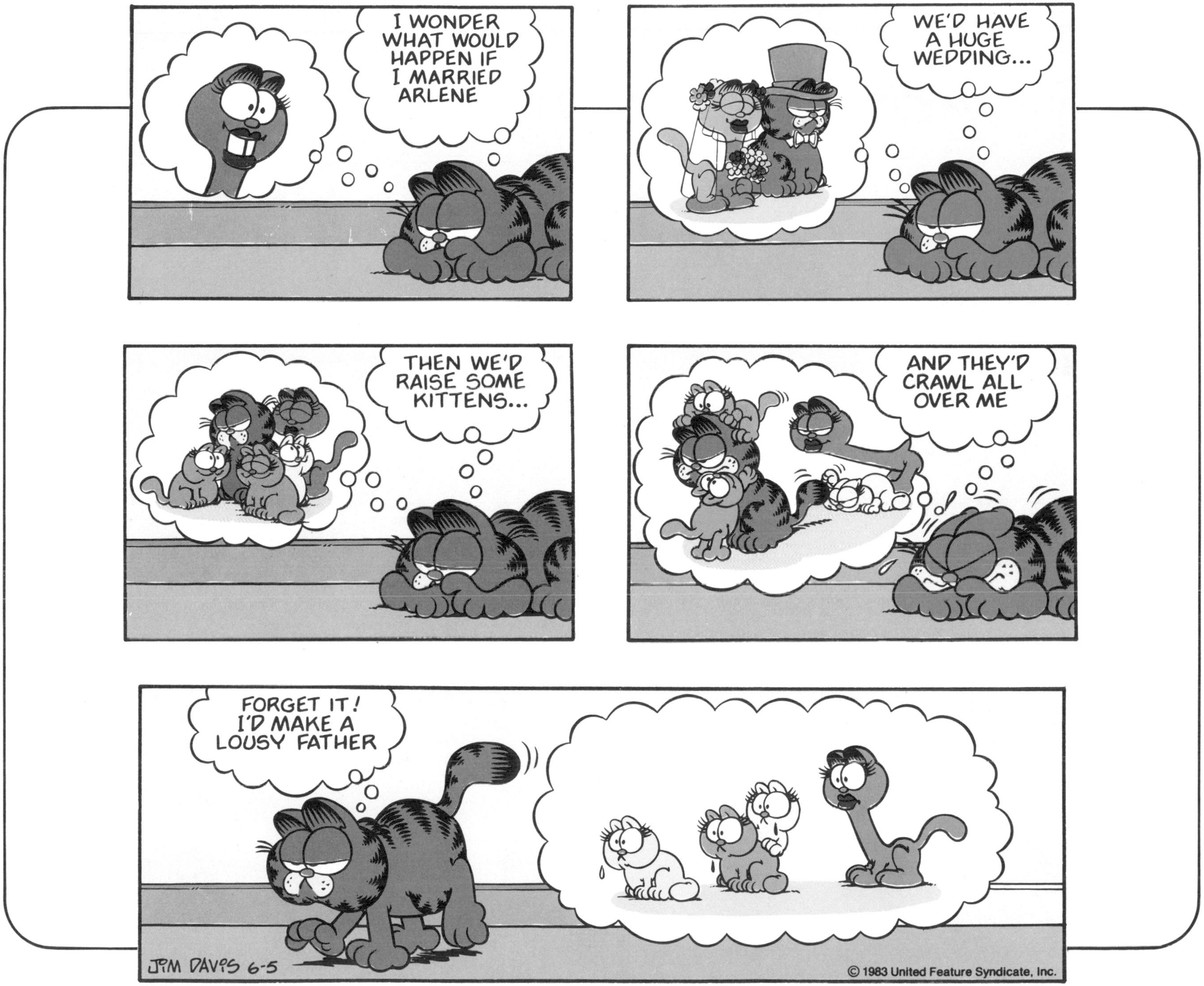
I WONDER WHAT WOULD HAPPEN IF I MARRIED ARLENE
WE'D HAVE A HUGE WEDDING...
THEN WE'D RAISE SOME KITTENS...
AND THEY'D CRAWL ALL OVER ME
FORGET IT! I'D MAKE A LOUSY FATHER
JIM DAVIS 6-5
© 1983 United Feature Syndicate, Inc.

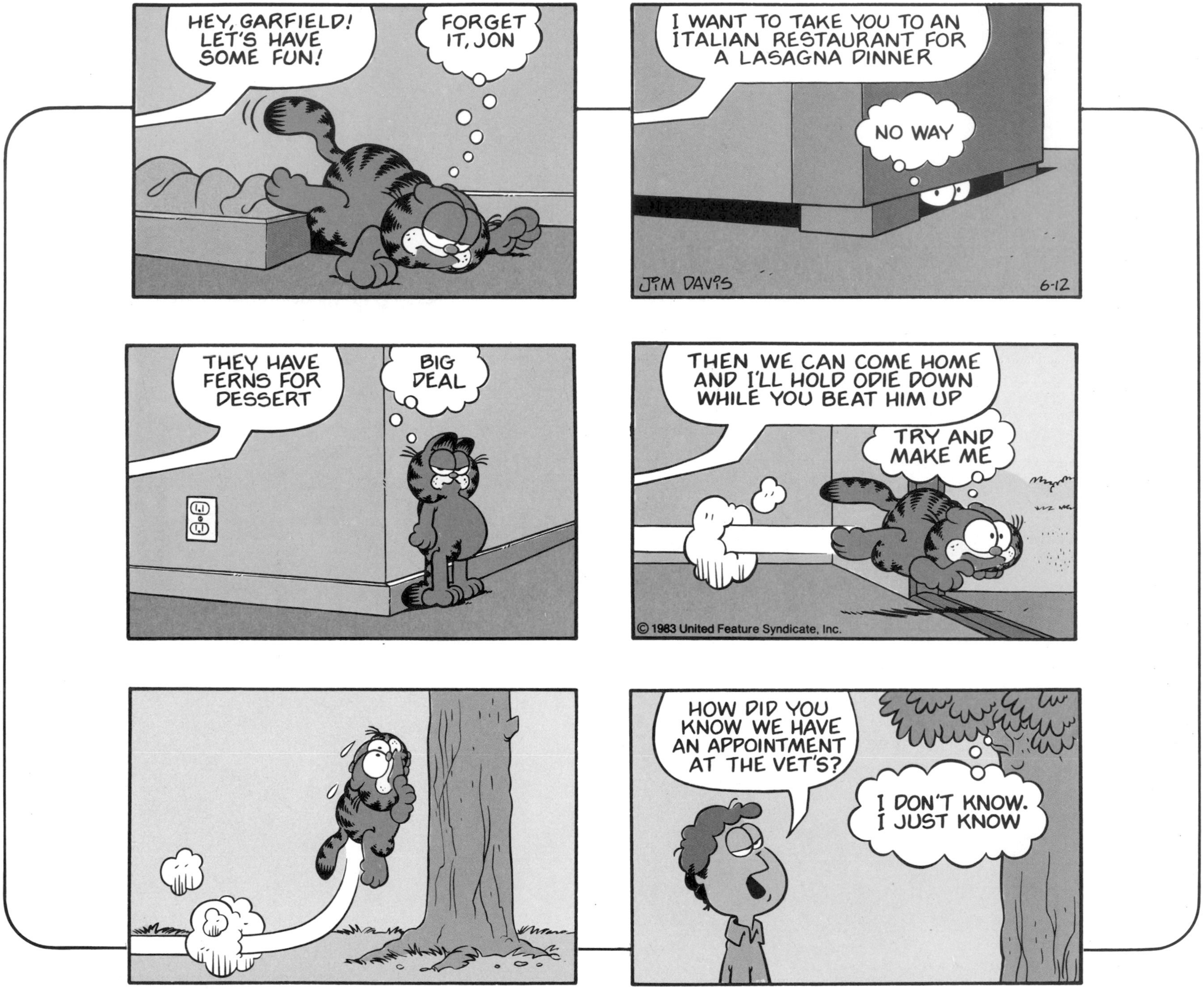
HEY, GARFIELD! LET'S HAVE SOME FUN!
FORGET IT, JON
I WANT TO TAKE YOU TO AN ITALIAN RESTAURANT FOR A LASAGNA DINNER
NO WAY
JIM DAVIS
6-12
THEY HAVE FERNS FOR DESSERT
BIG DEAL
THEN WE CAN COME HOME AND I'LL HOLD ODIE DOWN WHILE YOU BEAT HIM UP
TRY AND MAKE ME
© 1983 United Feature Syndicate, Inc.
HOW DID YOU KNOW WE HAVE AN APPOINTMENT AT THE VET'S?
I DON'T KNOW. I JUST KNOW

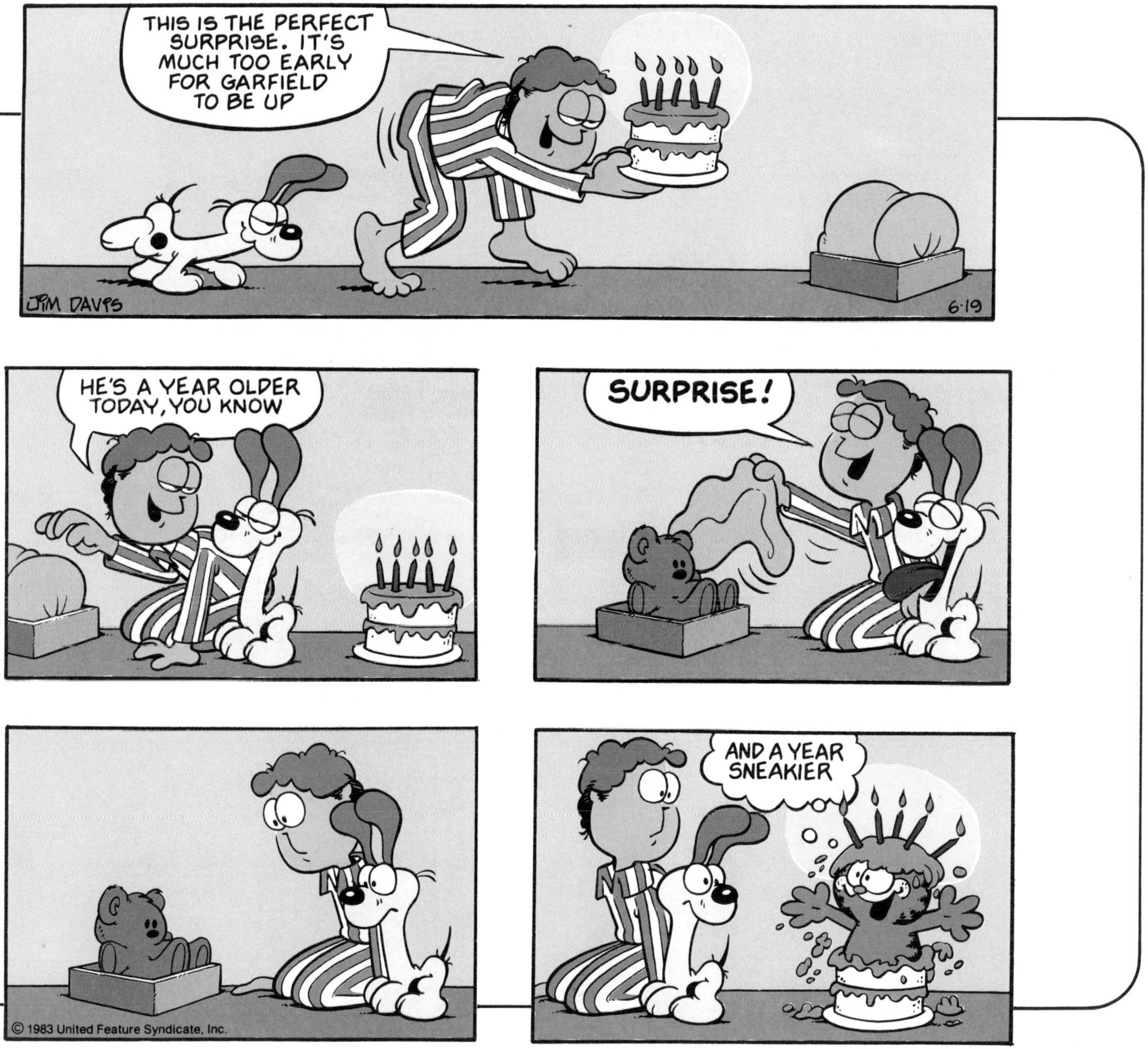
THIS IS THE PERFECT SURPRISE. IT'S MUCH TOO EARLY FOR GARFIELD TO BE UP
JIM DAVIS
6·19
HE'S A YEAR OLDER TODAY, YOU KNOW
SURPRISE!
© 1983 United Feature Syndicate, Inc.
AND A YEAR SNEAKIER

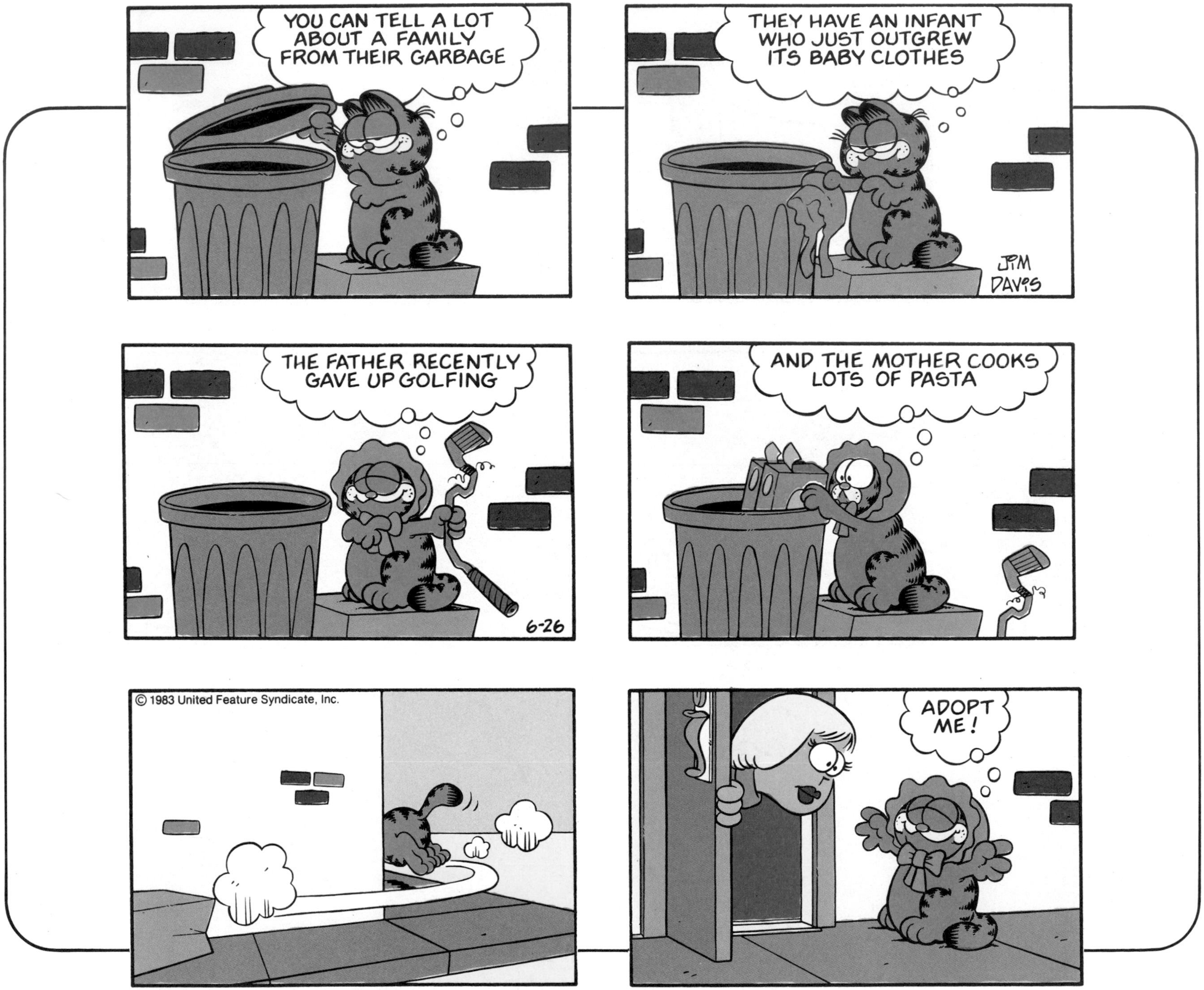
YOU CAN TELL A LOT ABOUT A FAMILY FROM THEIR GARBAGE
THEY HAVE AN INFANT WHO JUST OUTGREW ITS BABY CLOTHES
JIM DAVIS
THE FATHER RECENTLY GAVE UP GOLFING
6-26
AND THE MOTHER COOKS LOTS OF PASTA
© 1983 United Feature Syndicate, Inc.
ADOPT ME!

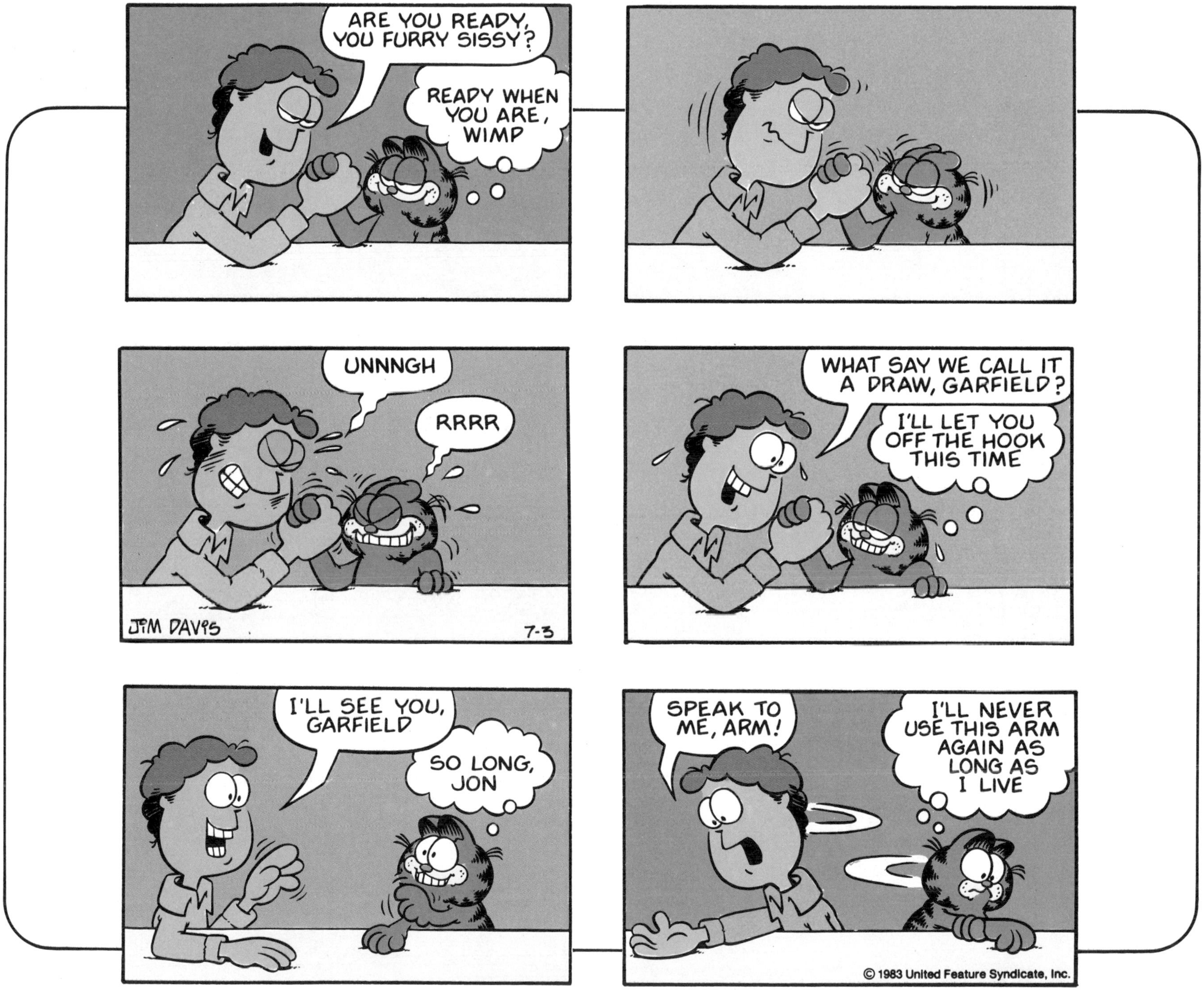
ARE YOU READY, YOU FURRY SISSY?
READY WHEN YOU ARE, WIMP
UNNNGH
RRRR
JIM DAVIS
7-3
WHAT SAY WE CALL IT A DRAW, GARFIELD?
I'LL LET YOU OFF THE HOOK THIS TIME
I'LL SEE YOU, GARFIELD
SO LONG, JON
SPEAK TO ME, ARM!
I'LL NEVER USE THIS ARM AGAIN AS LONG AS I LIVE
© 1983 United Feature Syndicate, Inc.

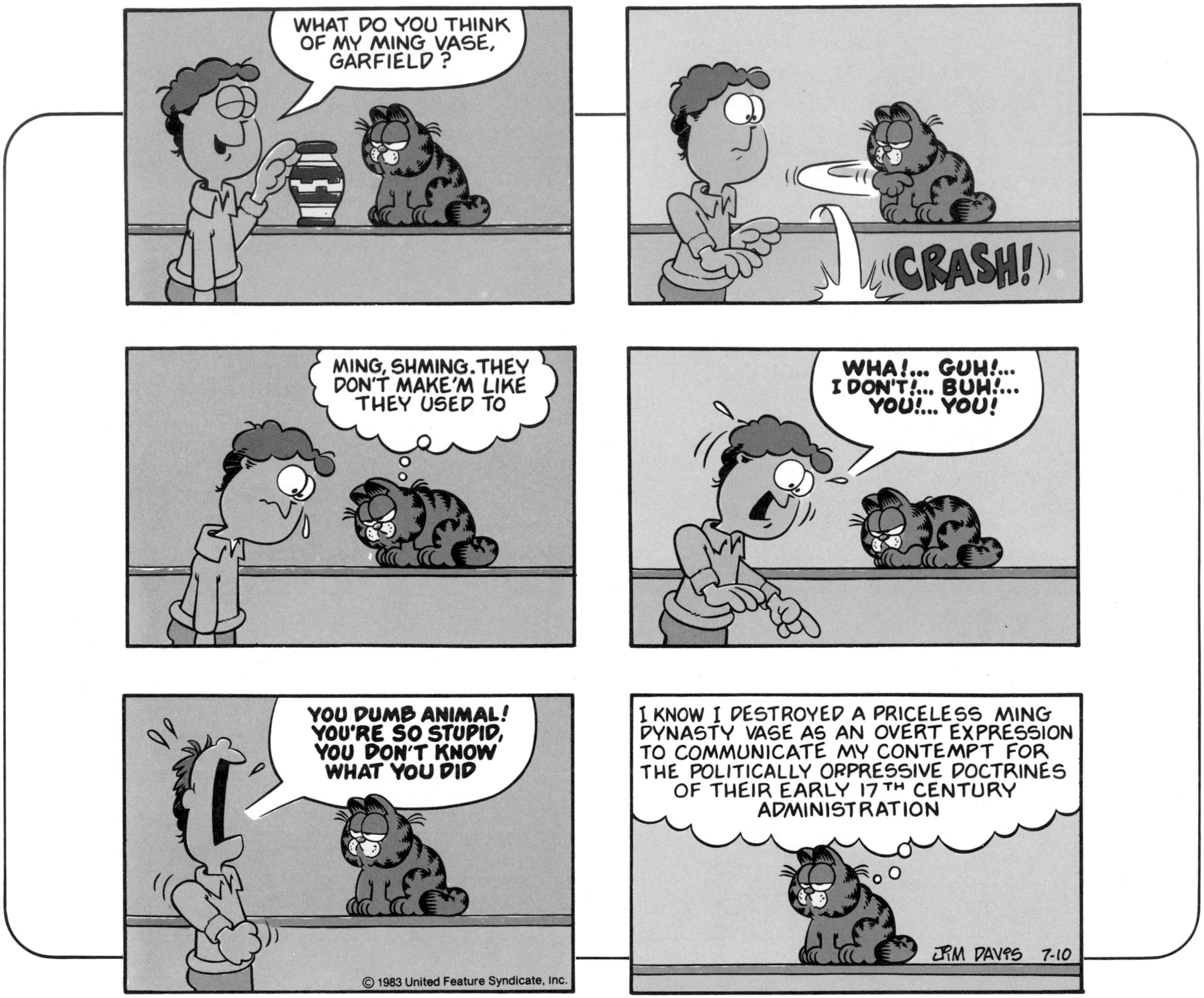
WHAT DO YOU THINK OF MY MING VASE, GARFIELD?
CRASH!
MING, SHMING. THEY DON'T MAKE'M LIKE THEY USED TO
WHA!... GUH!... I DON'T!... BUH!... YOU!... YOU!
YOU DUMB ANIMAL! YOU'RE SO STUPID, YOU DON'T KNOW WHAT YOU DID
© 1983 United Feature Syndicate, Inc.
I KNOW I DESTROYED A PRICELESS MING DYNASTY VASE AS AN OVERT EXPRESSION TO COMMUNICATE MY CONTEMPT FOR THE POLITICALLY ORPRESSIVE DOCTRINES OF THEIR EARLY 17TH CENTURY ADMINISTRATION
JIM DAVIS 7-10

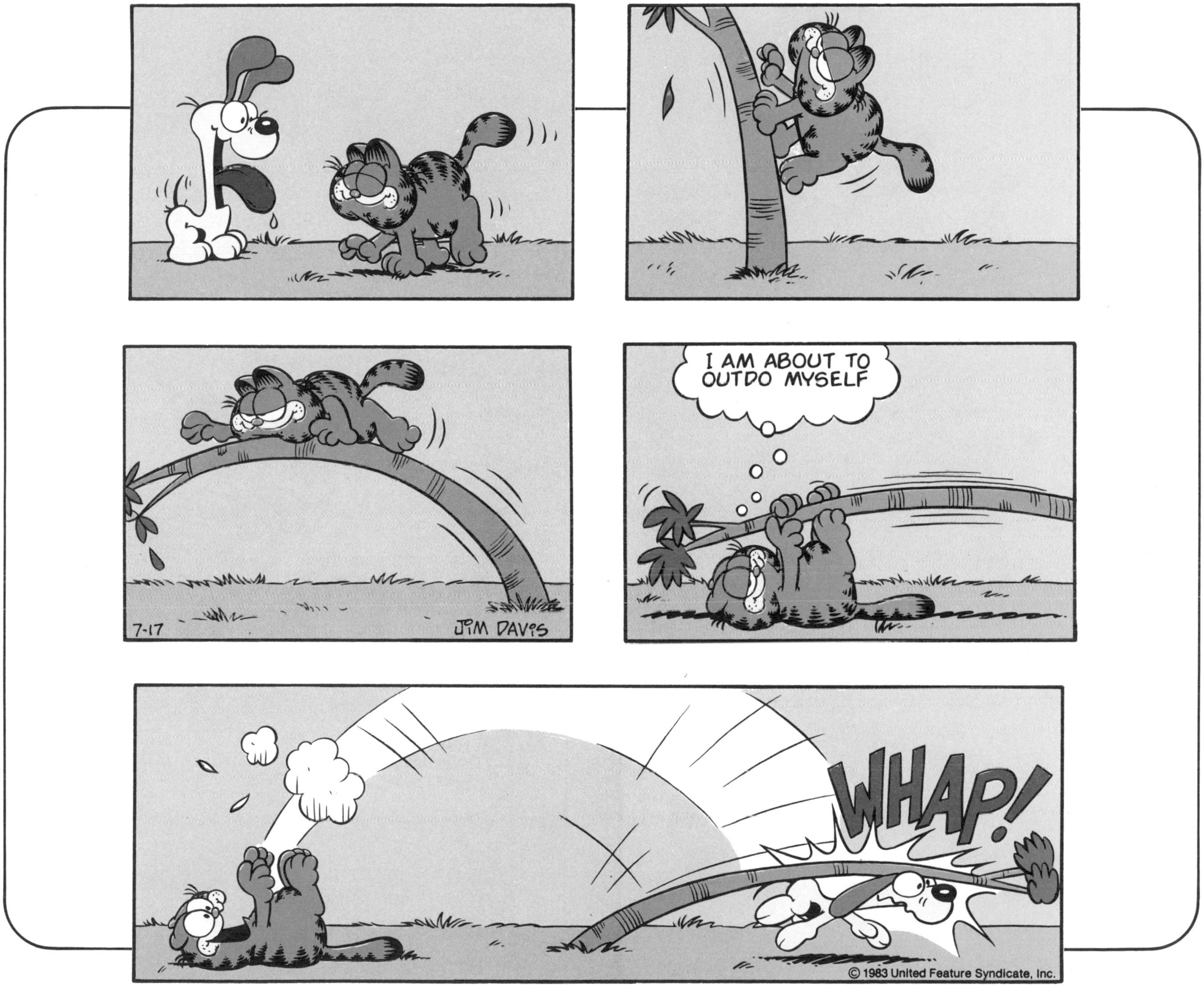
I AM ABOUT TO OUTDO MYSELF
WHAP!
7-17
JIM DAVIS
© 1983 United Feature Syndicate, Inc.

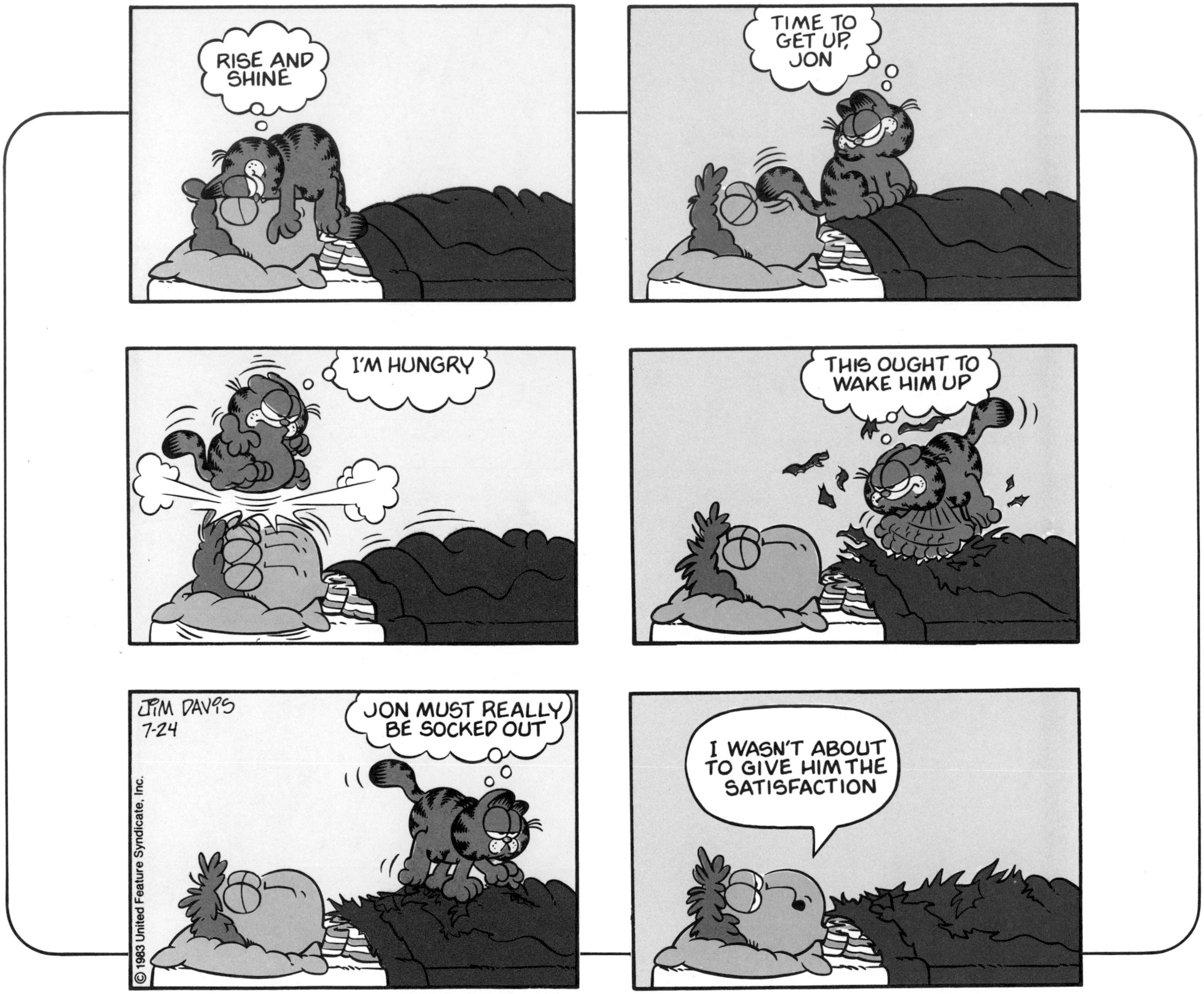
RISE AND SHINE
TIME TO GET UP, JON
I'M HUNGRY
THIS OUGHT TO WAKE HIM UP
JIM DAVIS 7-24
JON MUST REALLY BE SOCKED OUT
I WASN'T ABOUT TO GIVE HIM THE SATISFACTION
© 1983 United Feature Syndicate, Inc.

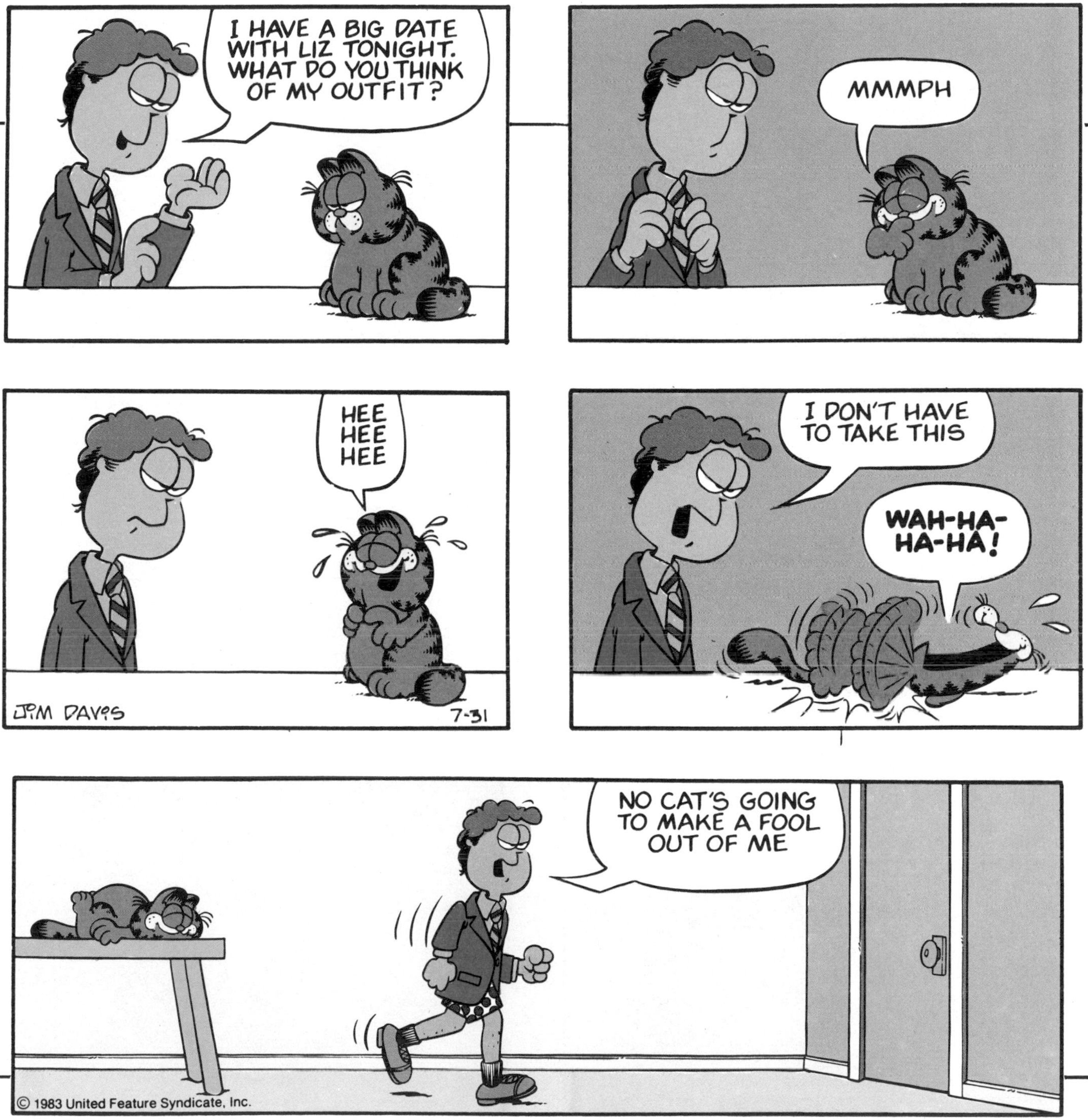
I HAVE A BIG DATE WITH LIZ TONIGHT. WHAT DO YOU THINK OF MY OUTFIT?
MMMPH
HEE HEE HEE
JIM DAVIS
7-31
I DON'T HAVE TO TAKE THIS
WAH-HA-HA-HA!
NO CAT'S GOING TO MAKE A FOOL OUT OF ME
© 1983 United Feature Syndicate, Inc.

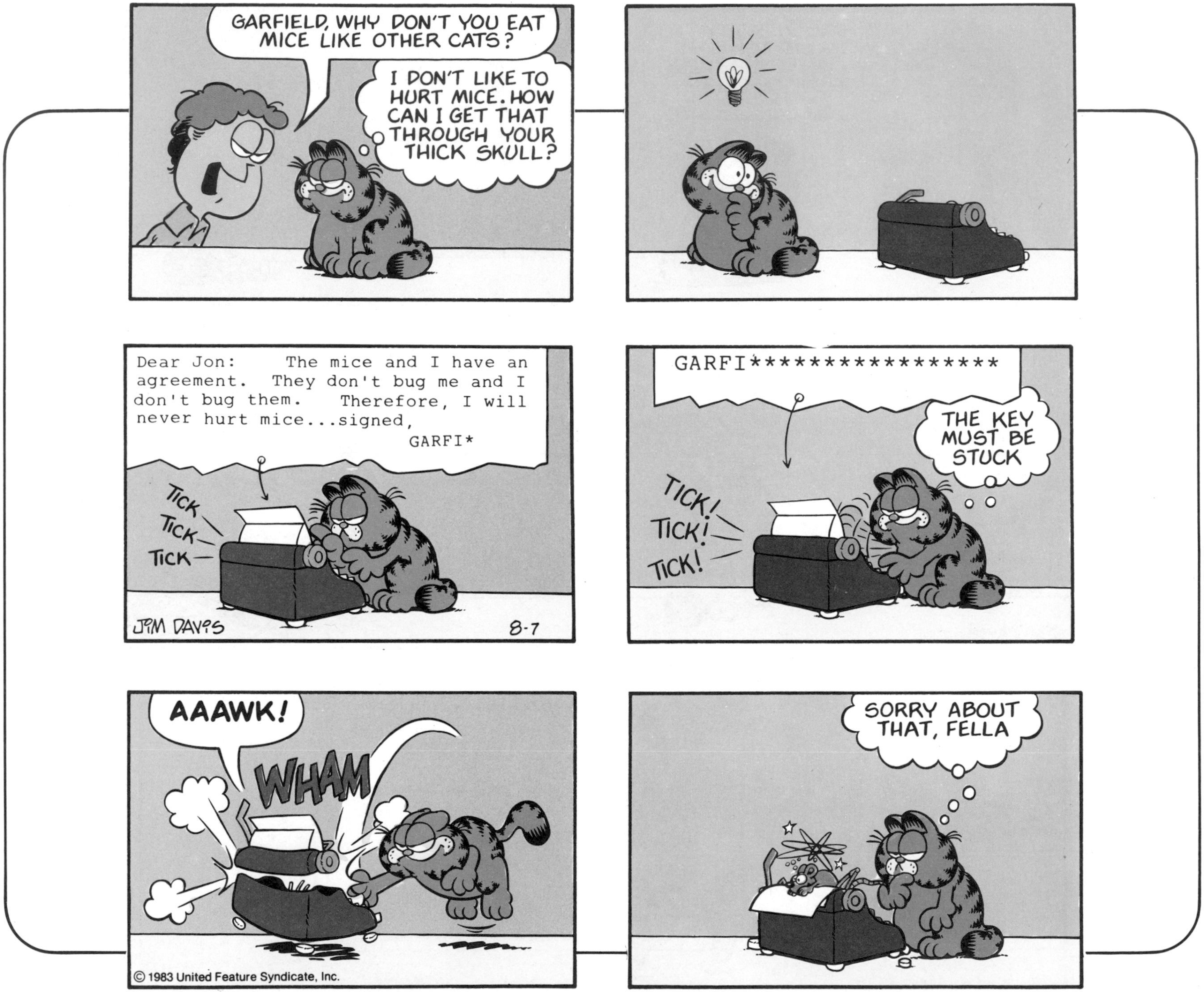
GARFIELD, WHY DON'T YOU EAT MICE LIKE OTHER CATS?
I DON'T LIKE TO HURT MICE. HOW CAN I GET THAT THROUGH YOUR THICK SKULL?
Dear Jon: The mice and I have an agreement. They don't bug me and I don't bug them. Therefore, I will never hurt mice...signed, GARFI*
TICK TICK TICK
JIM DAVIS
8-7
GARFI******************
TICK! TICK! TICK!
THE KEY MUST BE STUCK
AAAWK!
WHAM
SORRY ABOUT THAT, FELLA

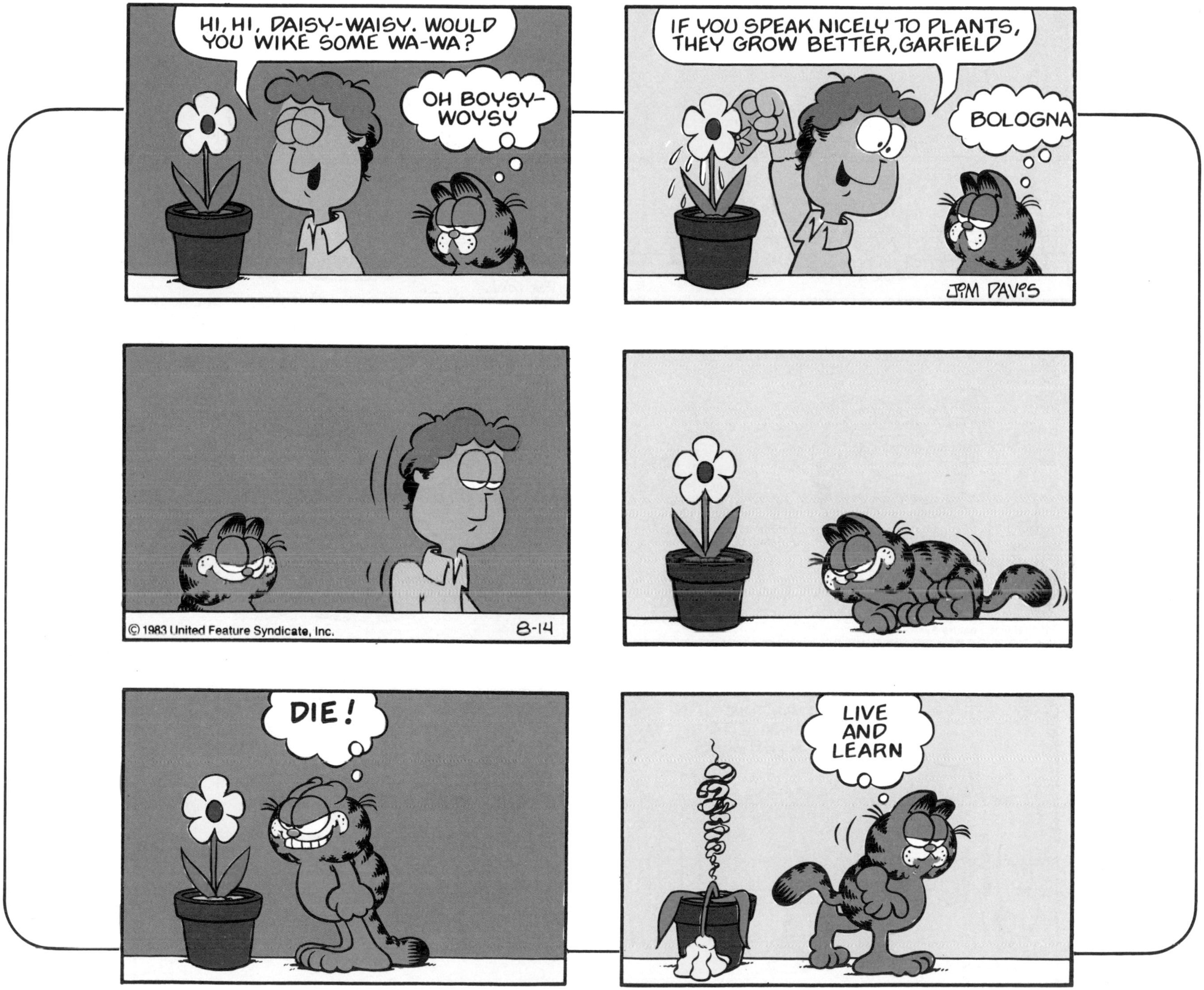
HI, HI, DAISY-WAISY. WOULD YOU WIKE SOME WA-WA?
OH BOYSY-WOYSY
IF YOU SPEAK NICELY TO PLANTS, THEY GROW BETTER, GARFIELD
BOLOGNA
JIM DAVIS
8-14
DIE!
LIVE AND LEARN

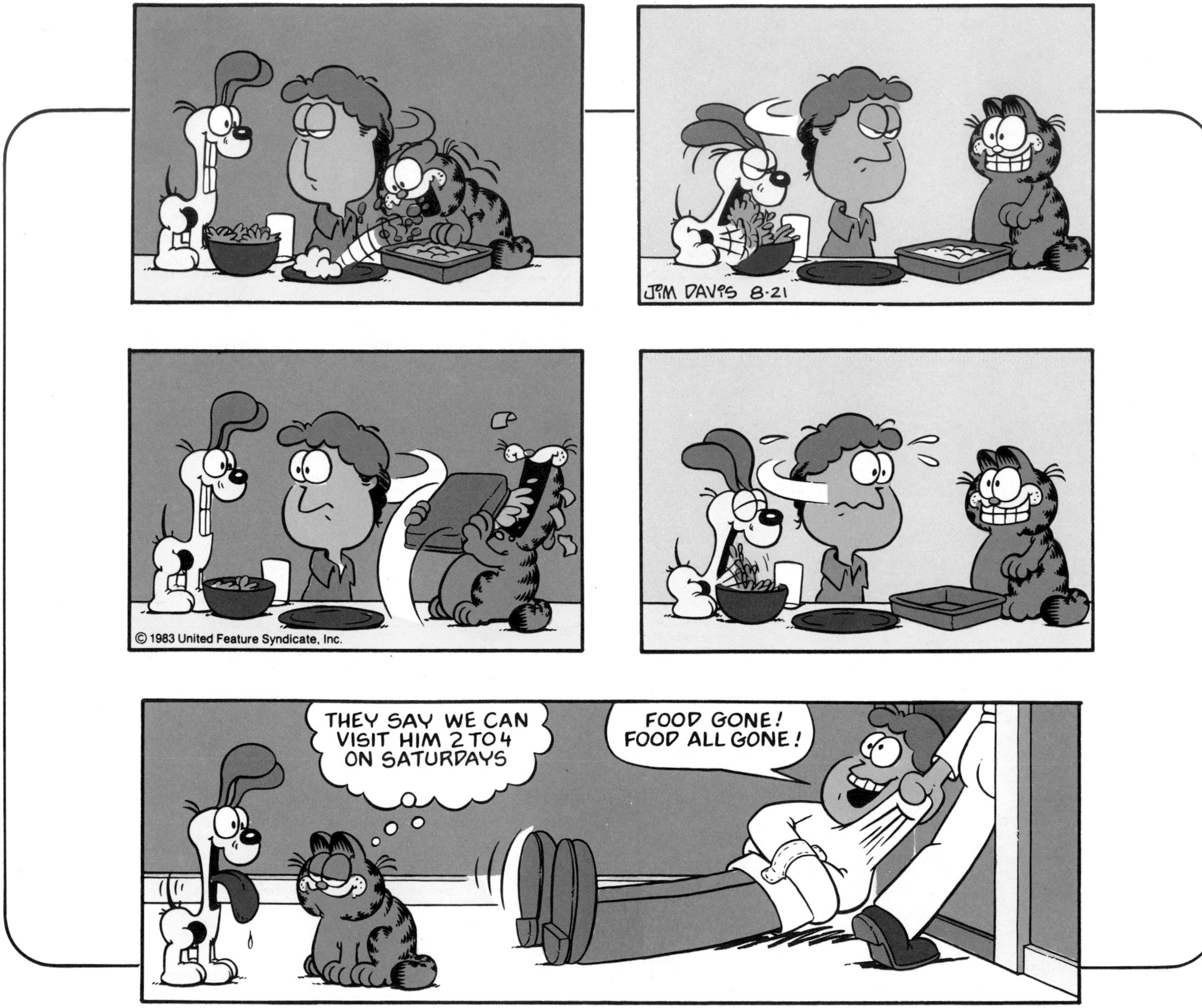
JIM DAVIS 8-21
© 1983 United Feature Syndicate, Inc.
THEY SAY WE CAN VISIT HIM 2 TO 4 ON SATURDAYS
FOOD GONE! FOOD ALL GONE!

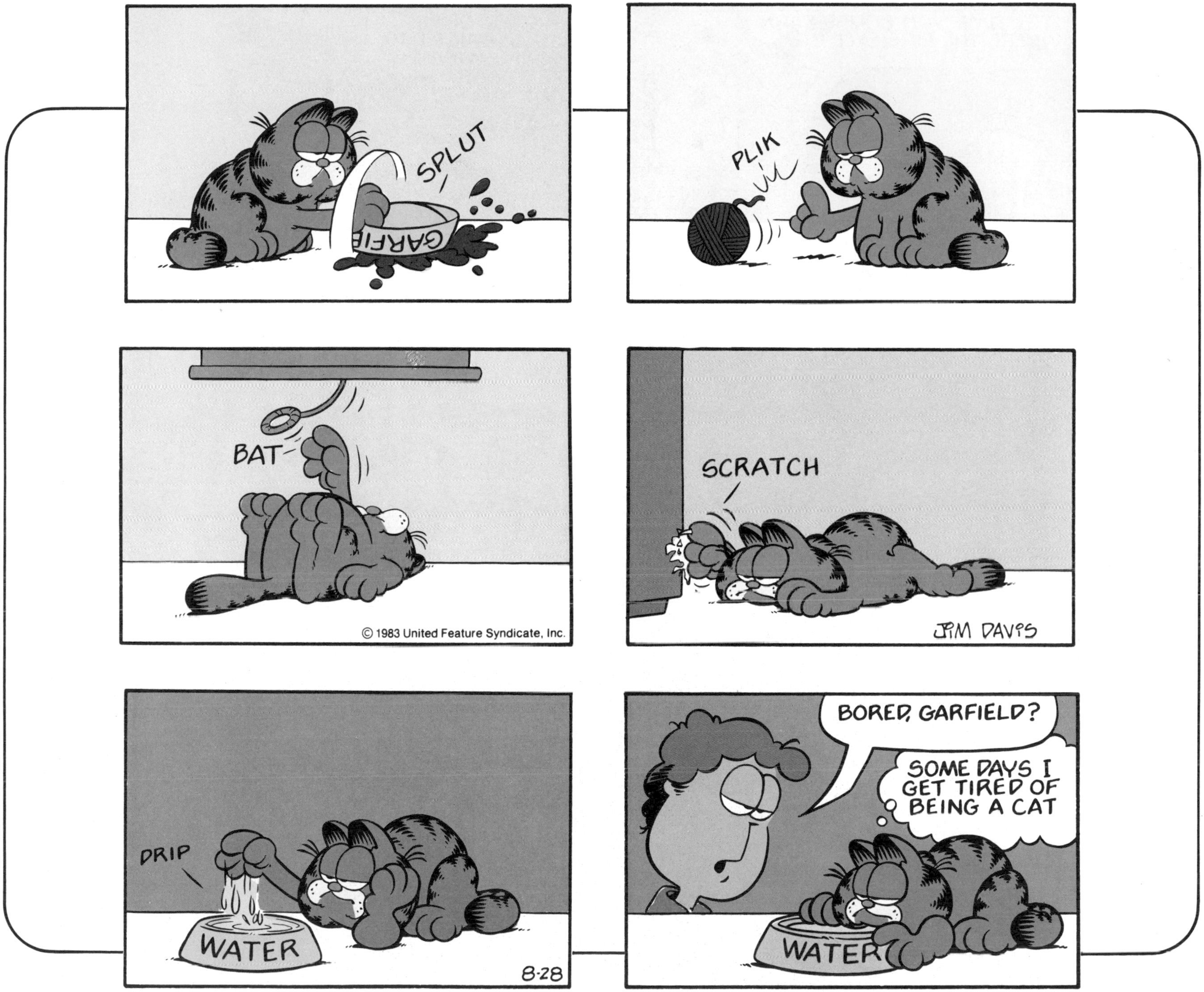
SPLUT
GARFIELD
PLIK
BAT
SCRATCH
© 1983 United Feature Syndicate, Inc.
JIM DAVIS
DRIP
WATER
8-28
BORED, GARFIELD?
SOME DAYS I GET TIRED OF BEING A CAT
WATER

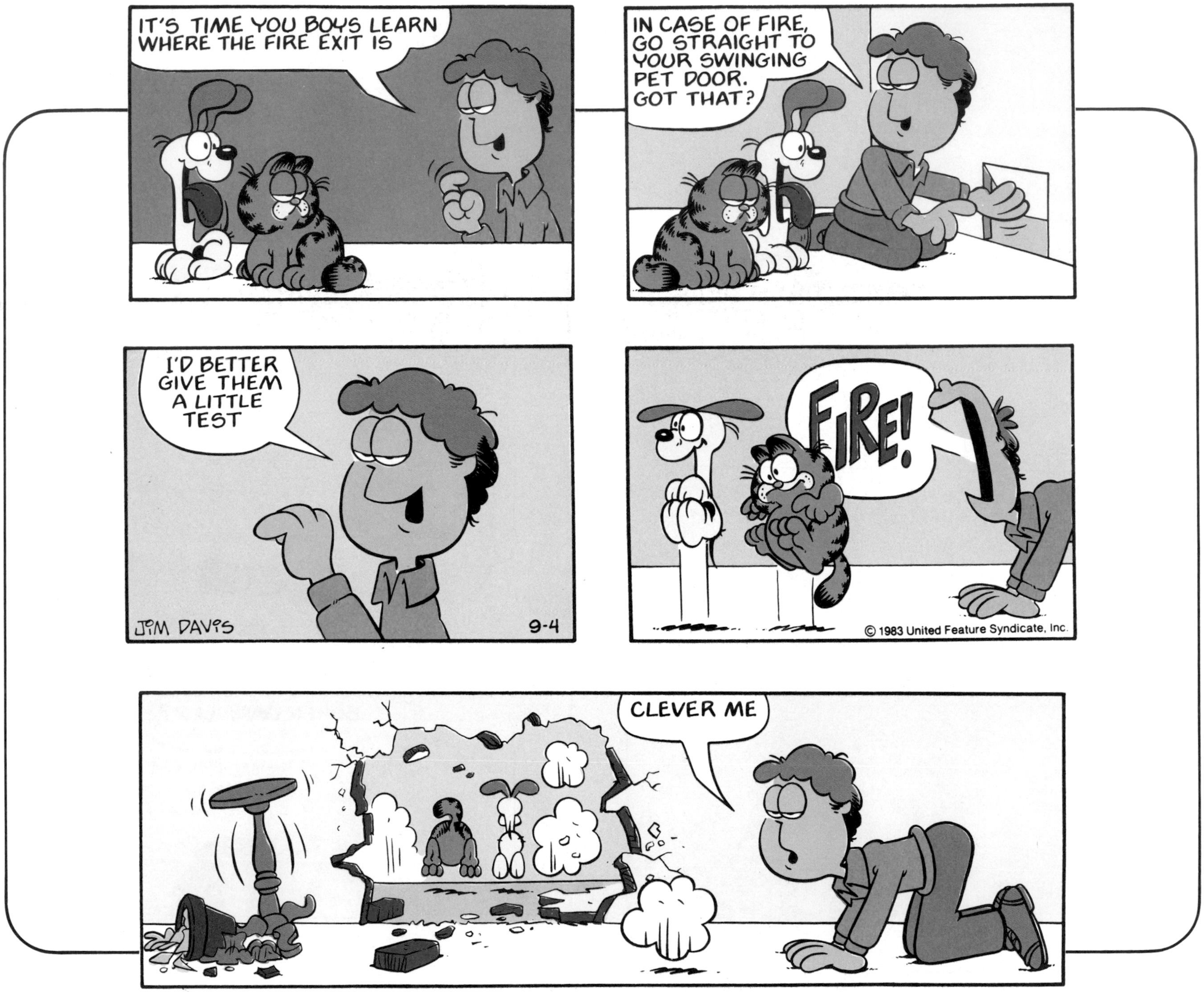
IT'S TIME YOU BOYS LEARN WHERE THE FIRE EXIT IS
IN CASE OF FIRE, GO STRAIGHT TO YOUR SWINGING PET DOOR. GOT THAT?
I'D BETTER GIVE THEM A LITTLE TEST
JIM DAVIS
9-4
FIRE!
© 1983 United Feature Syndicate, Inc.
CLEVER ME

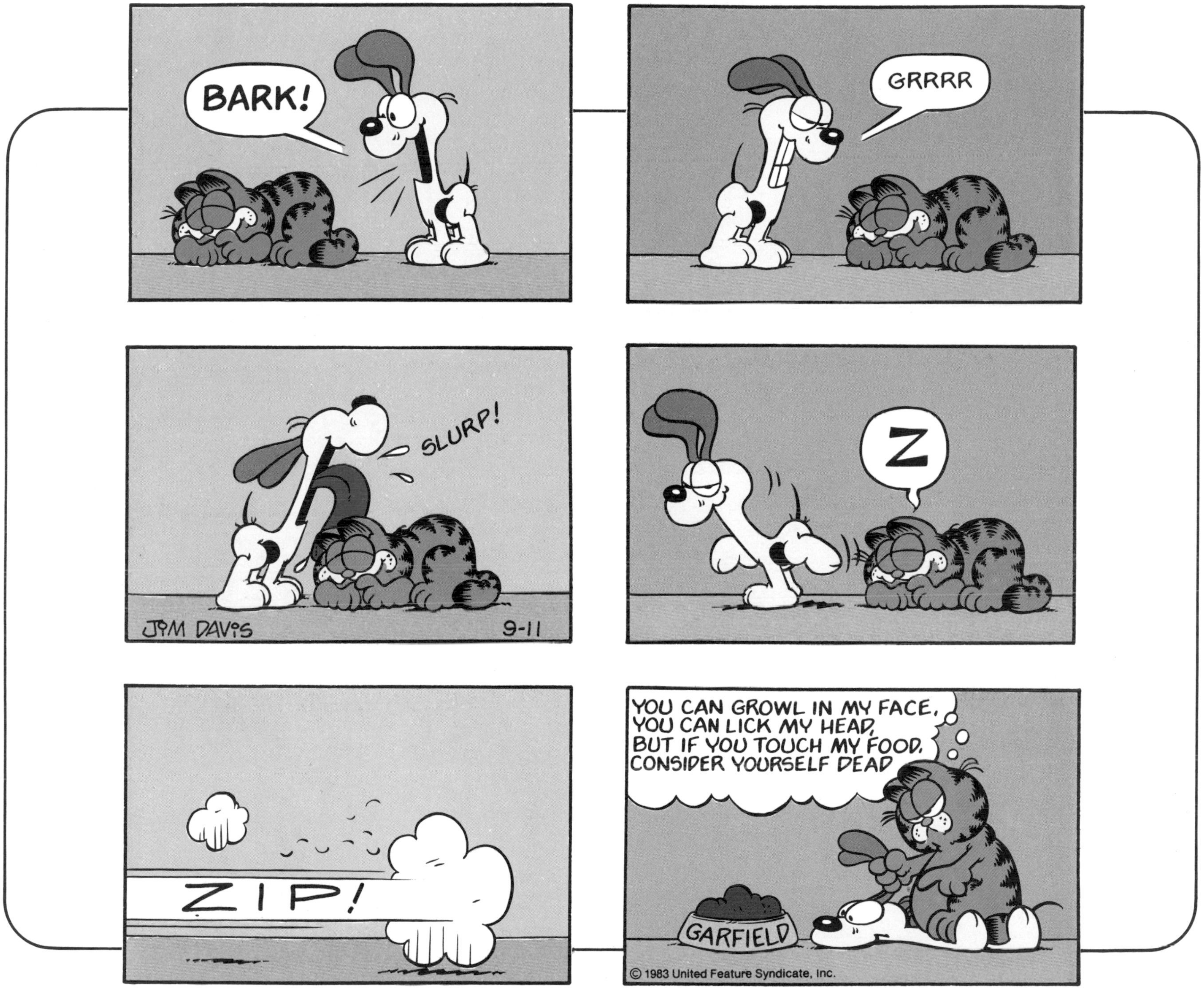
BARK!
GRRRR
SLURP!
JIM DAVIS
9-11
Z
ZIP!
YOU CAN GROWL IN MY FACE, YOU CAN LICK MY HEAD, BUT IF YOU TOUCH MY FOOD, CONSIDER YOURSELF DEAD
GARFIELD
© 1983 United Feature Syndicate, Inc.

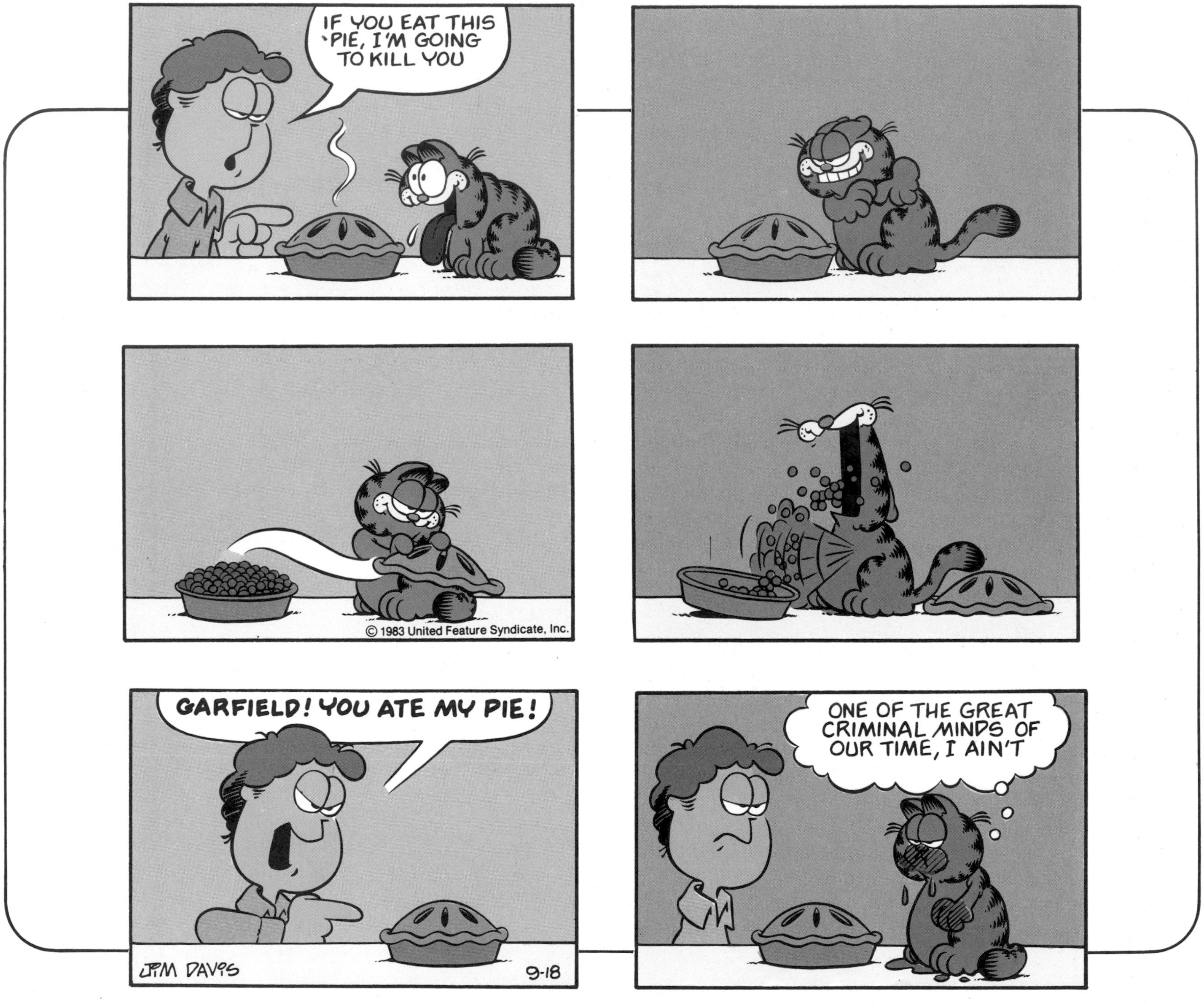
IF YOU EAT THIS PIE, I'M GOING TO KILL YOU
© 1983 United Feature Syndicate, Inc.
GARFIELD! YOU ATE MY PIE!
JIM DAVIS
9-18
ONE OF THE GREAT CRIMINAL MINDS OF OUR TIME, I AIN'T

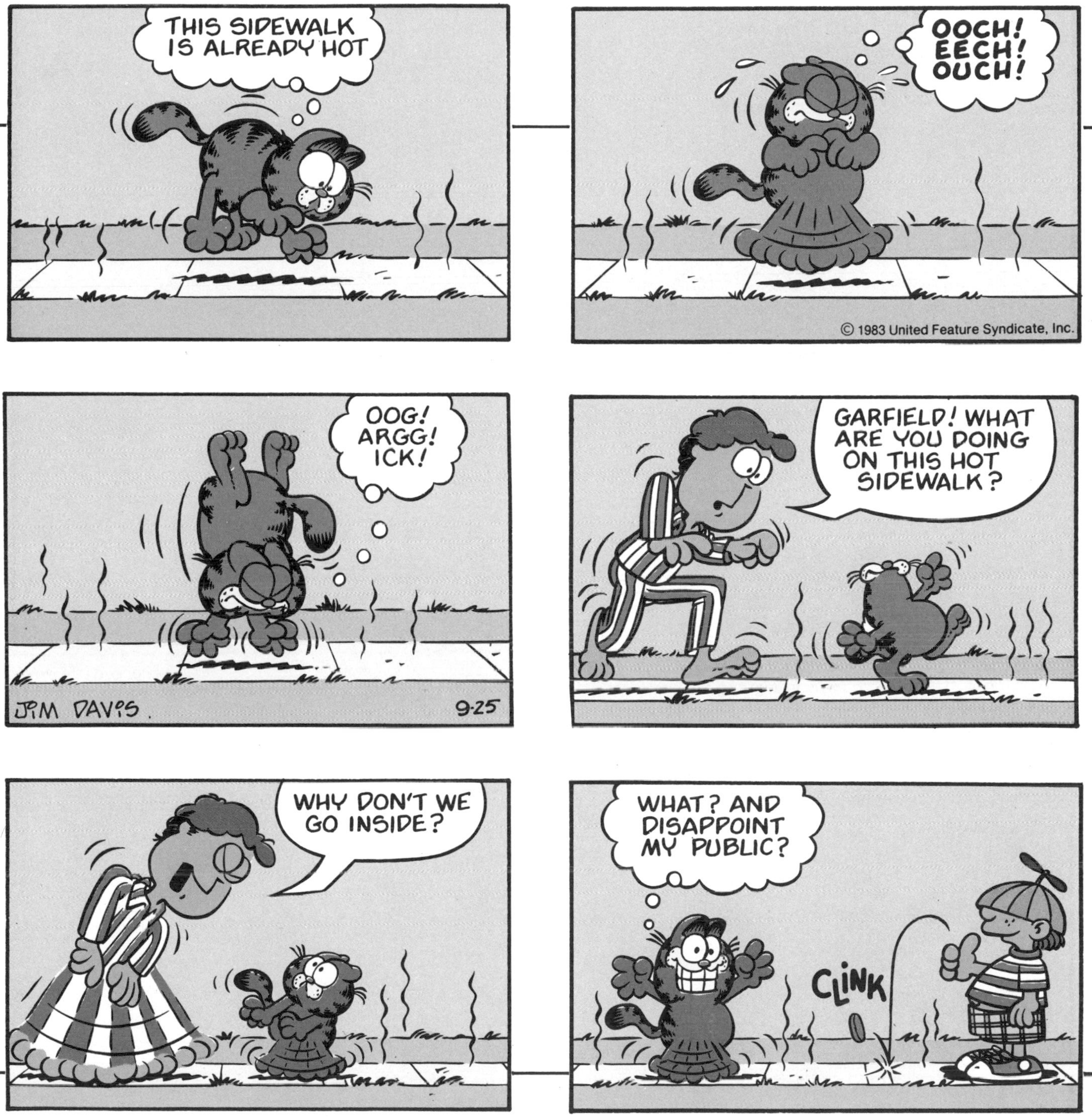
THIS SIDEWALK IS ALREADY HOT
OOCH! EECH! OUCH!
© 1983 United Feature Syndicate, Inc.
OOG! ARGG! ICK!
JIM DAVIS
9-25
GARFIELD! WHAT ARE YOU DOING ON THIS HOT SIDEWALK?
WHY DON'T WE GO INSIDE?
WHAT? AND DISAPPOINT MY PUBLIC?
CLINK

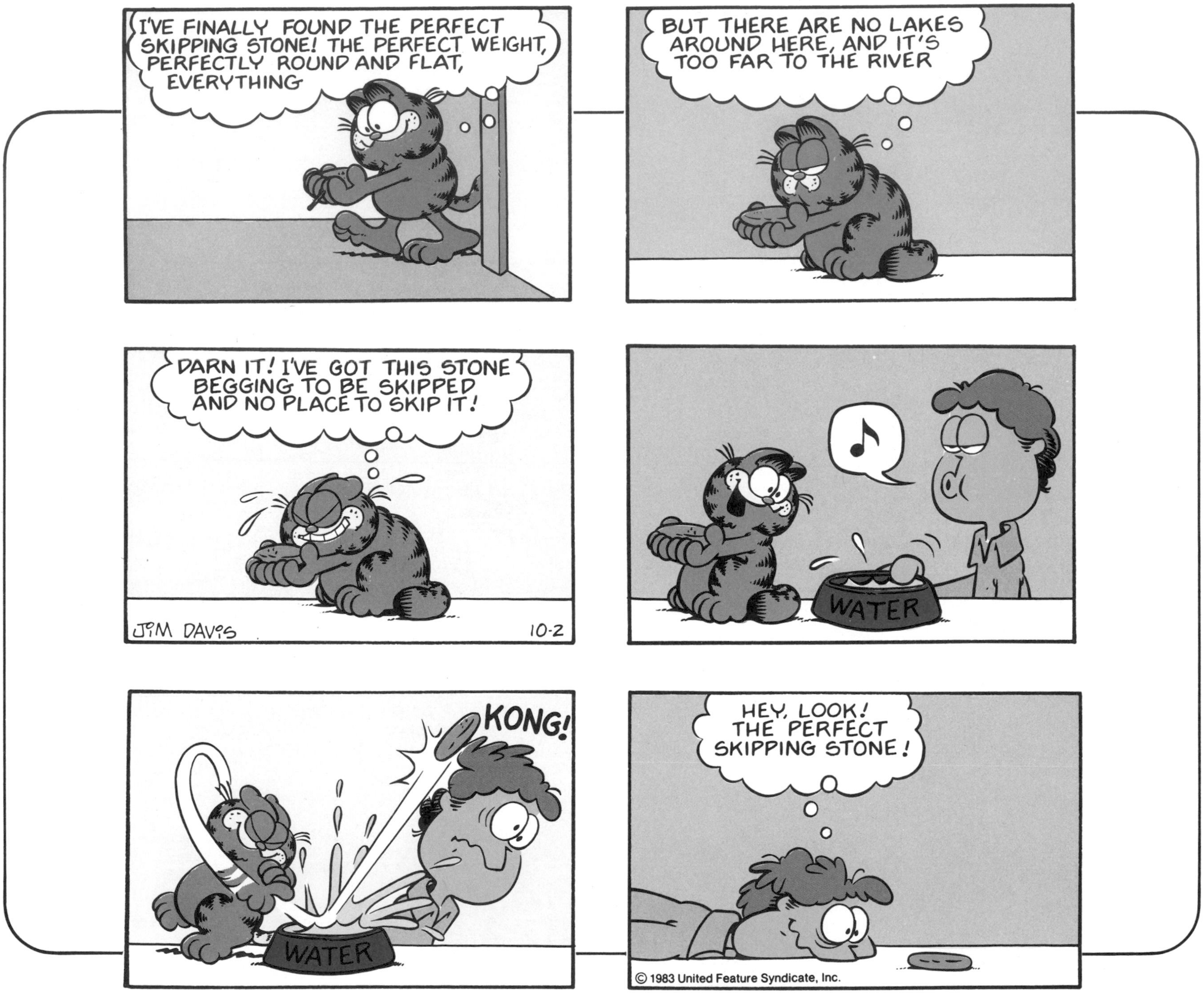
I'VE FINALLY FOUND THE PERFECT SKIPPING STONE! THE PERFECT WEIGHT, PERFECTLY ROUND AND FLAT, EVERYTHING
BUT THERE ARE NO LAKES AROUND HERE, AND IT'S TOO FAR TO THE RIVER
DARN IT! I'VE GOT THIS STONE BEGGING TO BE SKIPPED AND NO PLACE TO SKIP IT!
JIM DAVIS
10-2
♪
WATER
KONG!
WATER
HEY, LOOK! THE PERFECT SKIPPING STONE!
© 1983 United Feature Syndicate, Inc.

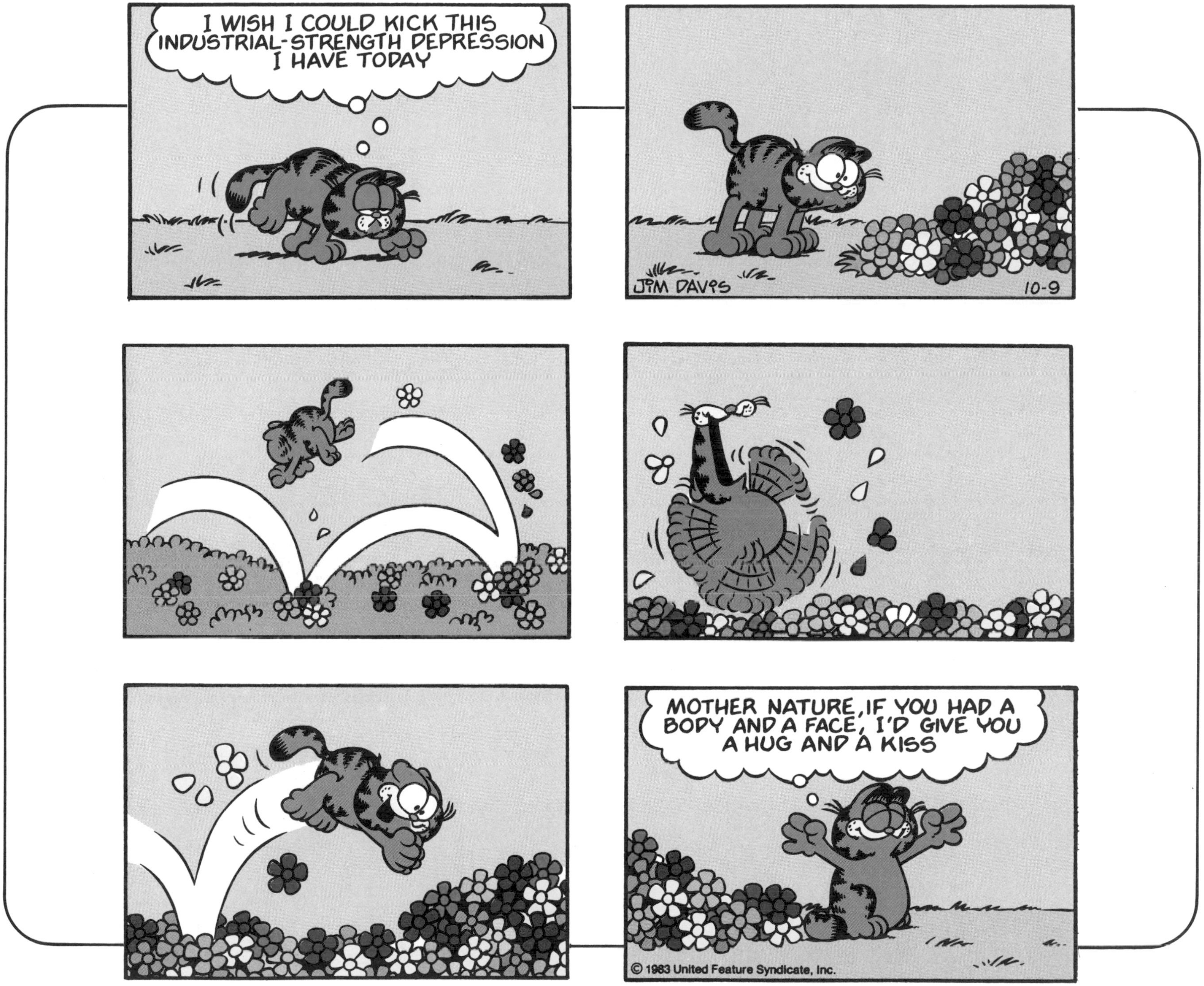
I WISH I COULD KICK THIS INDUSTRIAL-STRENGTH DEPRESSION I HAVE TODAY
JIM DAVIS
10-9
MOTHER NATURE, IF YOU HAD A BODY AND A FACE, I'D GIVE YOU A HUG AND A KISS
© 1983 United Feature Syndicate, Inc.

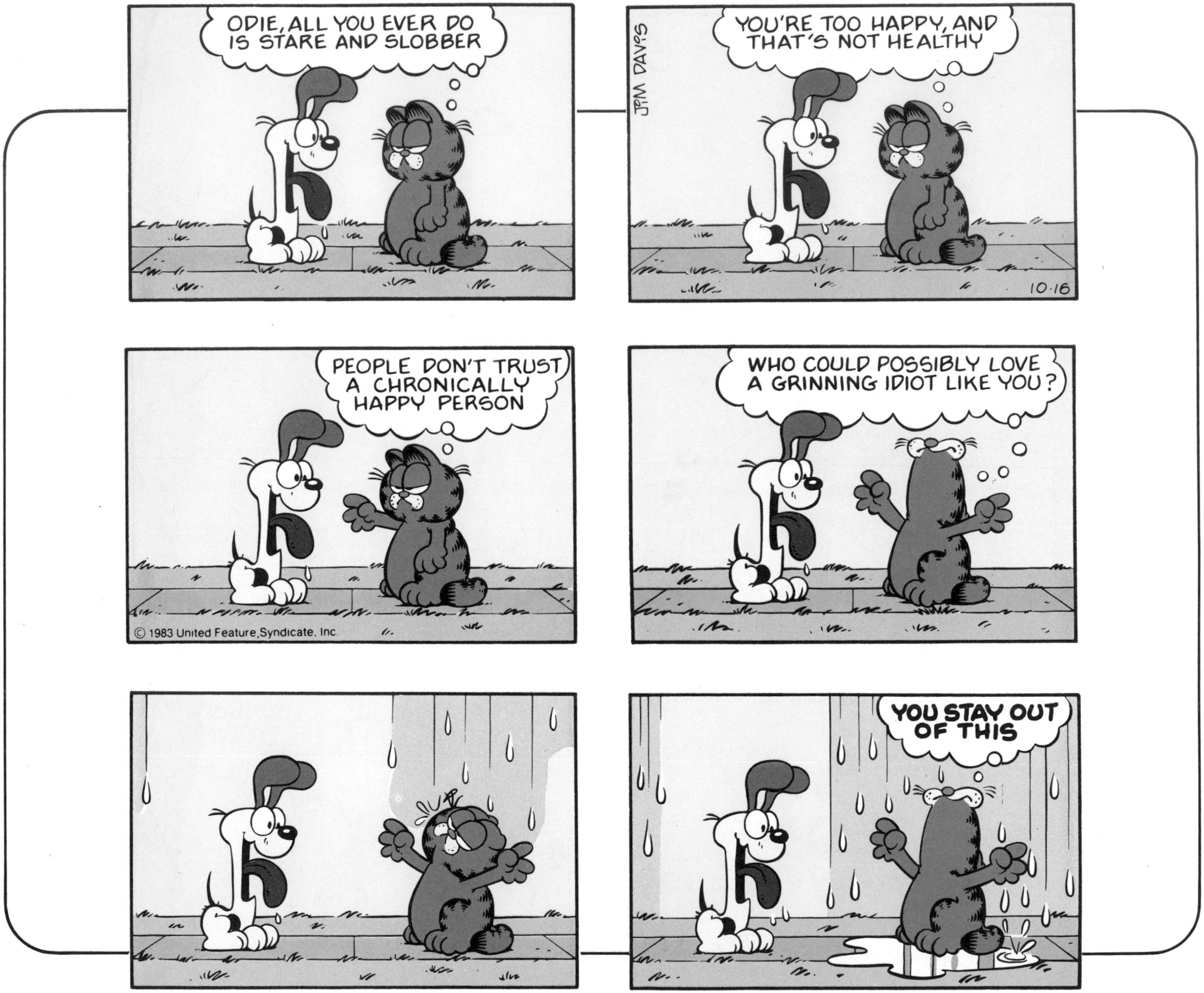
ODIE, ALL YOU EVER DO IS STARE AND SLOBBER
JIM DAVIS
YOU'RE TOO HAPPY, AND THAT'S NOT HEALTHY
10-16
PEOPLE DON'T TRUST A CHRONICALLY HAPPY PERSON
© 1983 United Feature Syndicate, Inc.
WHO COULD POSSIBLY LOVE A GRINNING IDIOT LIKE YOU?
YOU STAY OUT OF THIS

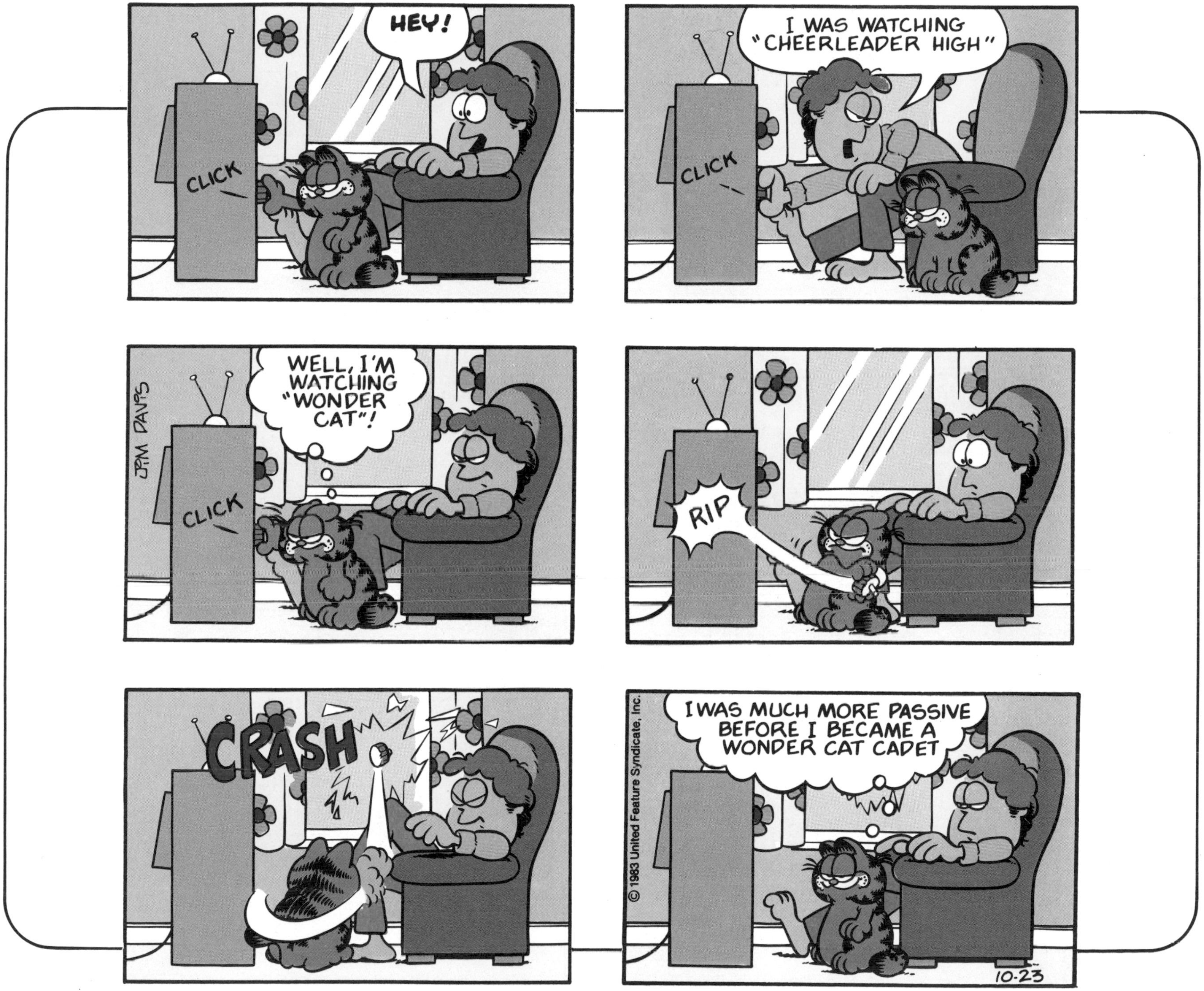

HEY!
CLICK
I WAS WATCHING "CHEERLEADER HIGH"
CLICK
WELL, I'M WATCHING "WONDER CAT"!
CLICK
JIM DAVIS
RIP
CRASH
I WAS MUCH MORE PASSIVE BEFORE I BECAME A WONDER CAT CADET
© 1983 United Feature Syndicate, Inc.
10-23

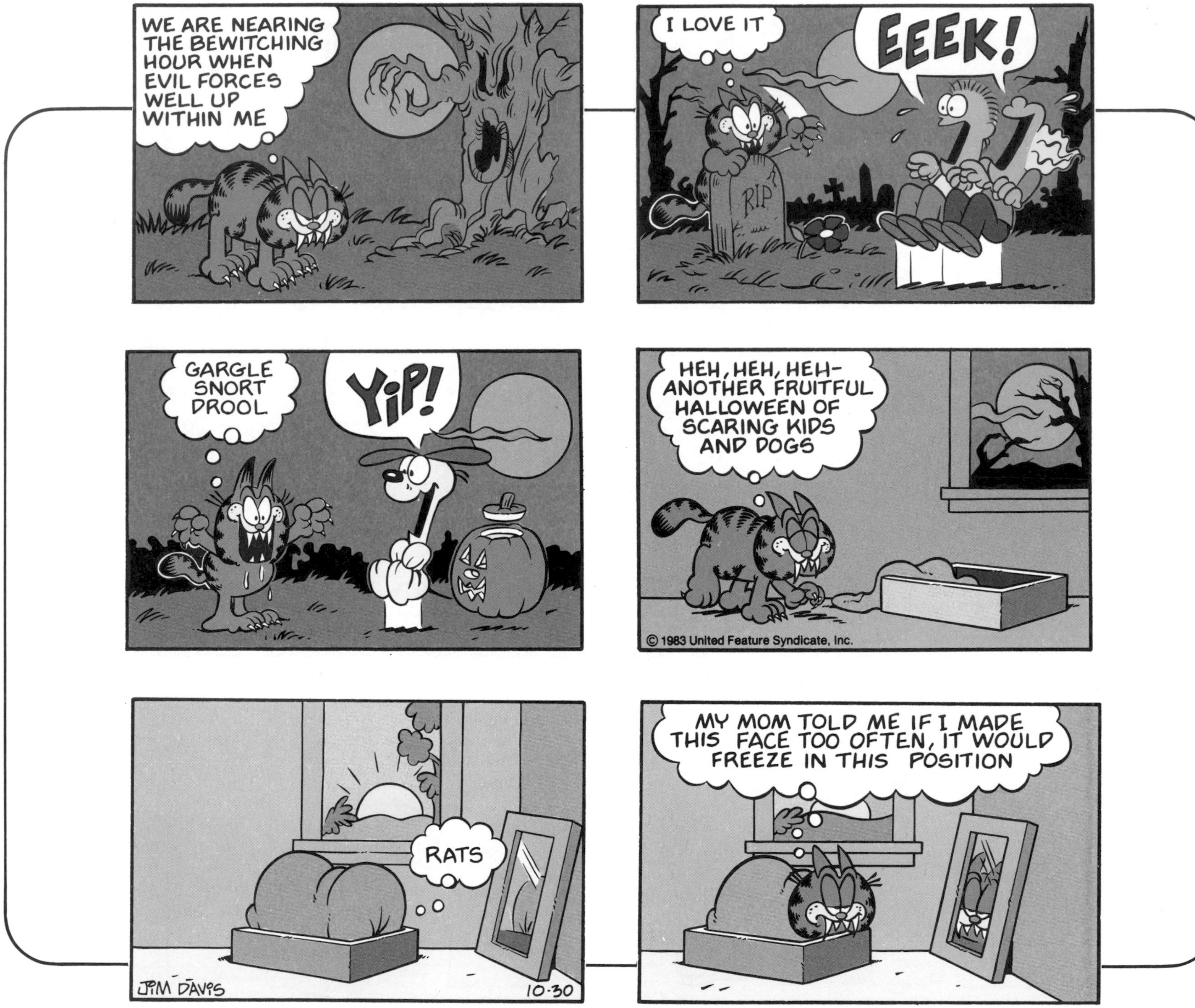
WE ARE NEARING THE BEWITCHING HOUR WHEN EVIL FORCES WELL UP WITHIN ME
I LOVE IT
EEEK!
RIP
GARGLE SNORT DROOL
YIP!
HEH, HEH, HEH- ANOTHER FRUITFUL HALLOWEEN OF SCARING KIDS AND DOGS
© 1983 United Feature Syndicate, Inc.
RATS
JIM DAVIS
10-30
MY MOM TOLD ME IF I MADE THIS FACE TOO OFTEN, IT WOULD FREEZE IN THIS POSITION

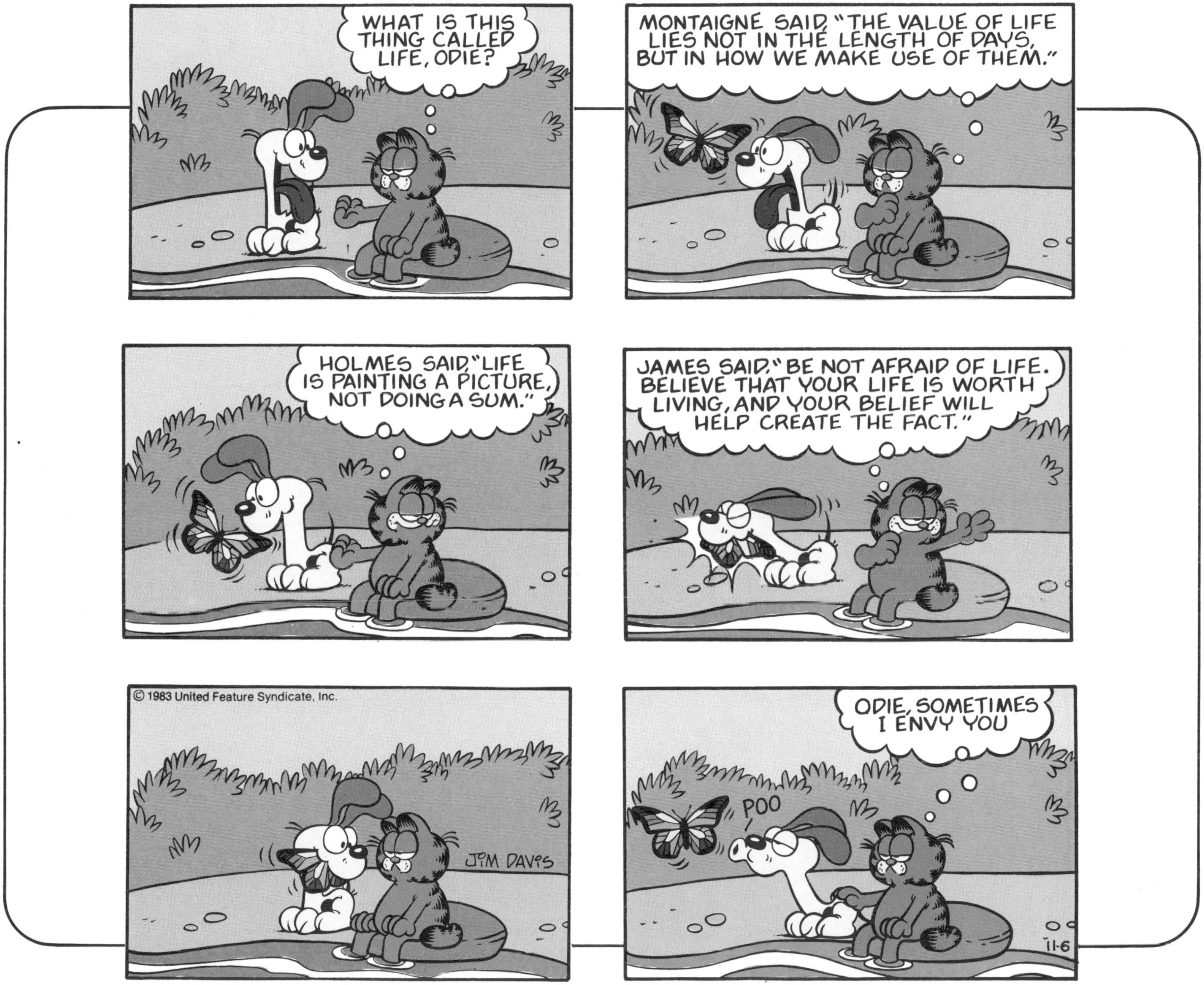
WHAT IS THIS THING CALLED LIFE, ODIE?
MONTAIGNE SAID, "THE VALUE OF LIFE LIES NOT IN THE LENGTH OF DAYS, BUT IN HOW WE MAKE USE OF THEM."
HOLMES SAID, "LIFE IS PAINTING A PICTURE, NOT DOING A SUM."
JAMES SAID, "BE NOT AFRAID OF LIFE. BELIEVE THAT YOUR LIFE IS WORTH LIVING, AND YOUR BELIEF WILL HELP CREATE THE FACT."
© 1983 United Feature Syndicate, Inc.
JIM DAVIS
ODIE, SOMETIMES I ENVY YOU
POO
11-6

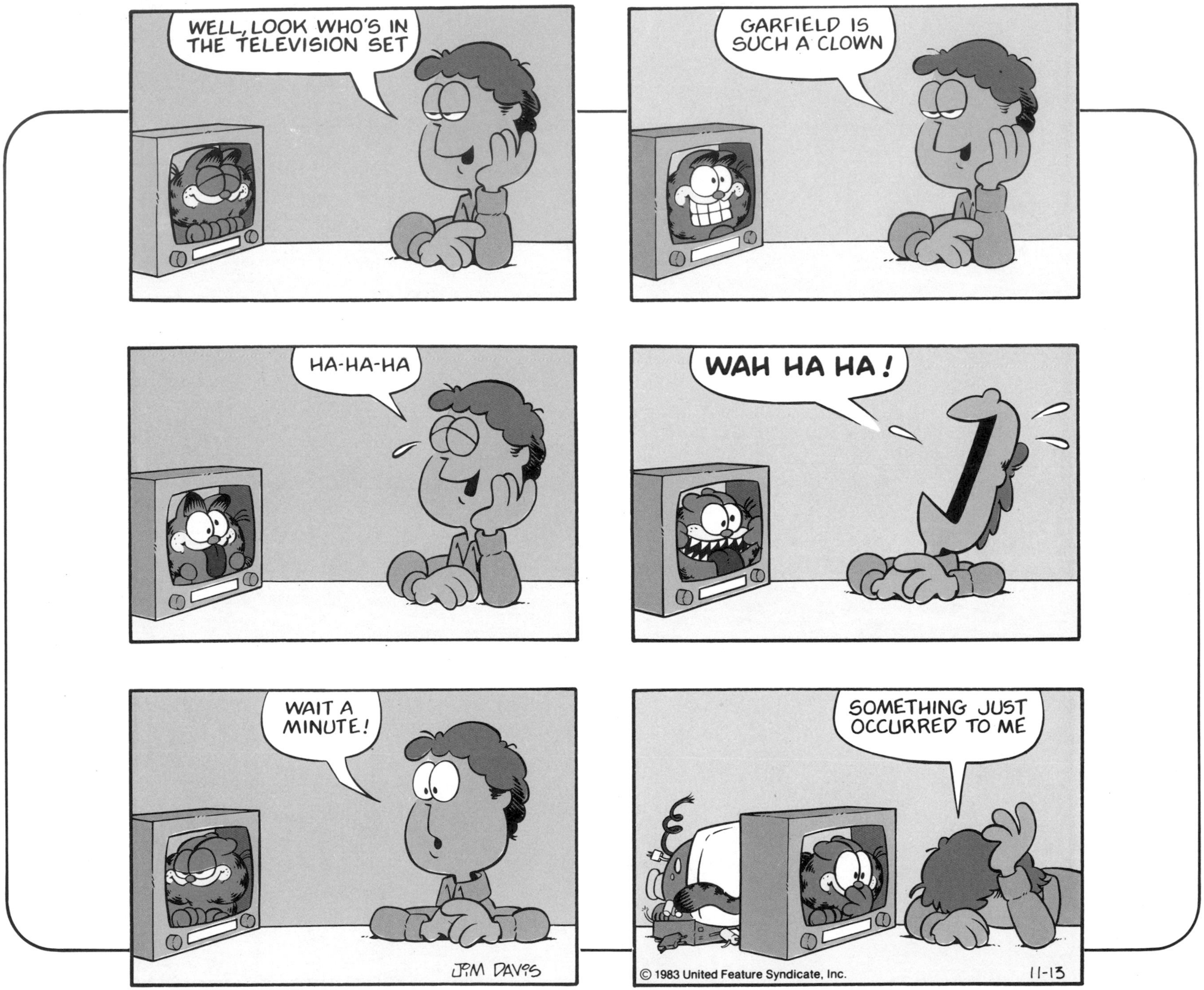
WELL, LOOK WHO'S IN THE TELEVISION SET
GARFIELD IS SUCH A CLOWN
HA-HA-HA
WAH HA HA!
WAIT A MINUTE!
SOMETHING JUST OCCURRED TO ME
JIM DAVIS
© 1983 United Feature Syndicate, Inc.
11-13

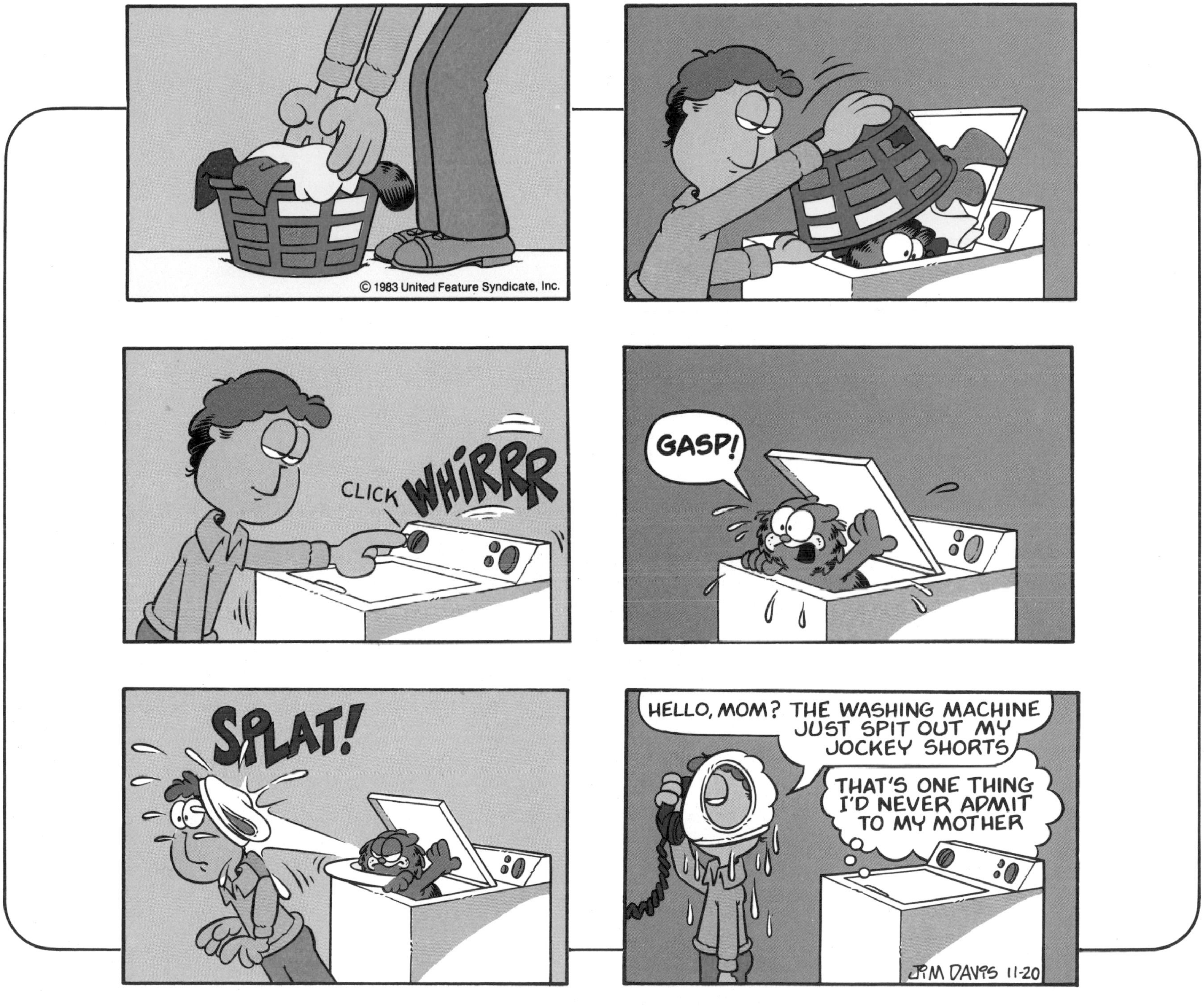
© 1983 United Feature Syndicate, Inc.
CLICK
WHIRRR
GASP!
SPLAT!
HELLO, MOM? THE WASHING MACHINE JUST SPIT OUT MY JOCKEY SHORTS
THAT'S ONE THING I'D NEVER ADMIT TO MY MOTHER
JIM DAVIS 11-20

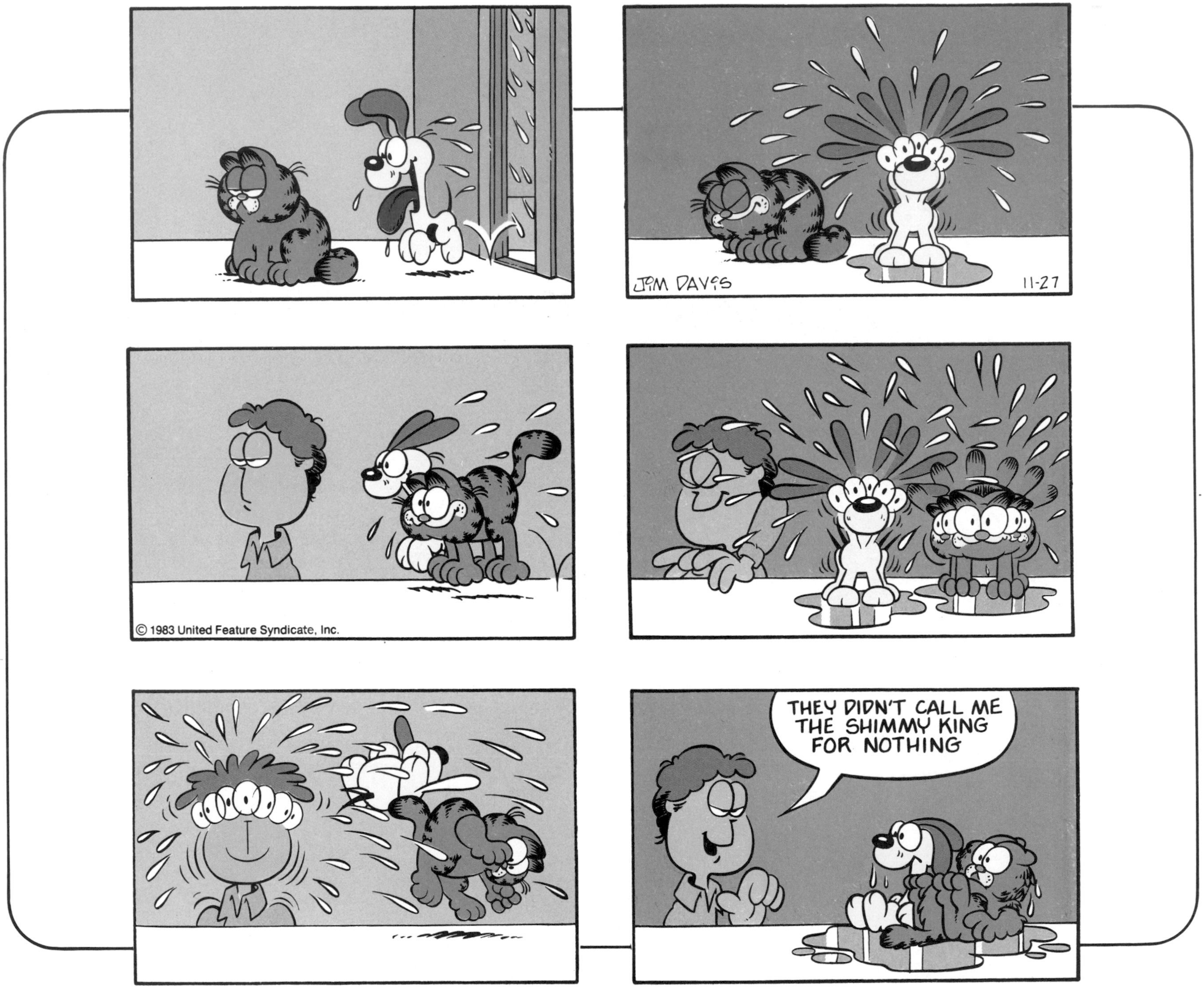
JIM DAVIS
11-27
© 1983 United Feature Syndicate, Inc.
THEY DIDN'T CALL ME THE SHIMMY KING FOR NOTHING

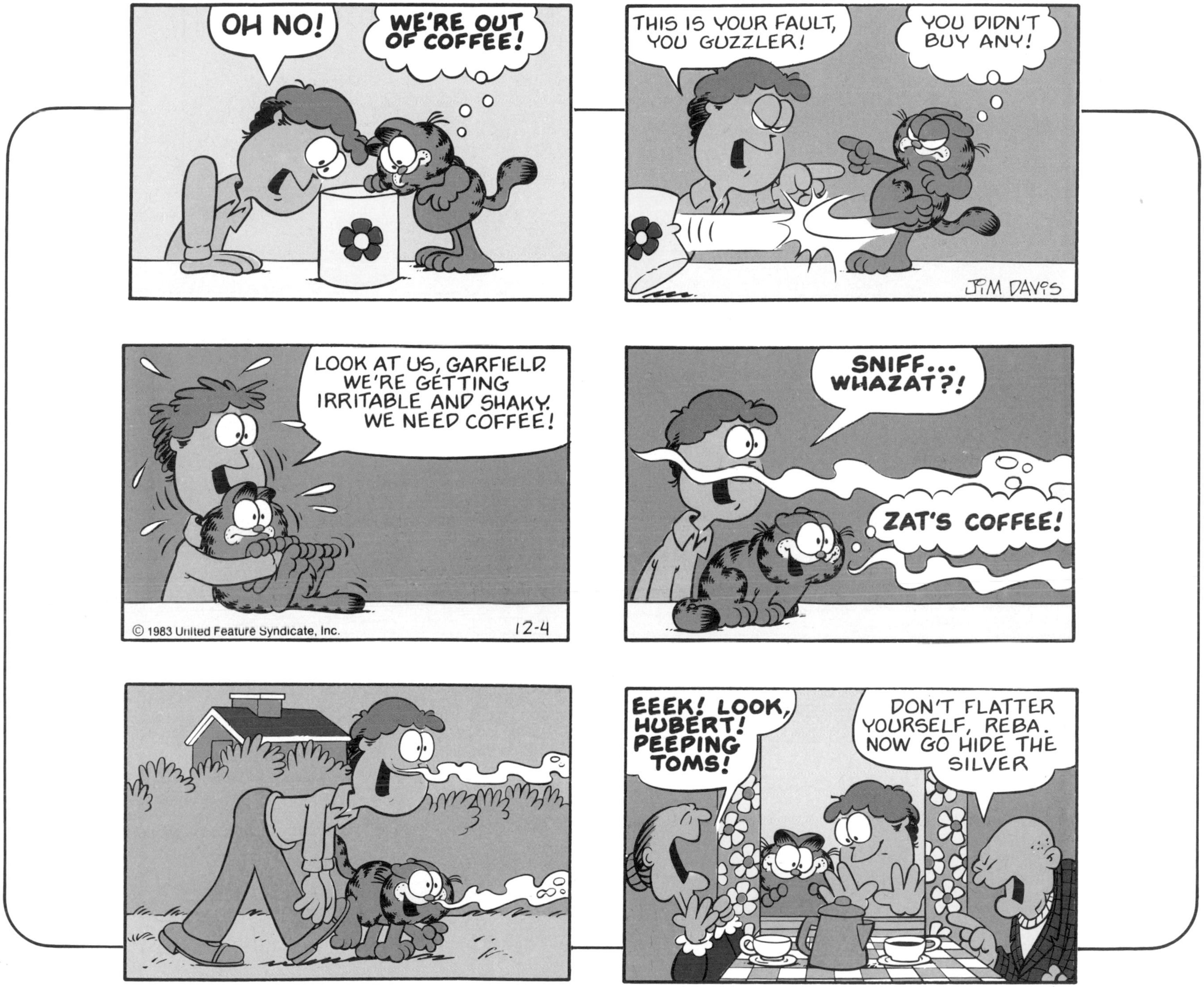
OH NO!
WE'RE OUT OF COFFEE!
THIS IS YOUR FAULT, YOU GUZZLER!
YOU DIDN'T BUY ANY!
JIM DAVIS
LOOK AT US, GARFIELD. WE'RE GETTING IRRITABLE AND SHAKY. WE NEED COFFEE!
© 1983 United Feature Syndicate, Inc.
12-4
SNIFF... WHAZAT?!
ZAT'S COFFEE!
EEEK! LOOK, HUBERT! PEEPING TOMS!
DON'T FLATTER YOURSELF, REBA. NOW GO HIDE THE SILVER

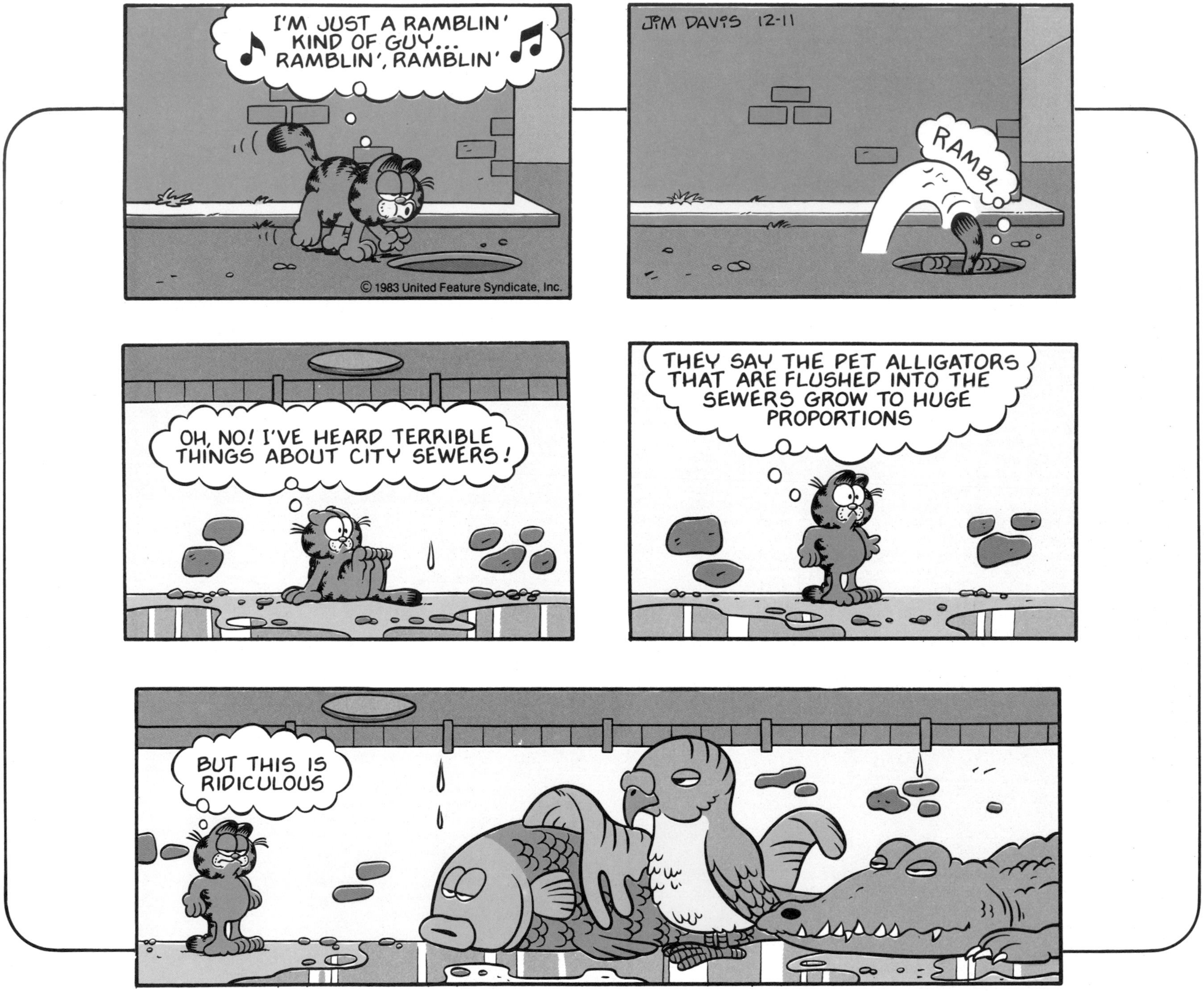
I'M JUST A RAMBLIN' KIND OF GUY... RAMBLIN', RAMBLIN'
© 1983 United Feature Syndicate, Inc.
JIM DAVIS 12-11
RAMBL
OH, NO! I'VE HEARD TERRIBLE THINGS ABOUT CITY SEWERS!
THEY SAY THE PET ALLIGATORS THAT ARE FLUSHED INTO THE SEWERS GROW TO HUGE PROPORTIONS
BUT THIS IS RIDICULOUS

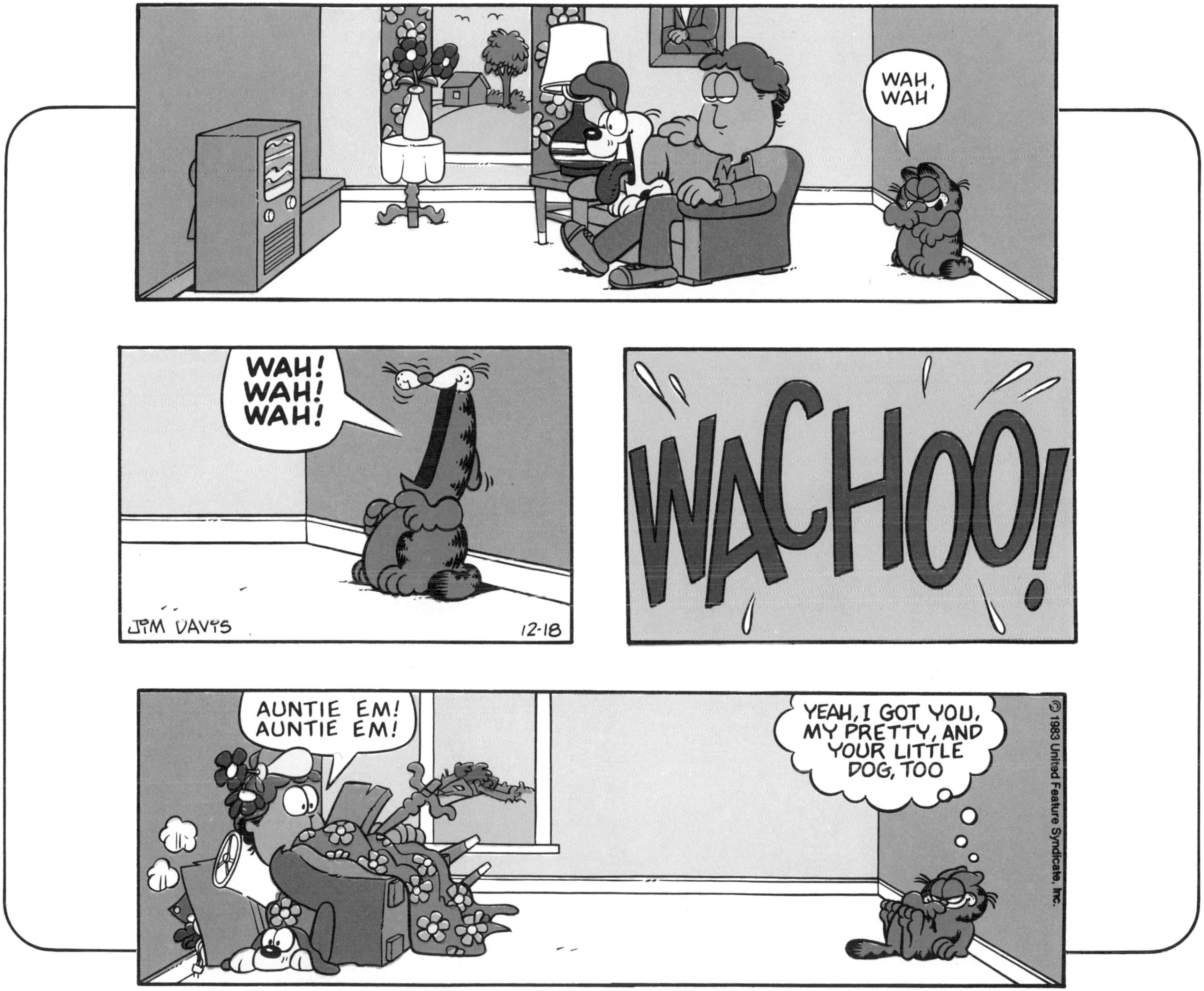
WAH, WAH
WAH! WAH! WAH!
JIM DAVIS
12-18
WACHOO!
AUNTIE EM! AUNTIE EM!
YEAH, I GOT YOU, MY PRETTY, AND YOUR LITTLE DOG, TOO
© 1983 United Feature Syndicate, Inc.

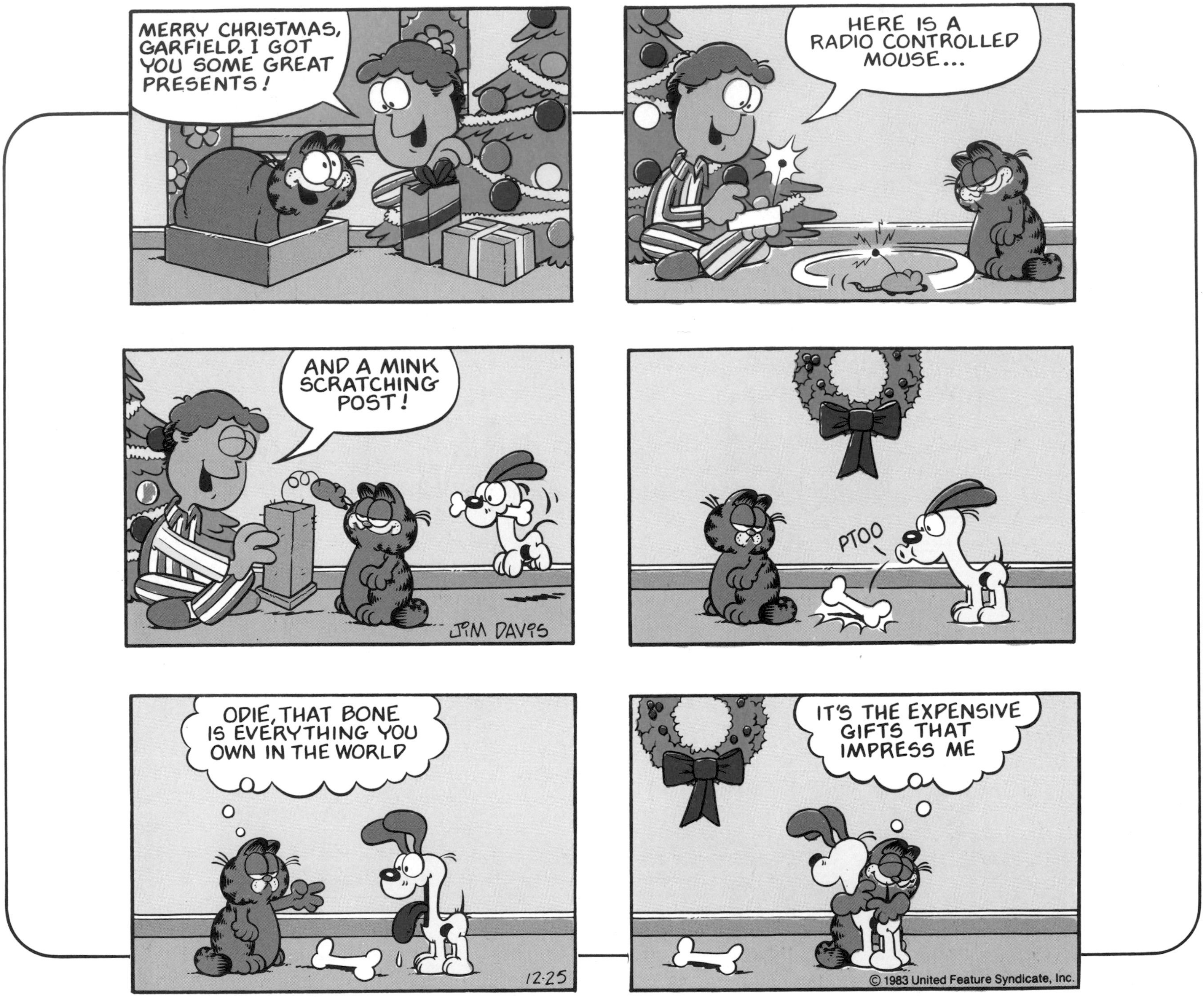

MERRY CHRISTMAS, GARFIELD. I GOT YOU SOME GREAT PRESENTS!
HERE IS A RADIO CONTROLLED MOUSE...
AND A MINK SCRATCHING POST!
JIM DAVIS
PTOO
ODIE, THAT BONE IS EVERYTHING YOU OWN IN THE WORLD
12-25
IT'S THE EXPENSIVE GIFTS THAT IMPRESS ME
© 1983 United Feature Syndicate, Inc.

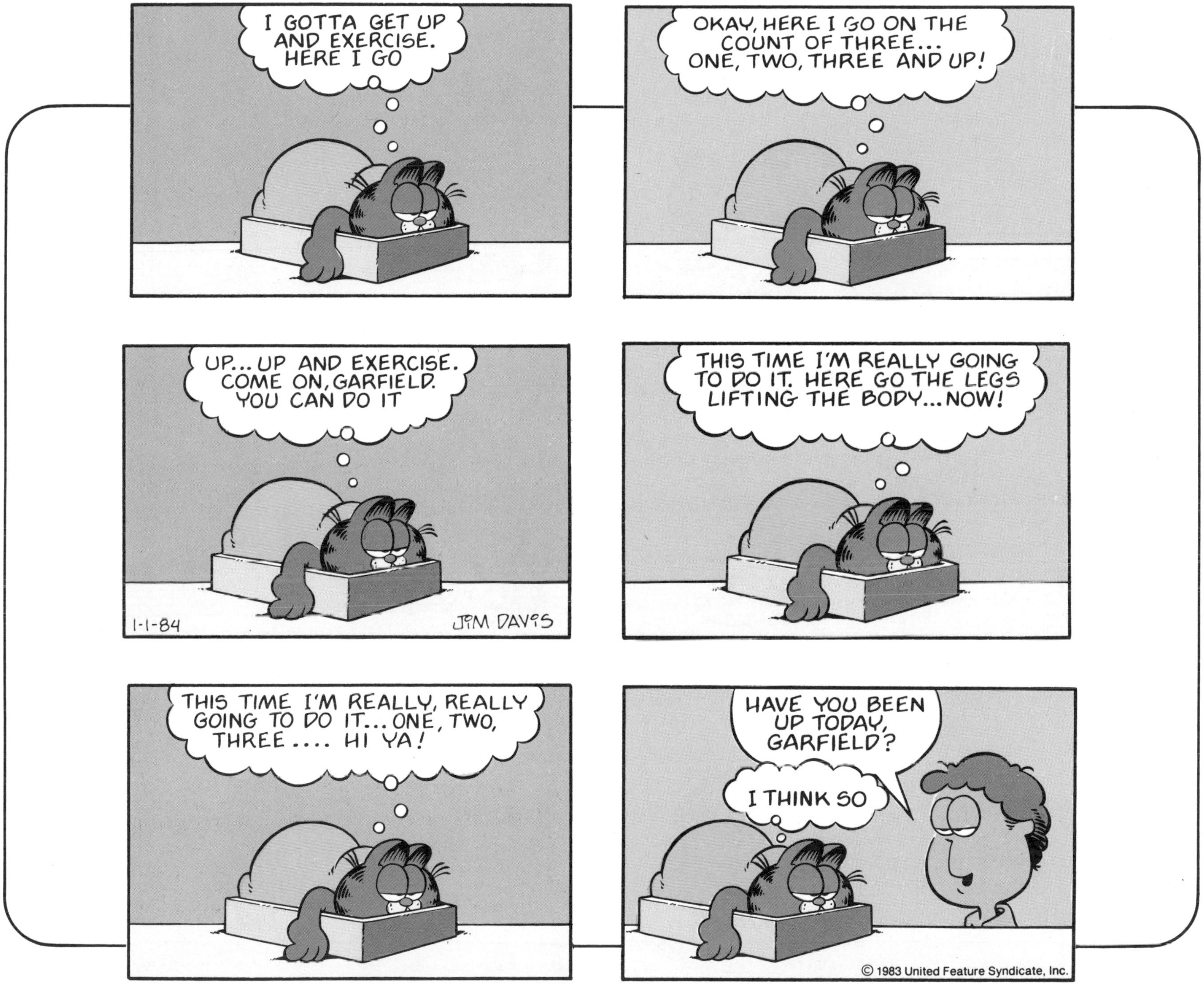
I GOTTA GET UP AND EXERCISE. HERE I GO
OKAY, HERE I GO ON THE COUNT OF THREE... ONE, TWO, THREE AND UP!
UP... UP AND EXERCISE. COME ON, GARFIELD. YOU CAN DO IT
1-1-84
JIM DAVIS
THIS TIME I'M REALLY GOING TO DO IT. HERE GO THE LEGS LIFTING THE BODY... NOW!
THIS TIME I'M REALLY, REALLY GOING TO DO IT... ONE, TWO, THREE.... HI YA!
HAVE YOU BEEN UP TODAY, GARFIELD?
I THINK SO
© 1983 United Feature Syndicate, Inc.

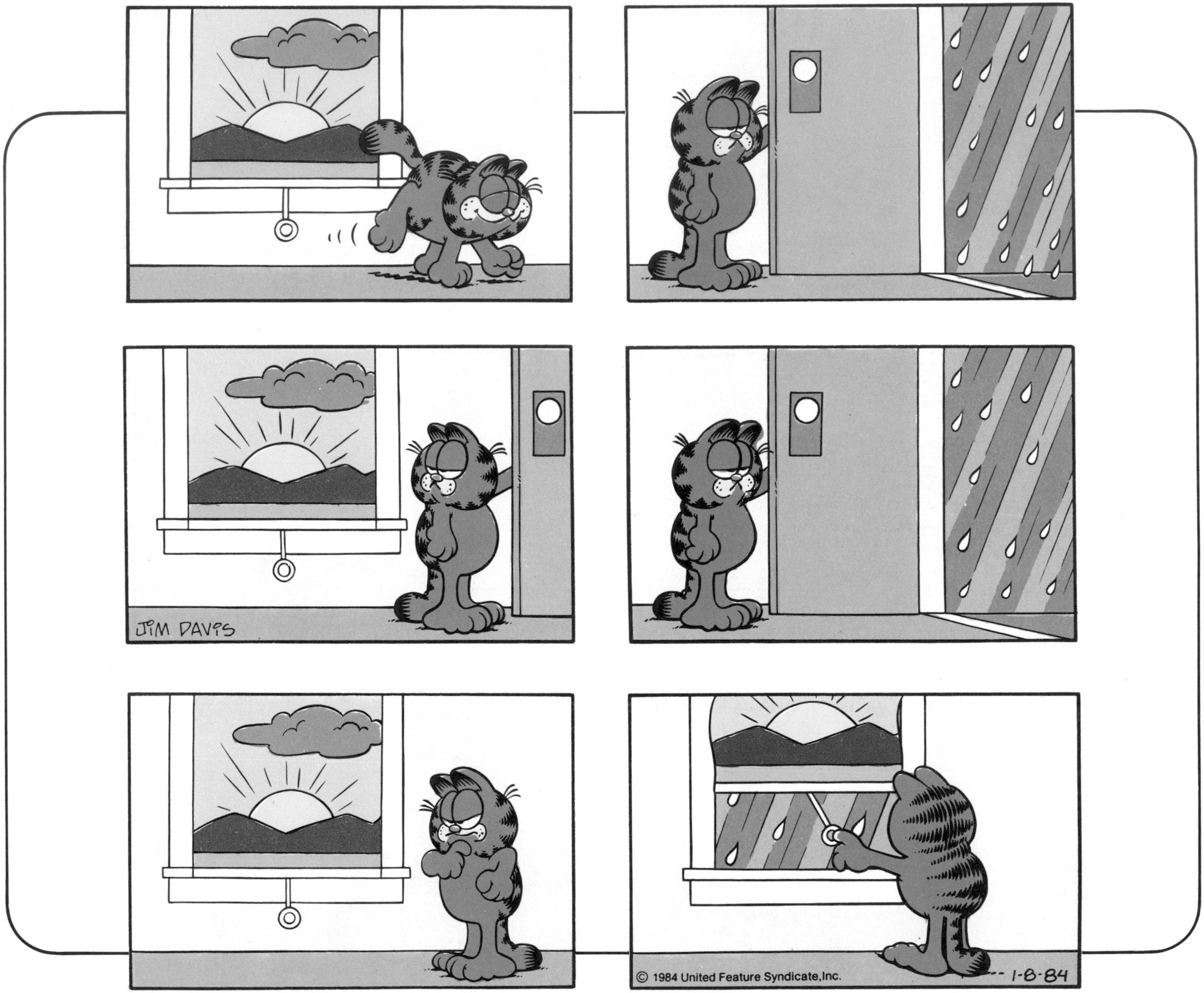
JIM DAVIS
© 1984 United Feature Syndicate, Inc.
1-8-84

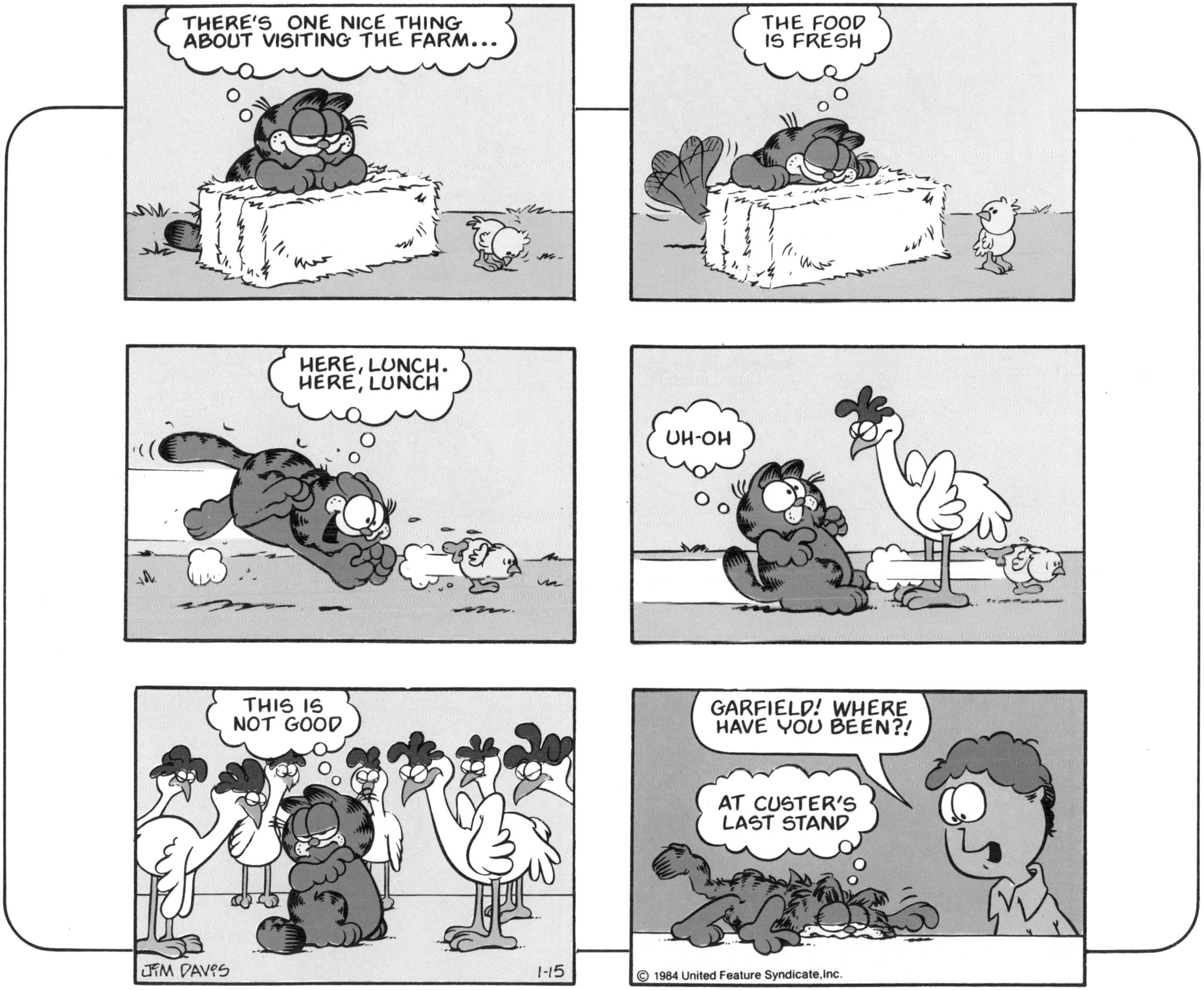
THERE'S ONE NICE THING ABOUT VISITING THE FARM...
THE FOOD IS FRESH
HERE, LUNCH. HERE, LUNCH
UH-OH
THIS IS NOT GOOD
JIM DAVIS
1-15
GARFIELD! WHERE HAVE YOU BEEN?!
AT CUSTER'S LAST STAND
© 1984 United Feature Syndicate, Inc.

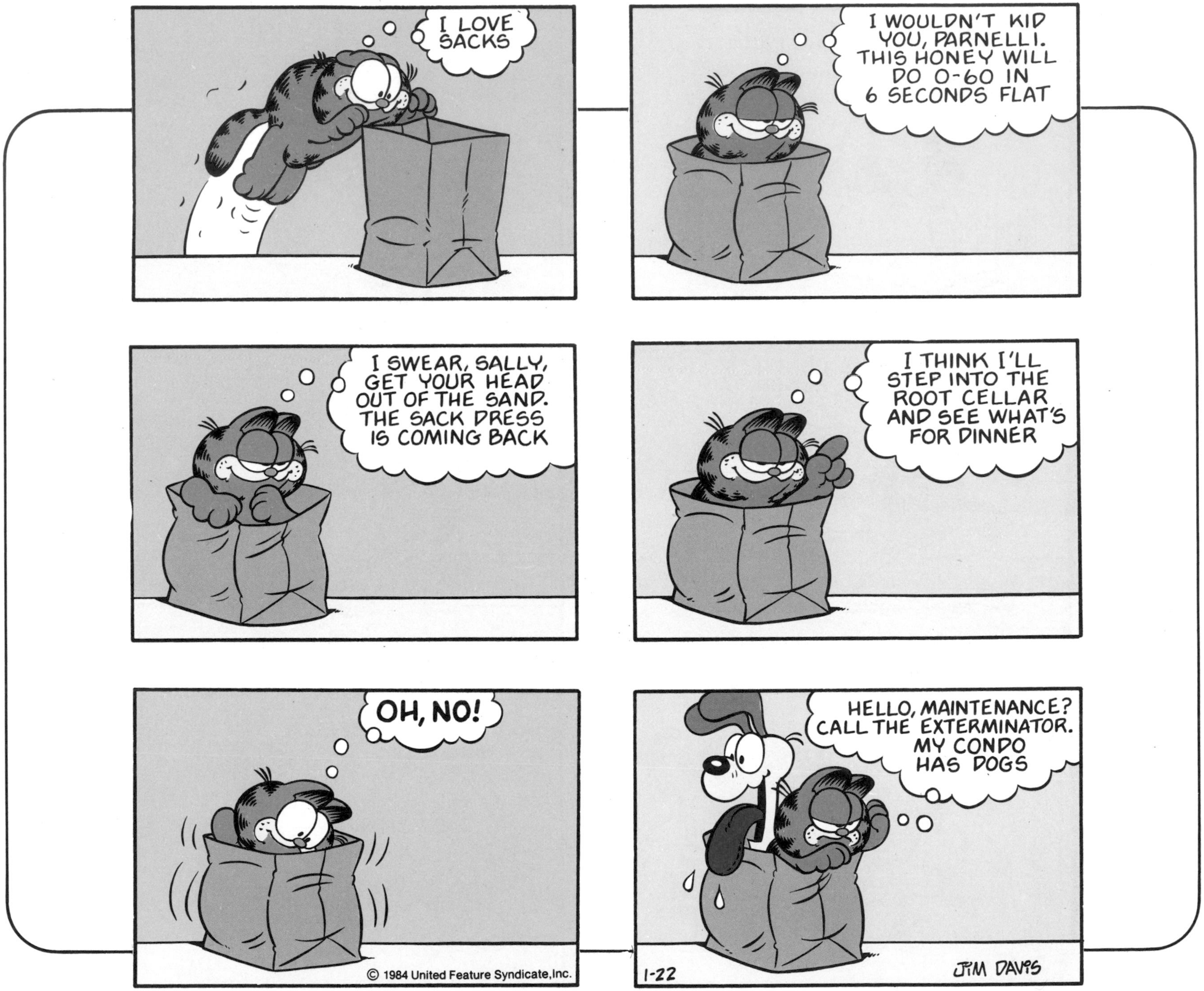
I LOVE SACKS
I WOULDN'T KID YOU, PARNELLI. THIS HONEY WILL DO 0-60 IN 6 SECONDS FLAT
I SWEAR, SALLY, GET YOUR HEAD OUT OF THE SAND. THE SACK DRESS IS COMING BACK
I THINK I'LL STEP INTO THE ROOT CELLAR AND SEE WHAT'S FOR DINNER
OH, NO!
HELLO, MAINTENANCE? CALL THE EXTERMINATOR. MY CONDO HAS DOGS
© 1984 United Feature Syndicate, Inc.
1-22
JIM DAVIS

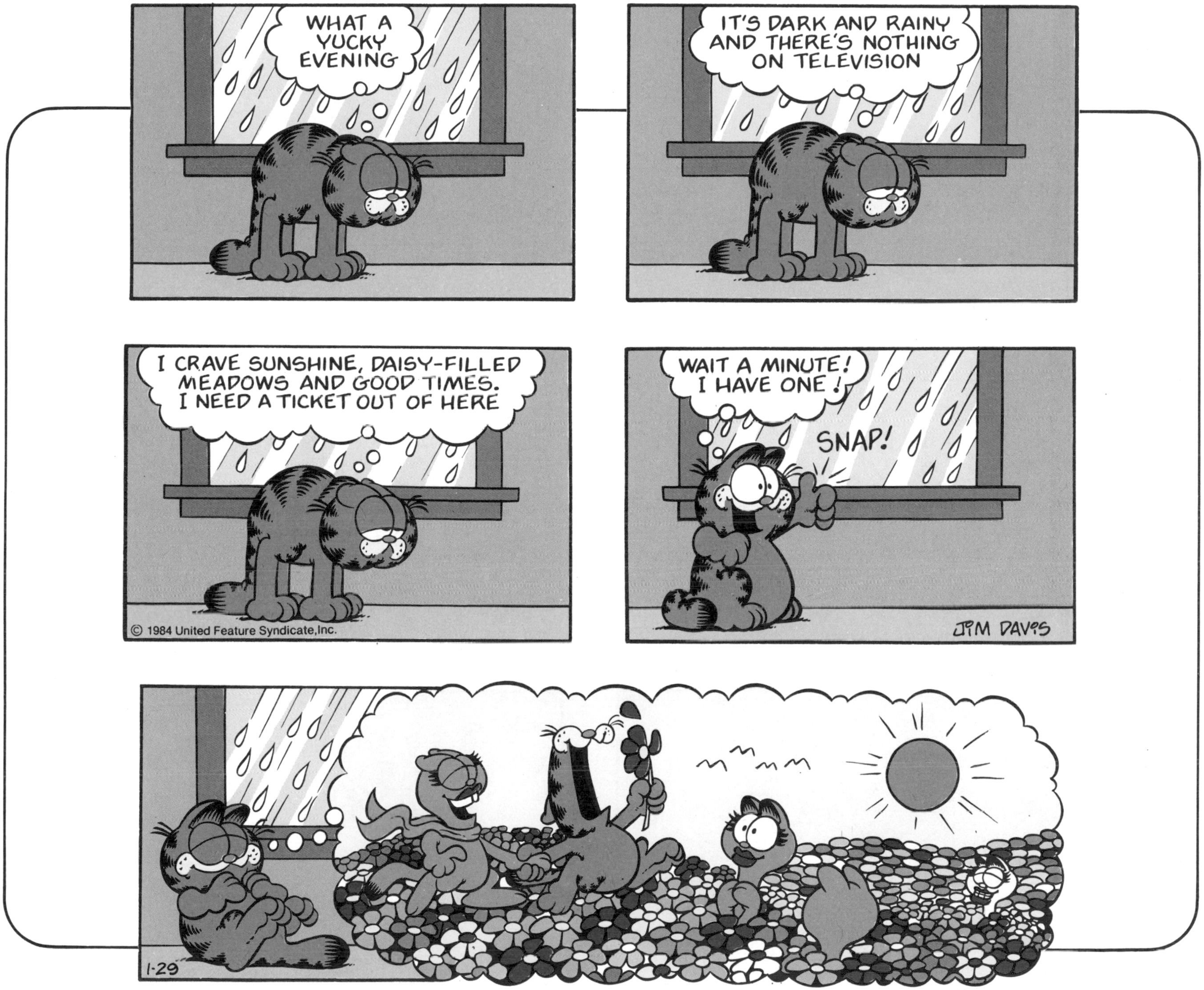
WHAT A YUCKY EVENING
IT'S DARK AND RAINY AND THERE'S NOTHING ON TELEVISION
I CRAVE SUNSHINE, DAISY-FILLED MEADOWS AND GOOD TIMES. I NEED A TICKET OUT OF HERE
WAIT A MINUTE! I HAVE ONE!
SNAP!
© 1984 United Feature Syndicate, Inc.
JIM DAVIS
1-29

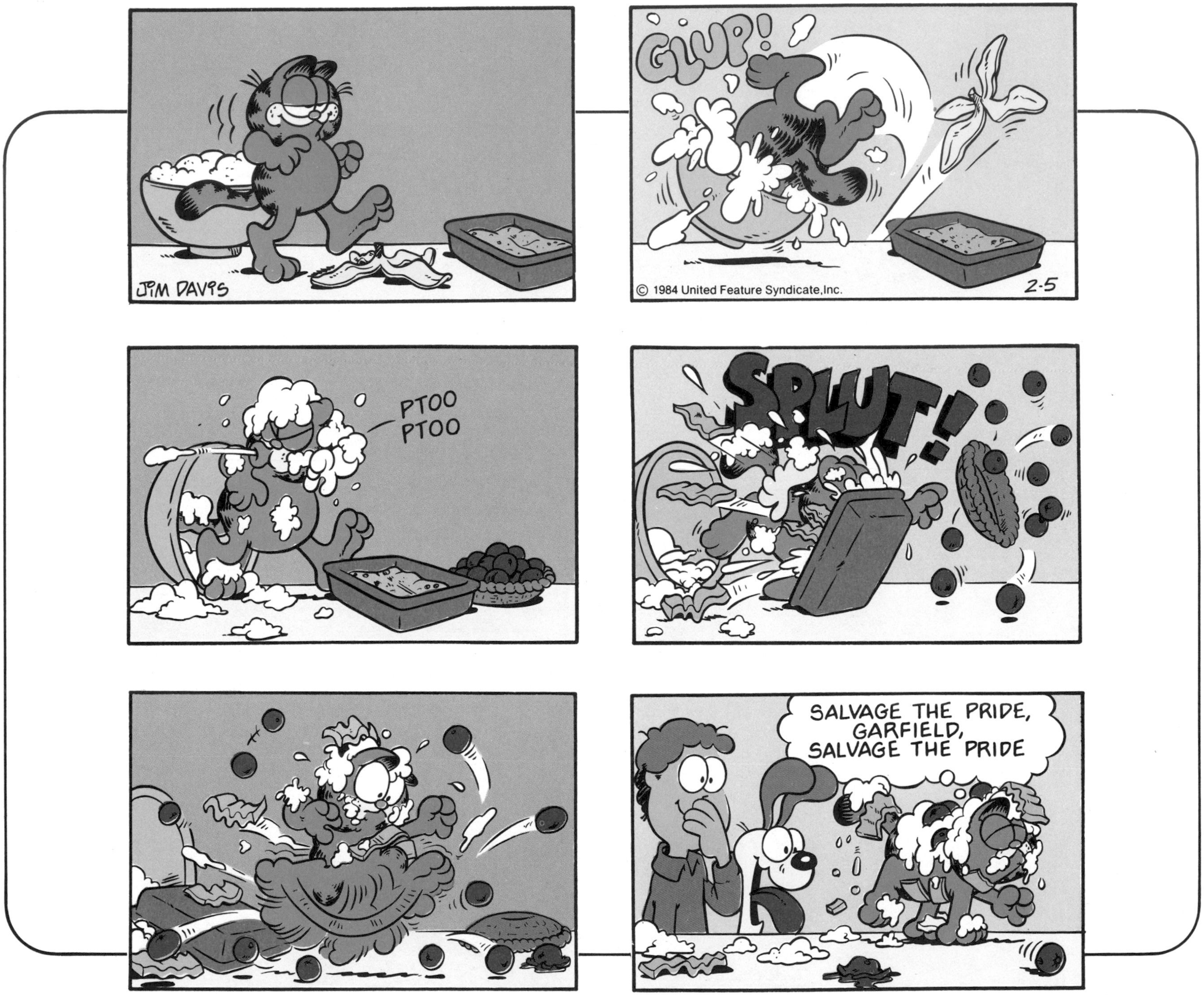
JIM DAVIS
GLUP!
© 1984 United Feature Syndicate, Inc.
2-5
PTOO PTOO
SPLUT!
SALVAGE THE PRIDE, GARFIELD, SALVAGE THE PRIDE

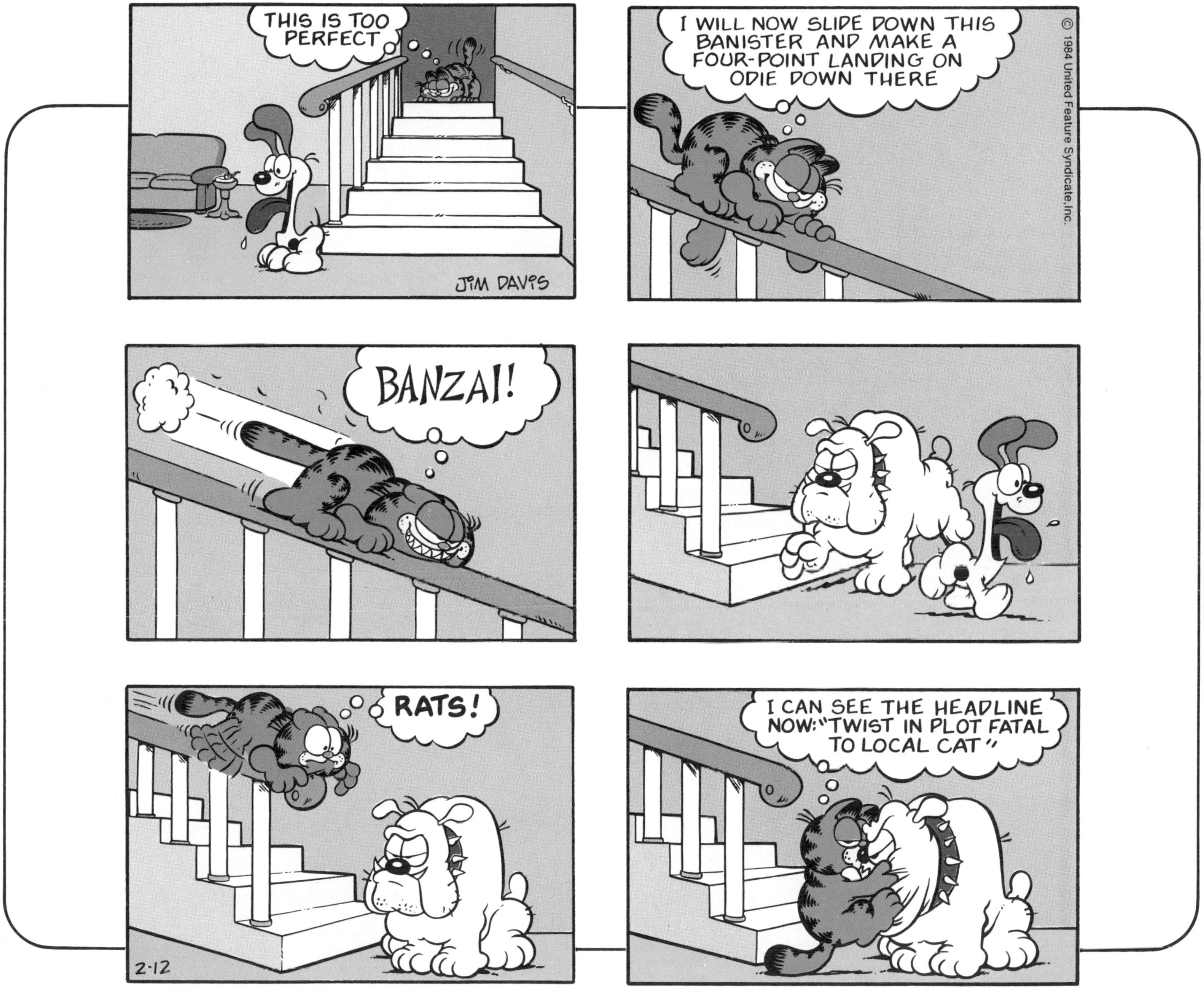
THIS IS TOO PERFECT
JIM DAVIS
I WILL NOW SLIDE DOWN THIS BANISTER AND MAKE A FOUR-POINT LANDING ON ODIE DOWN THERE
BANZAI!
RATS!
2-12
I CAN SEE THE HEADLINE NOW: "TWIST IN PLOT FATAL TO LOCAL CAT"

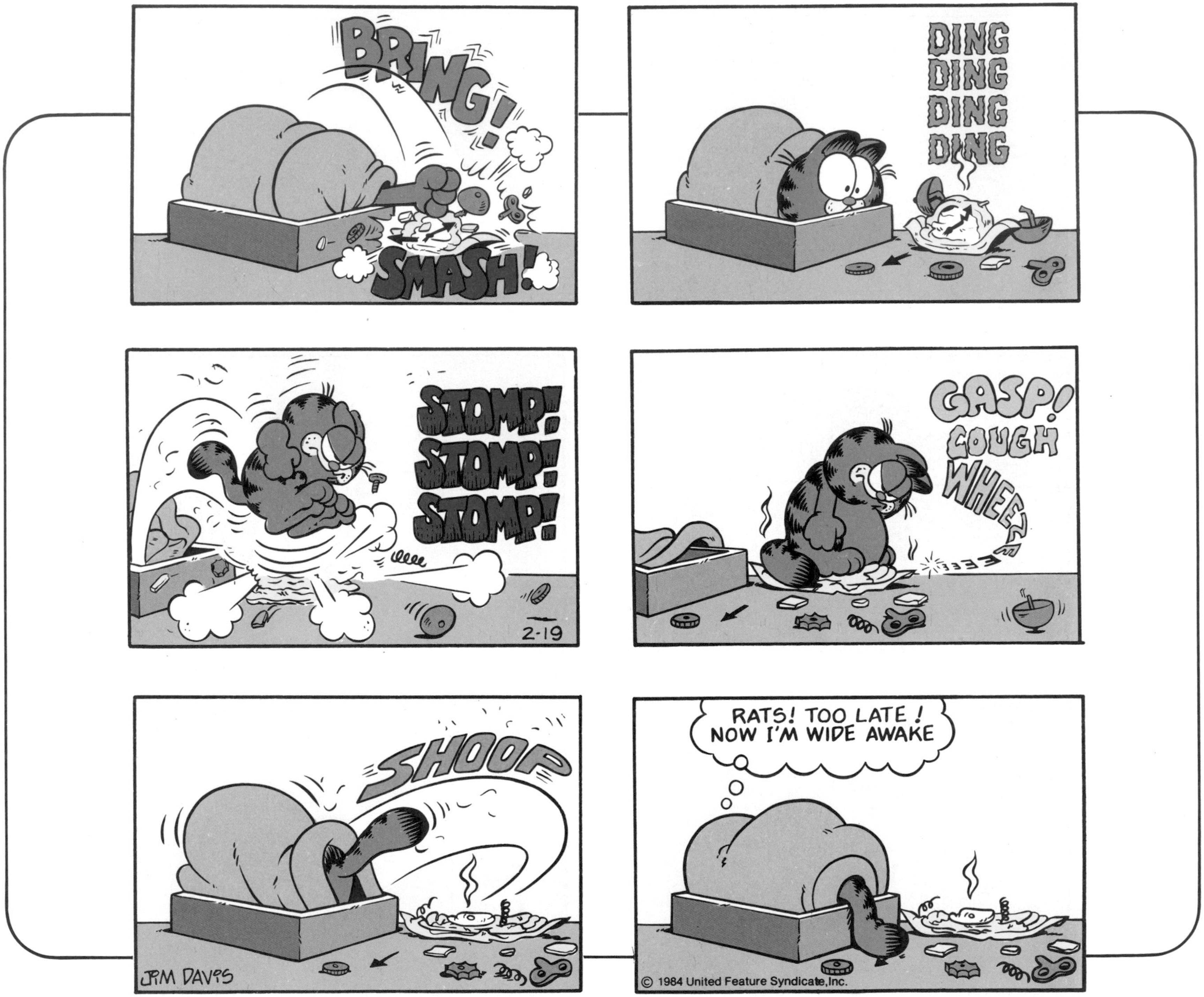
BRING!
SMASH!
DING DING DING DING
STOMP! STOMP! STOMP!
2-19
GASP! COUGH WHEEZE
SHOOP
JIM DAVIS
RATS! TOO LATE! NOW I'M WIDE AWAKE
© 1984 United Feature Syndicate, Inc.

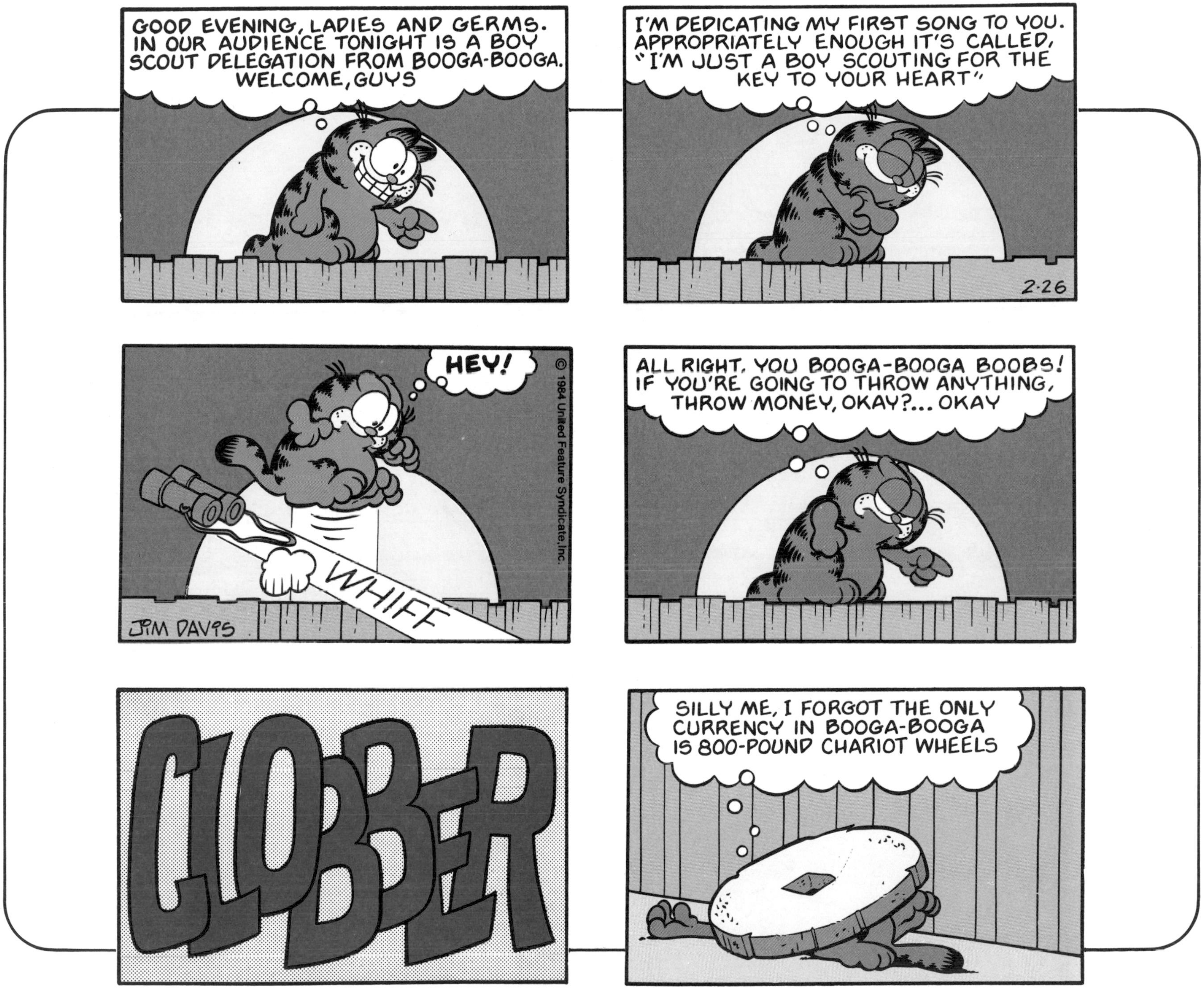
GOOD EVENING, LADIES AND GERMS. IN OUR AUDIENCE TONIGHT IS A BOY SCOUT DELEGATION FROM BOOGA-BOOGA. WELCOME, GUYS
I'M DEDICATING MY FIRST SONG TO YOU. APPROPRIATELY ENOUGH IT'S CALLED, "I'M JUST A BOY SCOUTING FOR THE KEY TO YOUR HEART"
2-26
HEY!
WHIFF
JIM DAVIS
© 1984 United Feature Syndicate, Inc.
ALL RIGHT, YOU BOOGA-BOOGA BOOBS! IF YOU'RE GOING TO THROW ANYTHING, THROW MONEY, OKAY?... OKAY
CLOBBER
SILLY ME, I FORGOT THE ONLY CURRENCY IN BOOGA-BOOGA IS 800-POUND CHARIOT WHEELS

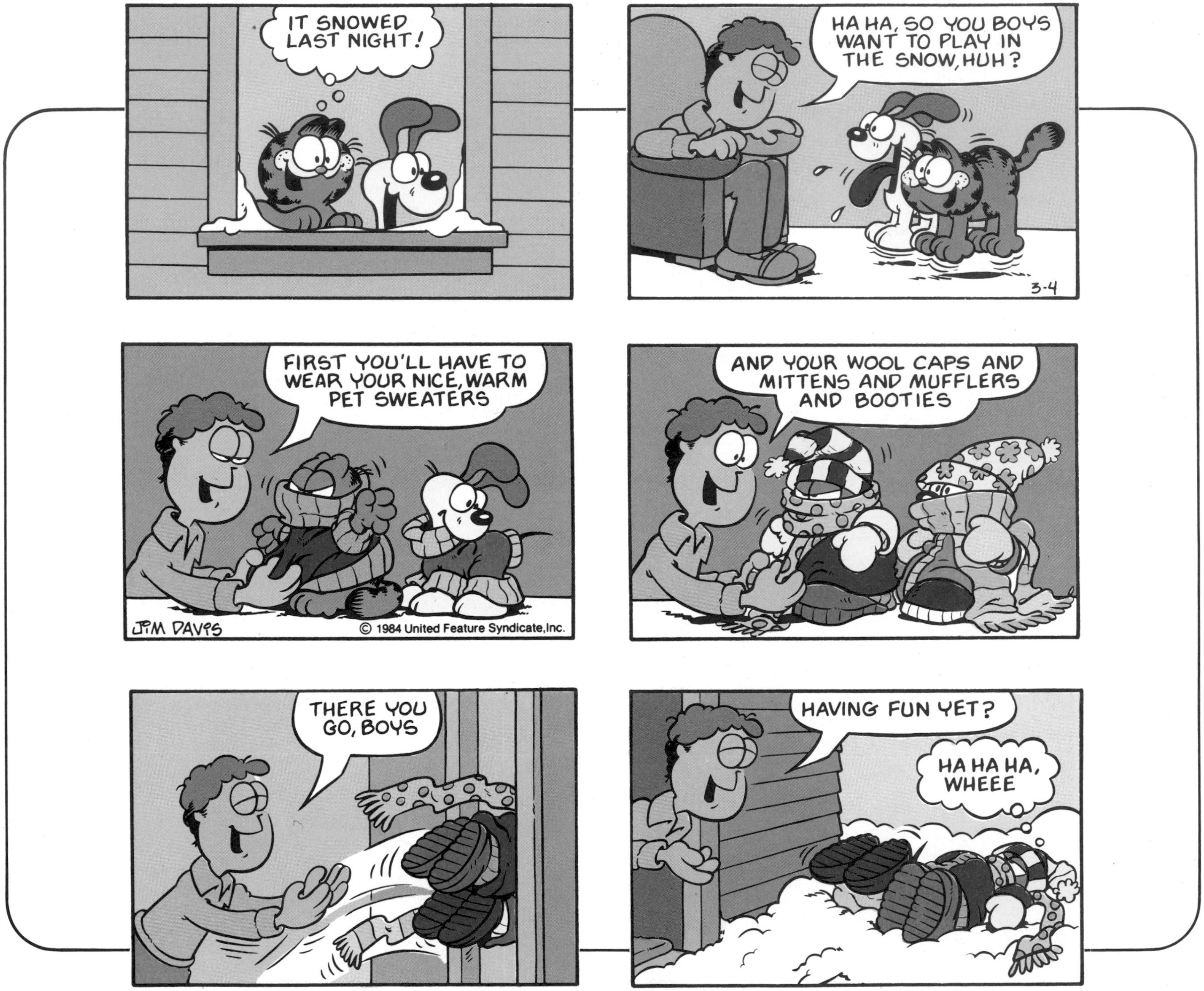
IT SNOWED LAST NIGHT!
HA HA, SO YOU BOYS WANT TO PLAY IN THE SNOW, HUH?
3-4
FIRST YOU'LL HAVE TO WEAR YOUR NICE, WARM PET SWEATERS
JIM DAVIS
© 1984 United Feature Syndicate, Inc.
AND YOUR WOOL CAPS AND MITTENS AND MUFFLERS AND BOOTIES
THERE YOU GO, BOYS
HAVING FUN YET?
HA HA HA, WHEEE

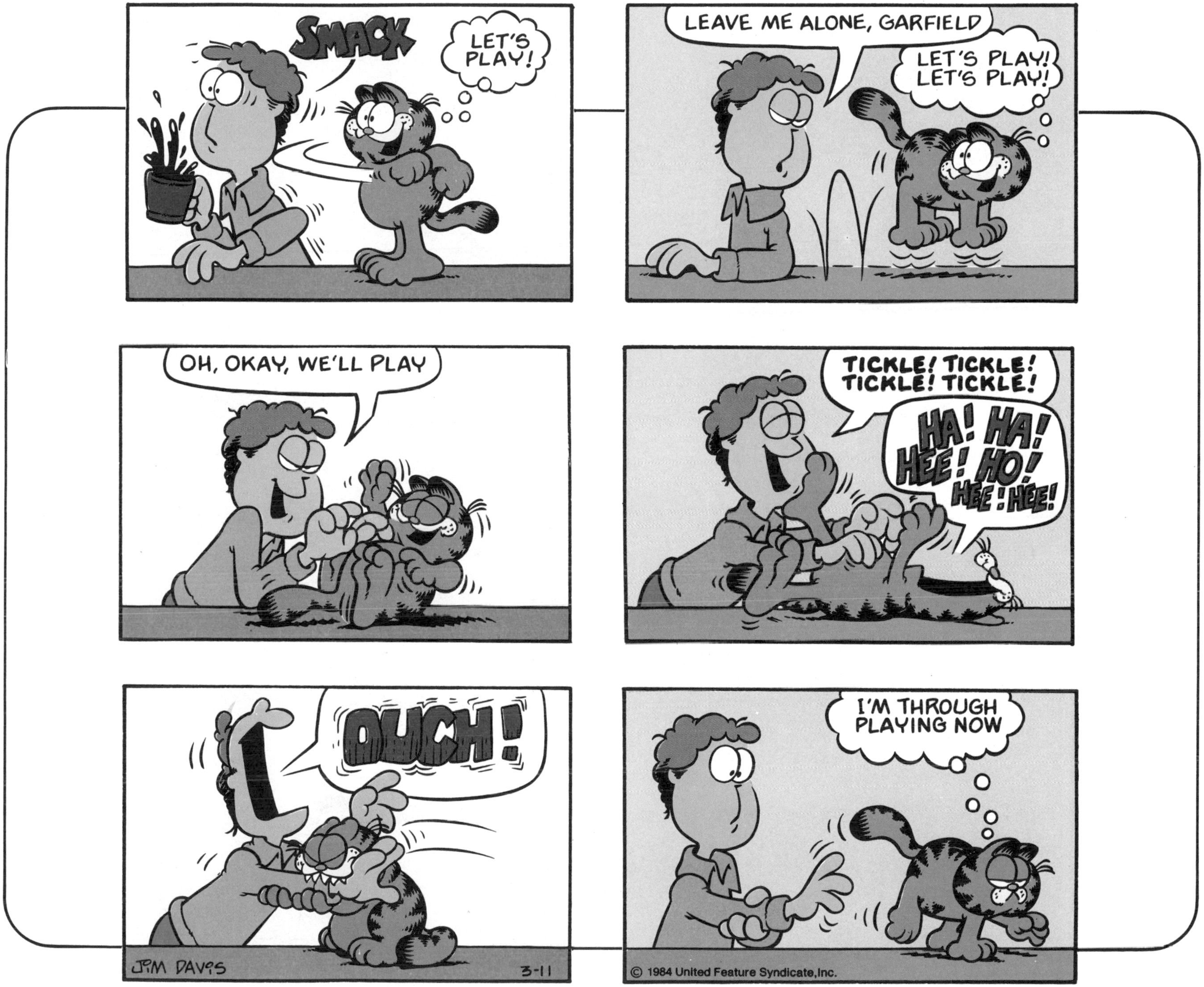

SMACK
LET'S PLAY!
LEAVE ME ALONE, GARFIELD
LET'S PLAY! LET'S PLAY!
OH, OKAY, WE'LL PLAY
TICKLE! TICKLE! TICKLE! TICKLE!
HA! HA! HEE! HO! HEE! HEE!
OUCH!
I'M THROUGH PLAYING NOW
JIM DAVIS
3-11

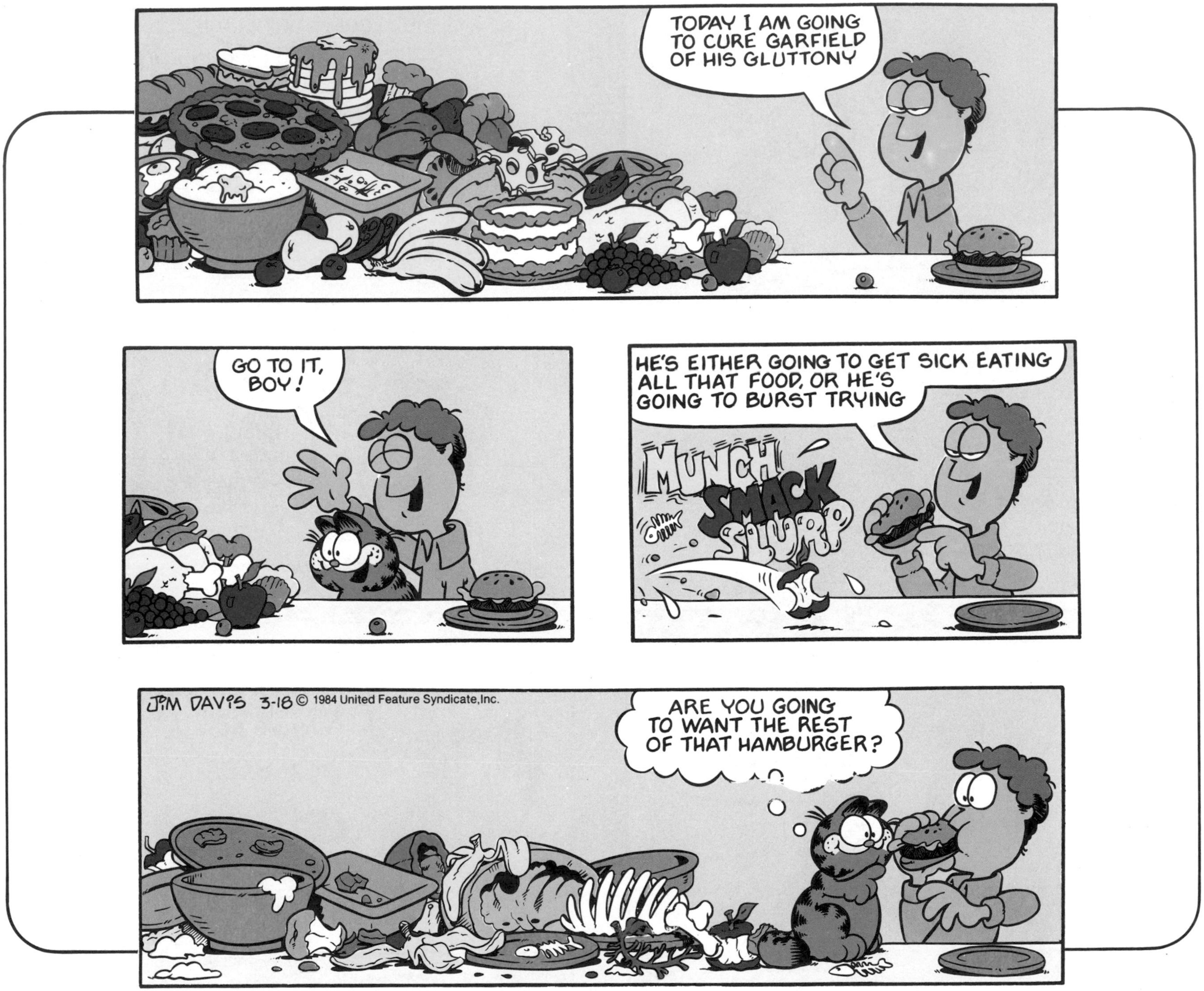
TODAY I AM GOING TO CURE GARFIELD OF HIS GLUTTONY
GO TO IT, BOY!
HE'S EITHER GOING TO GET SICK EATING ALL THAT FOOD, OR HE'S GOING TO BURST TRYING
MUNCH
SMACK
SLURP
JIM DAVIS 3-18 © 1984 United Feature Syndicate,Inc.
ARE YOU GOING TO WANT THE REST OF THAT HAMBURGER?

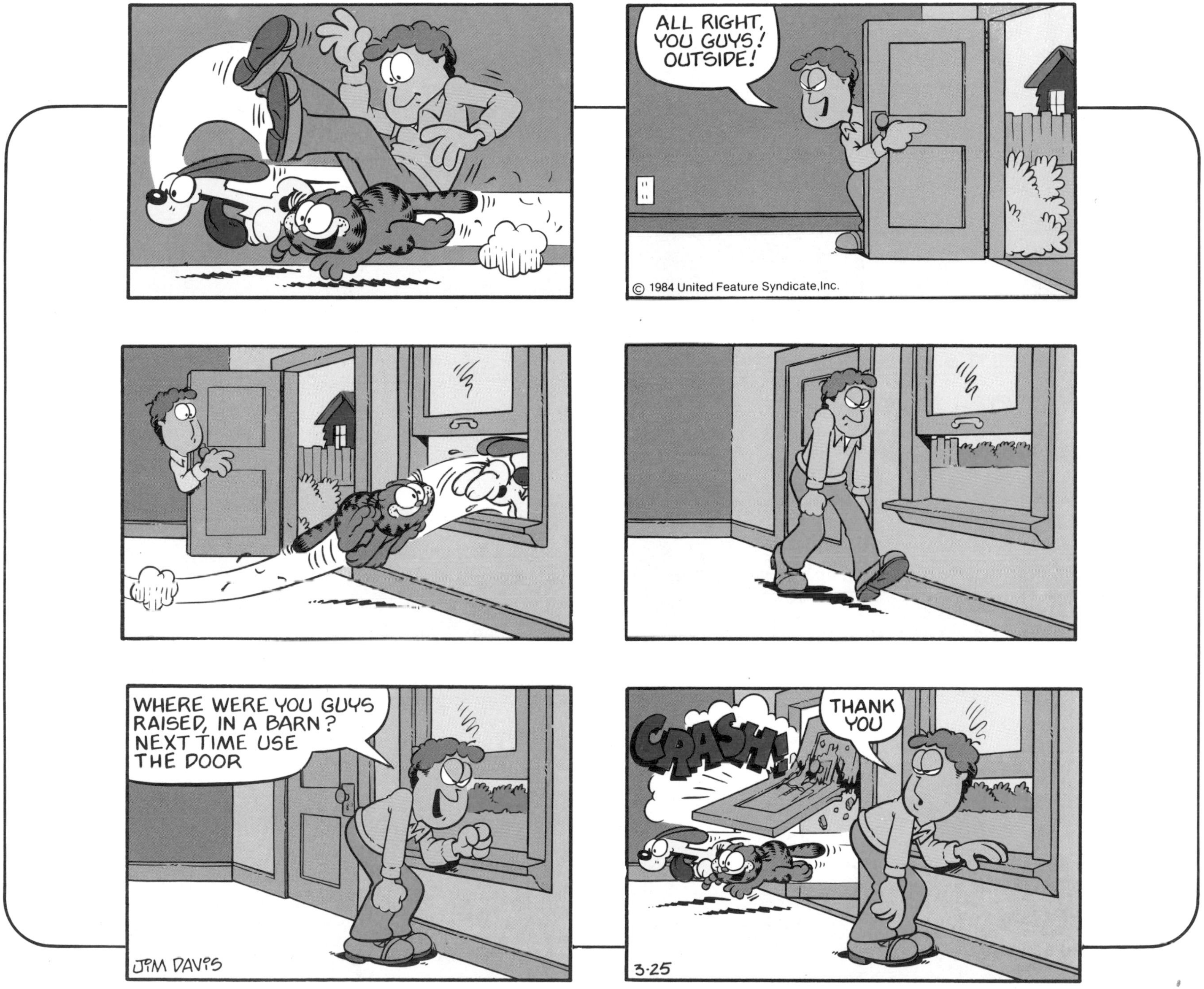

ALL RIGHT, YOU GUYS! OUTSIDE!
© 1984 United Feature Syndicate, Inc.
WHERE WERE YOU GUYS RAISED, IN A BARN? NEXT TIME USE THE DOOR
JIM DAVIS
CRASH!
THANK YOU
3-25

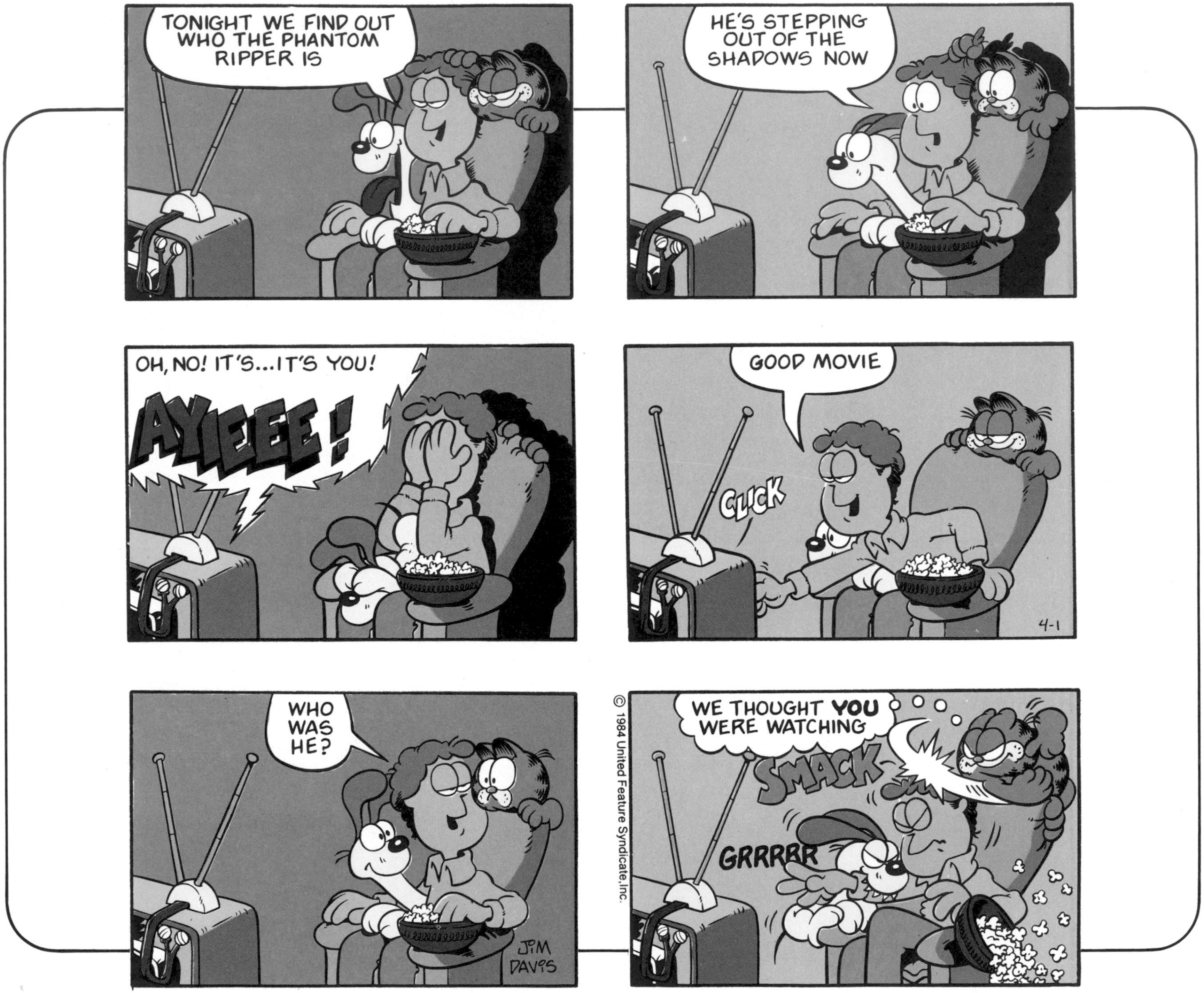
TONIGHT WE FIND OUT WHO THE PHANTOM RIPPER IS
HE'S STEPPING OUT OF THE SHADOWS NOW
OH, NO! IT'S...IT'S YOU!
AYIEEE!
GOOD MOVIE
CLICK
4-1
WHO WAS HE?
JIM DAVIS
WE THOUGHT YOU WERE WATCHING
SMACK
GRRRRR

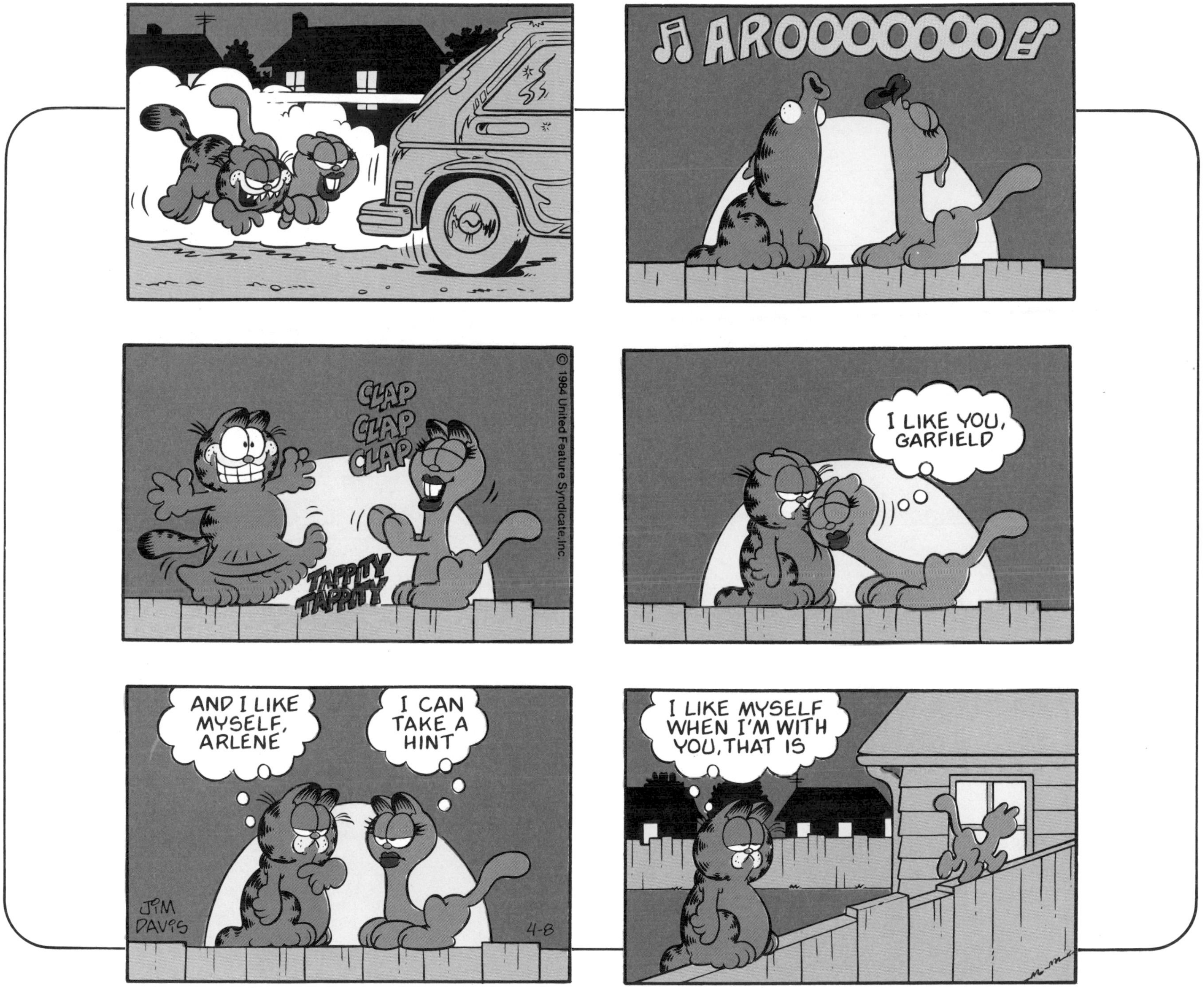
AROOOOOOO
CLAP
CLAP
CLAP
TAPPITY
TAPPITY
© 1984 United Feature Syndicate, Inc.
I LIKE YOU, GARFIELD
AND I LIKE MYSELF, ARLENE
I CAN TAKE A HINT
JIM DAVIS
4-8
I LIKE MYSELF WHEN I'M WITH YOU, THAT IS

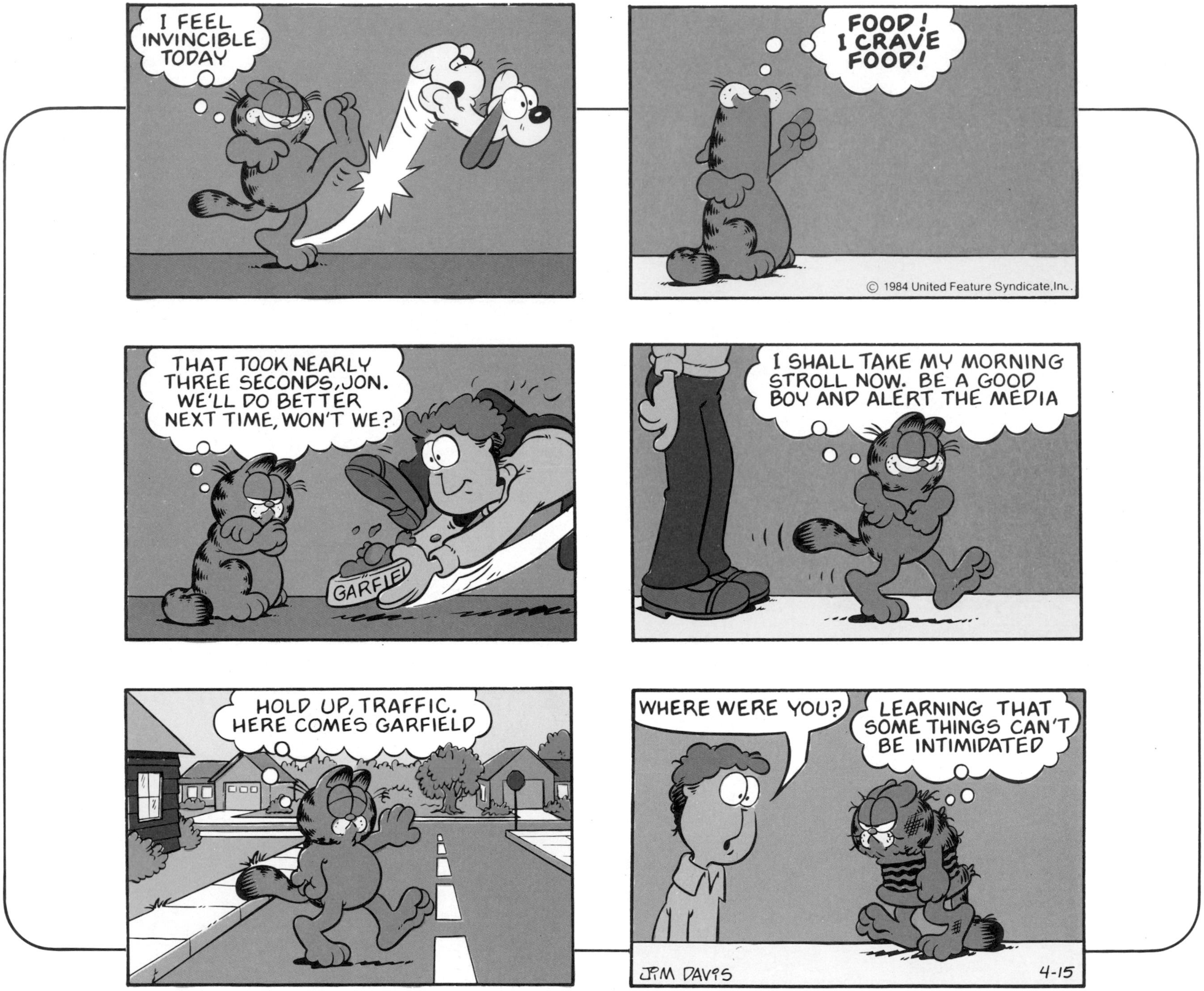
I FEEL INVINCIBLE TODAY
FOOD! I CRAVE FOOD!
© 1984 United Feature Syndicate, Inc.
THAT TOOK NEARLY THREE SECONDS, JON. WE'LL DO BETTER NEXT TIME, WON'T WE?
GARFIELD
I SHALL TAKE MY MORNING STROLL NOW. BE A GOOD BOY AND ALERT THE MEDIA
HOLD UP, TRAFFIC. HERE COMES GARFIELD
WHERE WERE YOU?
LEARNING THAT SOME THINGS CAN'T BE INTIMIDATED
JIM DAVIS
4-15

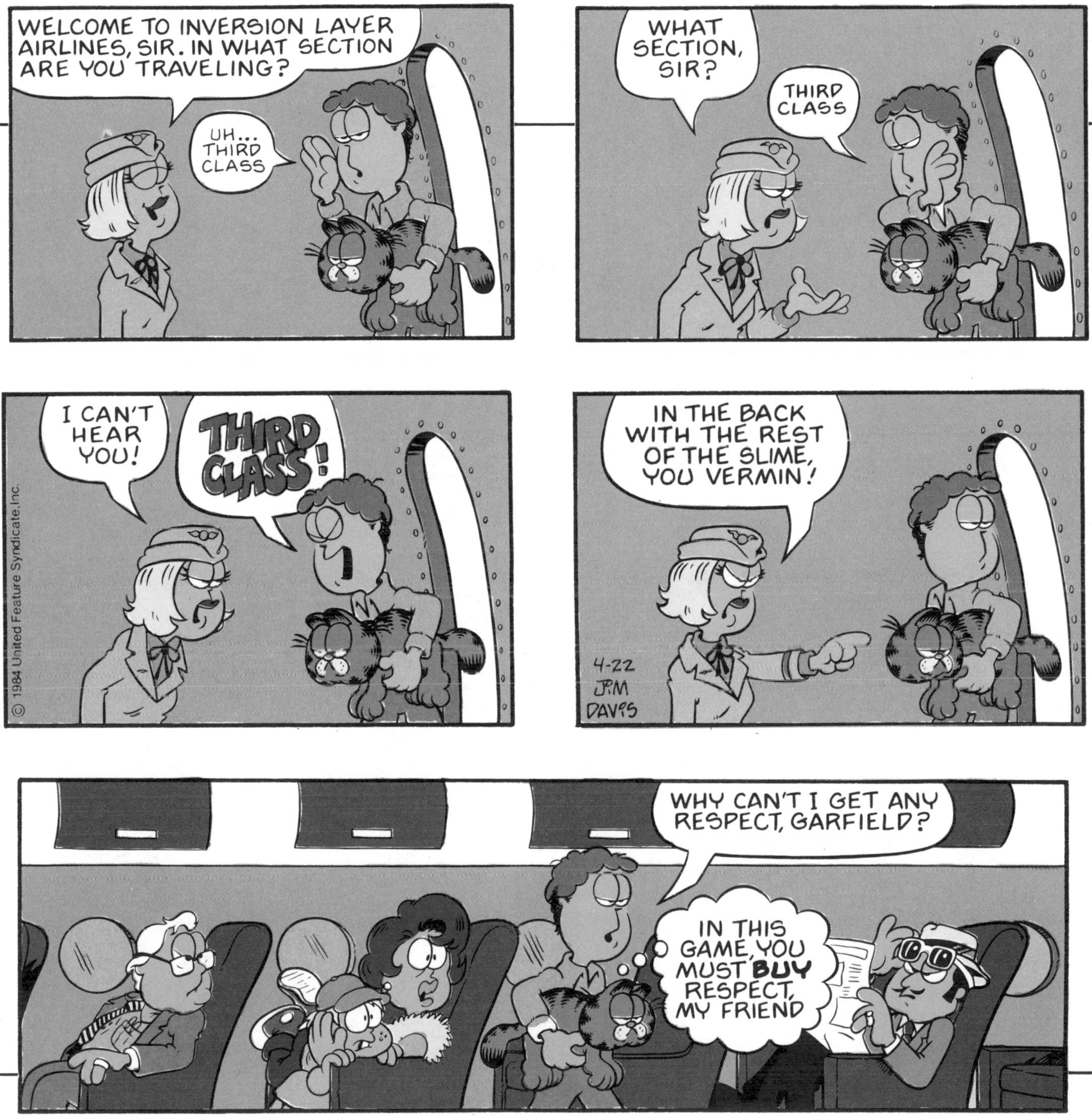
WELCOME TO INVERSION LAYER AIRLINES, SIR. IN WHAT SECTION ARE YOU TRAVELING?
UH... THIRD CLASS
WHAT SECTION, SIR?
THIRD CLASS
I CAN'T HEAR YOU!
THIRD CLASS!
IN THE BACK WITH THE REST OF THE SLIME, YOU VERMIN!
WHY CAN'T I GET ANY RESPECT, GARFIELD?
IN THIS GAME, YOU MUST **BUY** RESPECT, MY FRIEND
4-22 JIM DAVIS
© 1984 United Feature Syndicate, Inc.

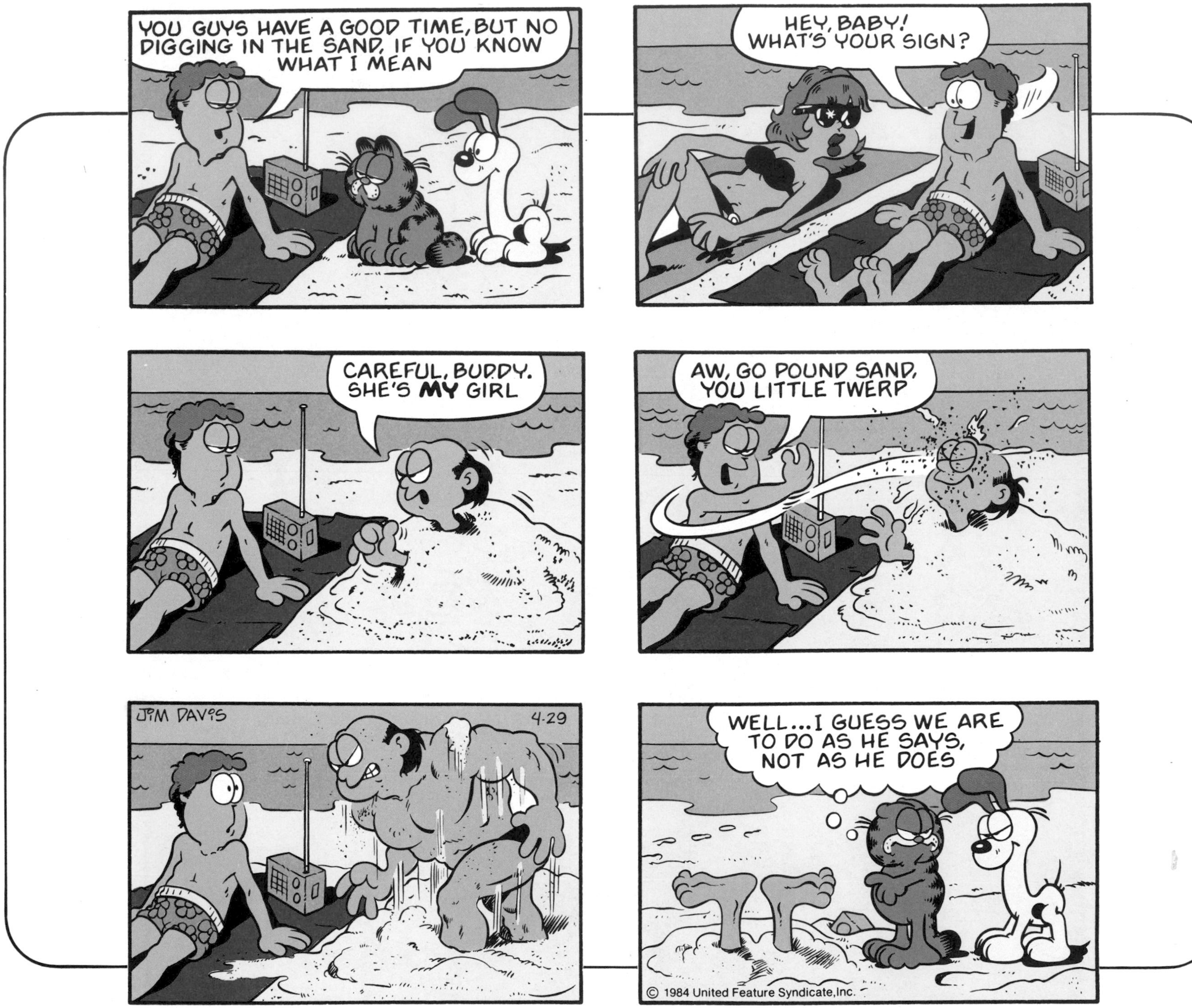
YOU GUYS HAVE A GOOD TIME, BUT NO DIGGING IN THE SAND, IF YOU KNOW WHAT I MEAN
HEY, BABY! WHAT'S YOUR SIGN?
CAREFUL, BUDDY. SHE'S MY GIRL
AW, GO POUND SAND, YOU LITTLE TWERP
JIM DAVIS
4-29
WELL...I GUESS WE ARE TO DO AS HE SAYS, NOT AS HE DOES
© 1984 United Feature Syndicate, Inc.

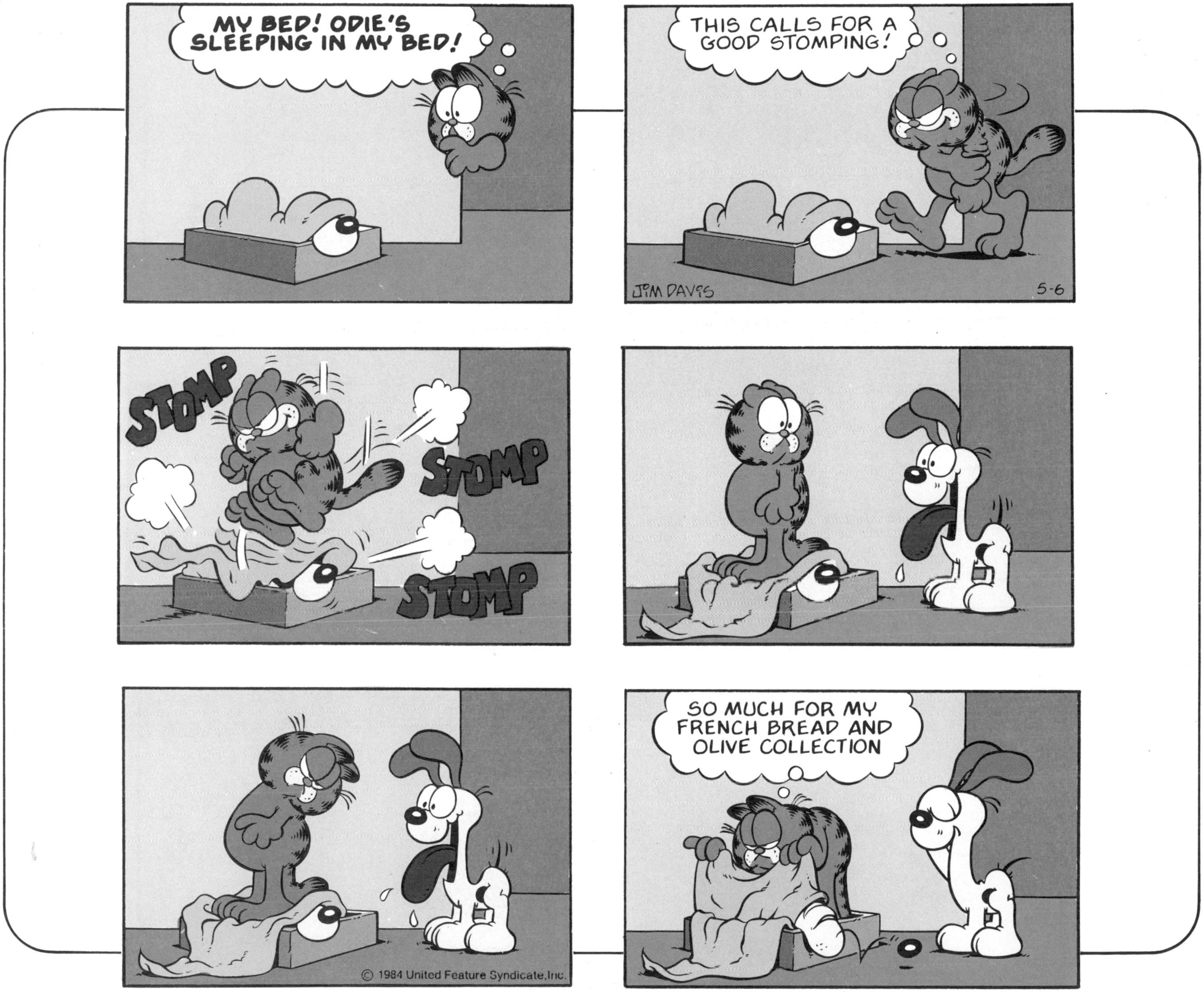
MY BED! ODIE'S SLEEPING IN MY BED!
THIS CALLS FOR A GOOD STOMPING!
JIM DAVIS
5-6
STOMP
STOMP
STOMP
© 1984 United Feature Syndicate, Inc.
SO MUCH FOR MY FRENCH BREAD AND OLIVE COLLECTION

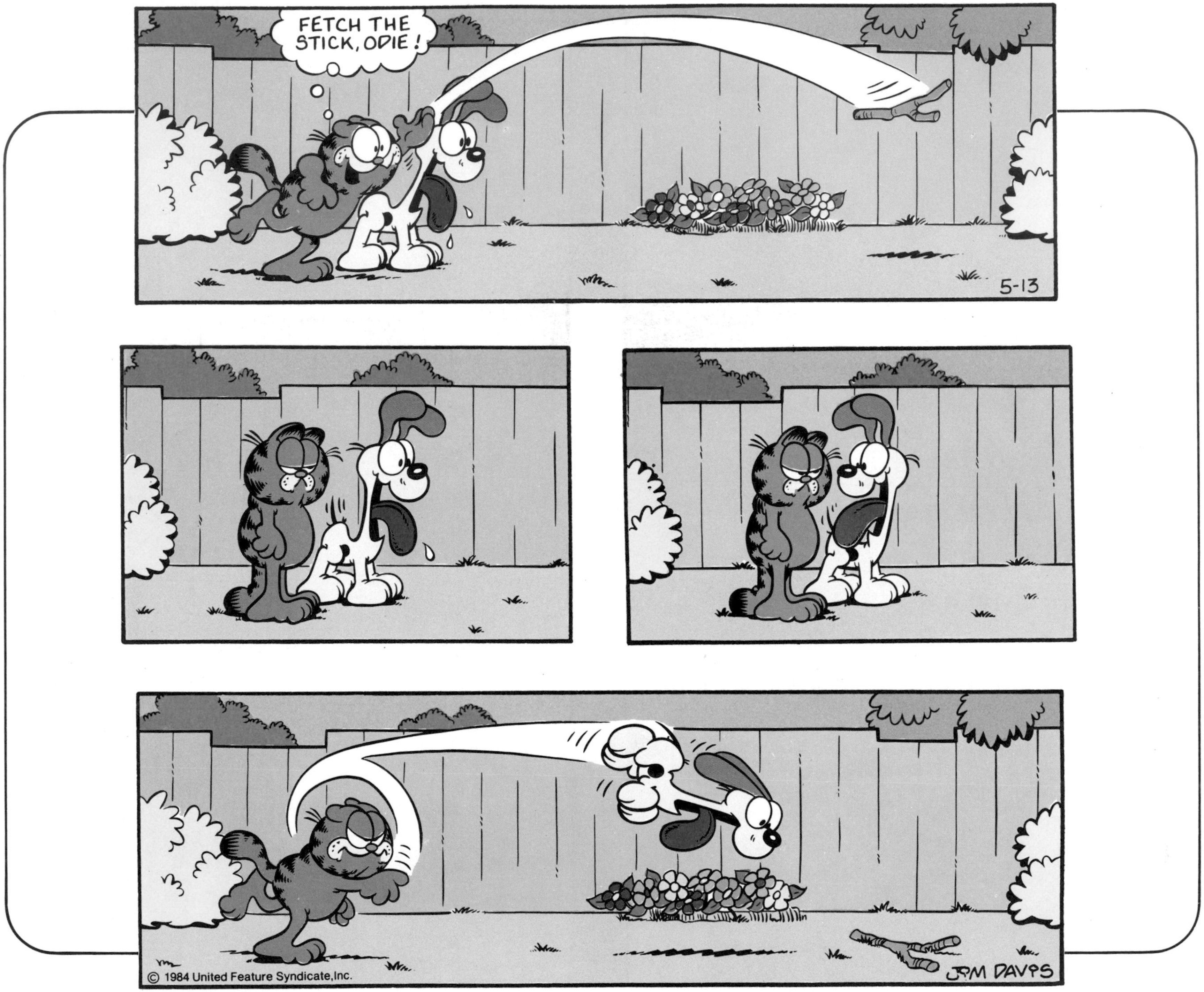
FETCH THE STICK, ODIE!
5-13
© 1984 United Feature Syndicate, Inc.
JPM DAVPS

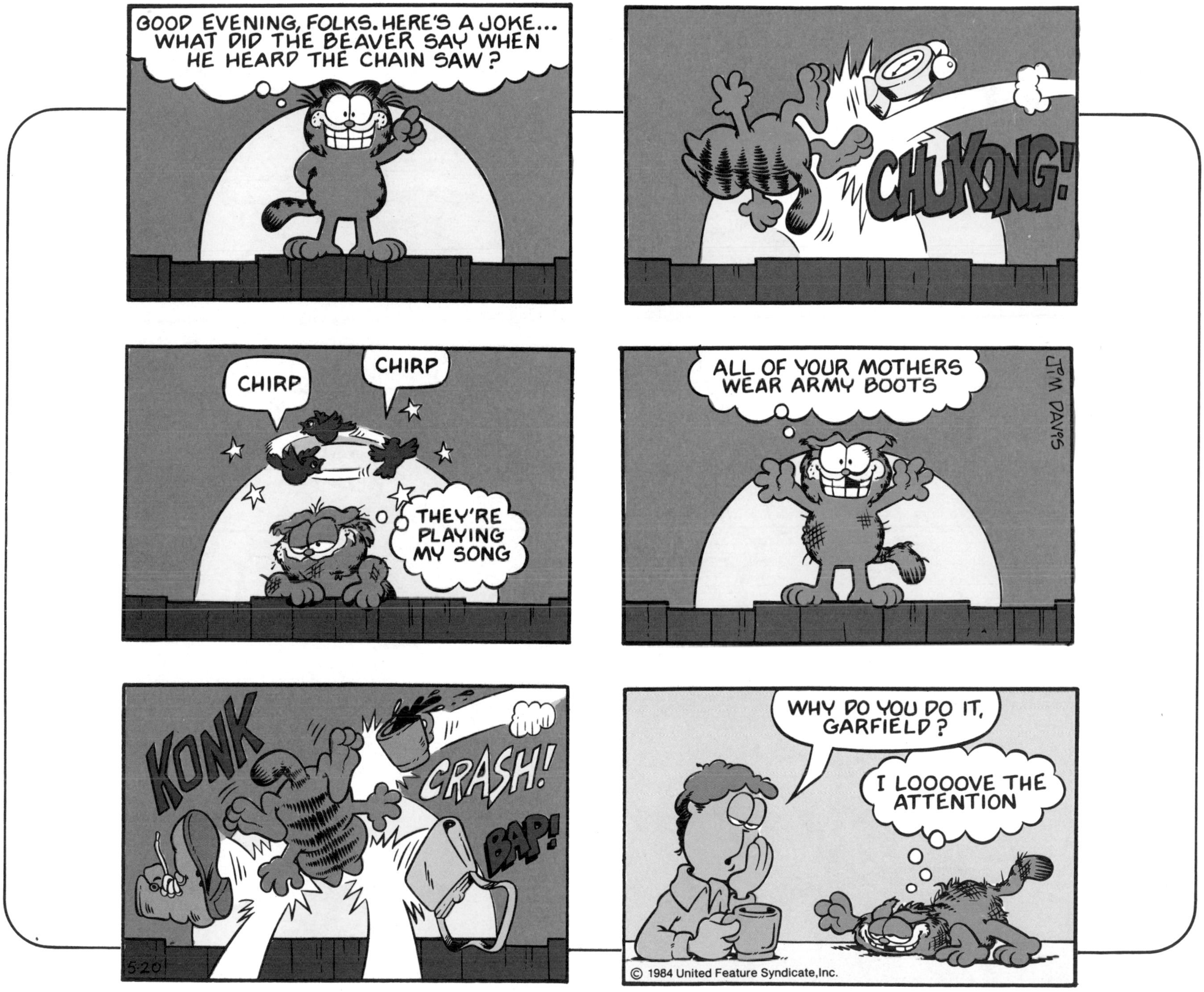
GOOD EVENING, FOLKS. HERE'S A JOKE... WHAT DID THE BEAVER SAY WHEN HE HEARD THE CHAIN SAW?
CHUKONG!
CHIRP
CHIRP
THEY'RE PLAYING MY SONG
ALL OF YOUR MOTHERS WEAR ARMY BOOTS
JIM DAVIS
KONK
CRASH!
BAP!
5-20
WHY DO YOU DO IT, GARFIELD?
I LOOOOVE THE ATTENTION
© 1984 United Feature Syndicate, Inc.

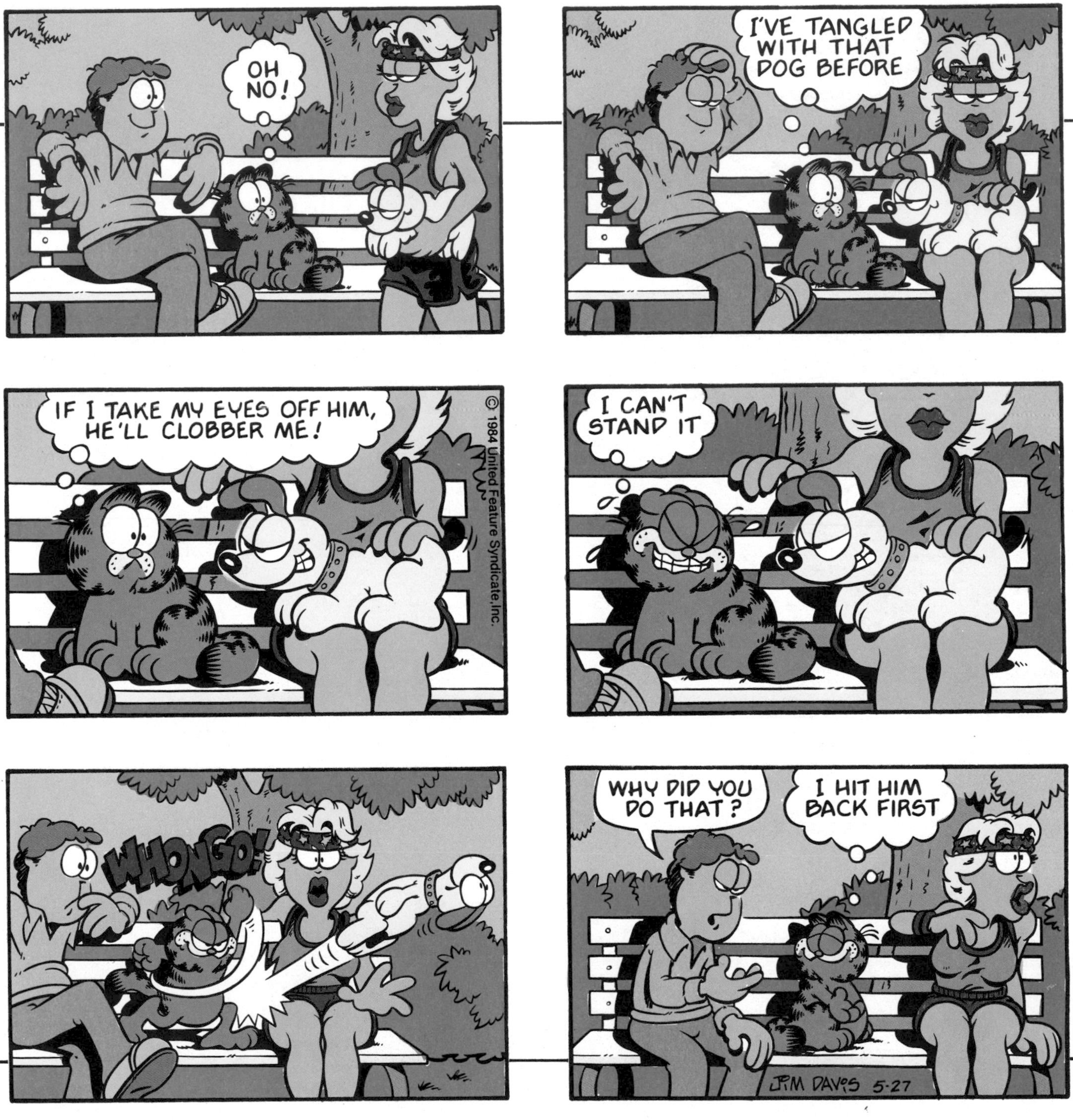
OH NO!
I'VE TANGLED WITH THAT DOG BEFORE
IF I TAKE MY EYES OFF HIM, HE'LL CLOBBER ME!
© 1984 United Feature Syndicate, Inc.
I CAN'T STAND IT
WHONGO!
WHY DID YOU DO THAT?
I HIT HIM BACK FIRST
JIM DAVIS 5-27

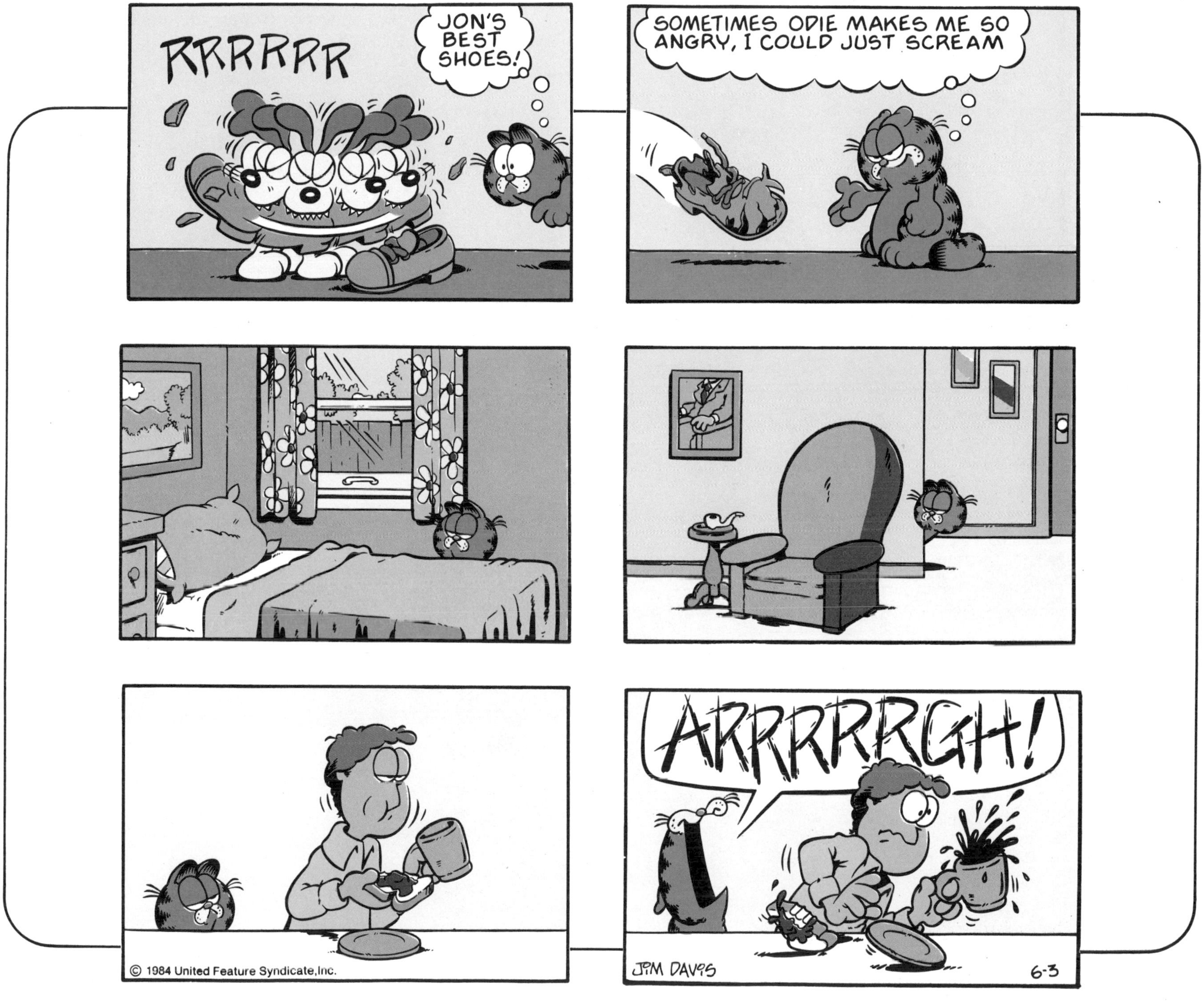

RRRRRR
JON'S BEST SHOES!
SOMETIMES ODIE MAKES ME SO ANGRY, I COULD JUST SCREAM
ARRRRRRGH!
JIM DAVIS
6-3

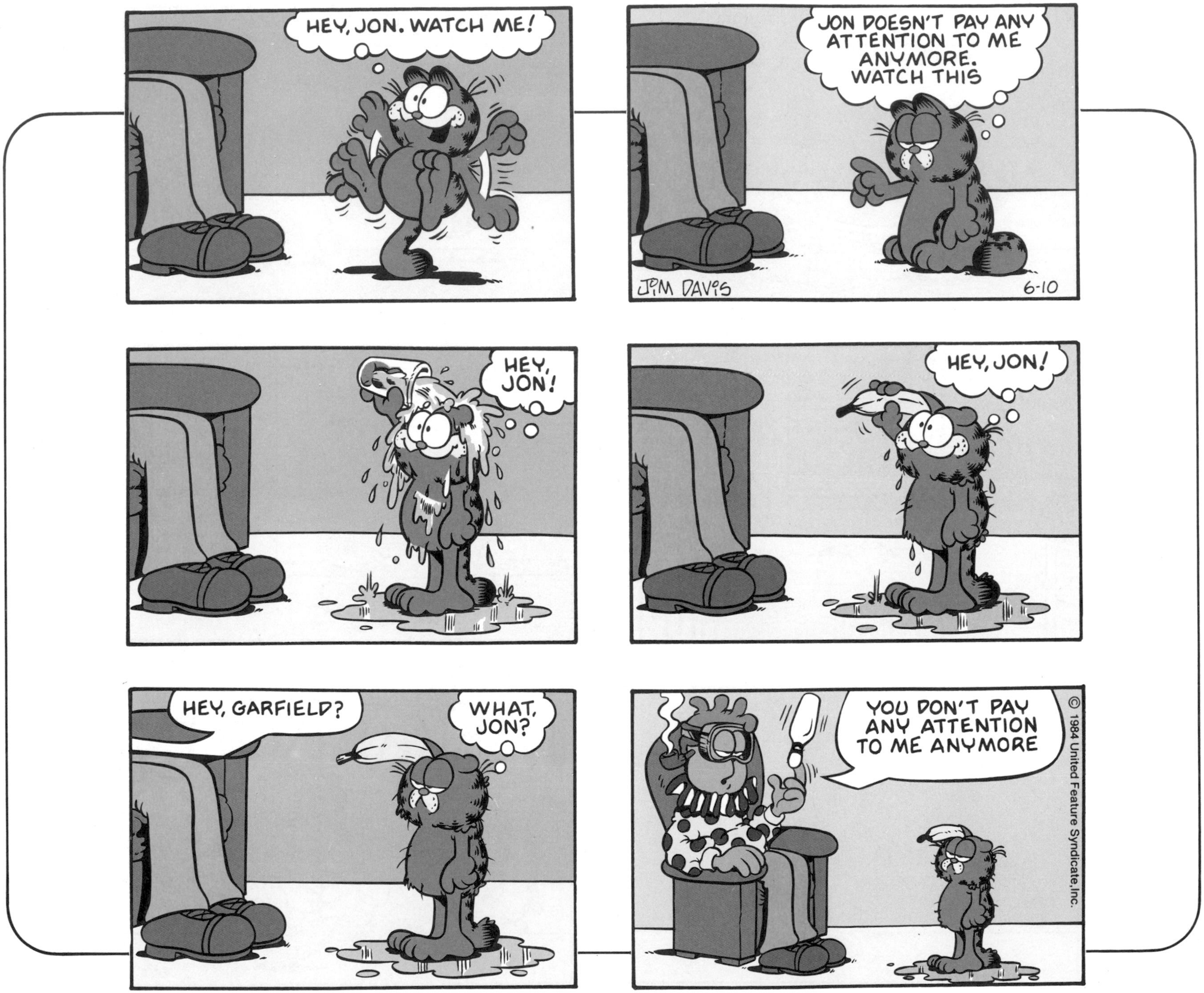
HEY, JON. WATCH ME!
JON DOESN'T PAY ANY ATTENTION TO ME ANYMORE. WATCH THIS
JIM DAVIS
6-10
HEY, JON!
HEY, JON!
HEY, GARFIELD?
WHAT, JON?
YOU DON'T PAY ANY ATTENTION TO ME ANYMORE
© 1984 United Feature Syndicate, Inc.

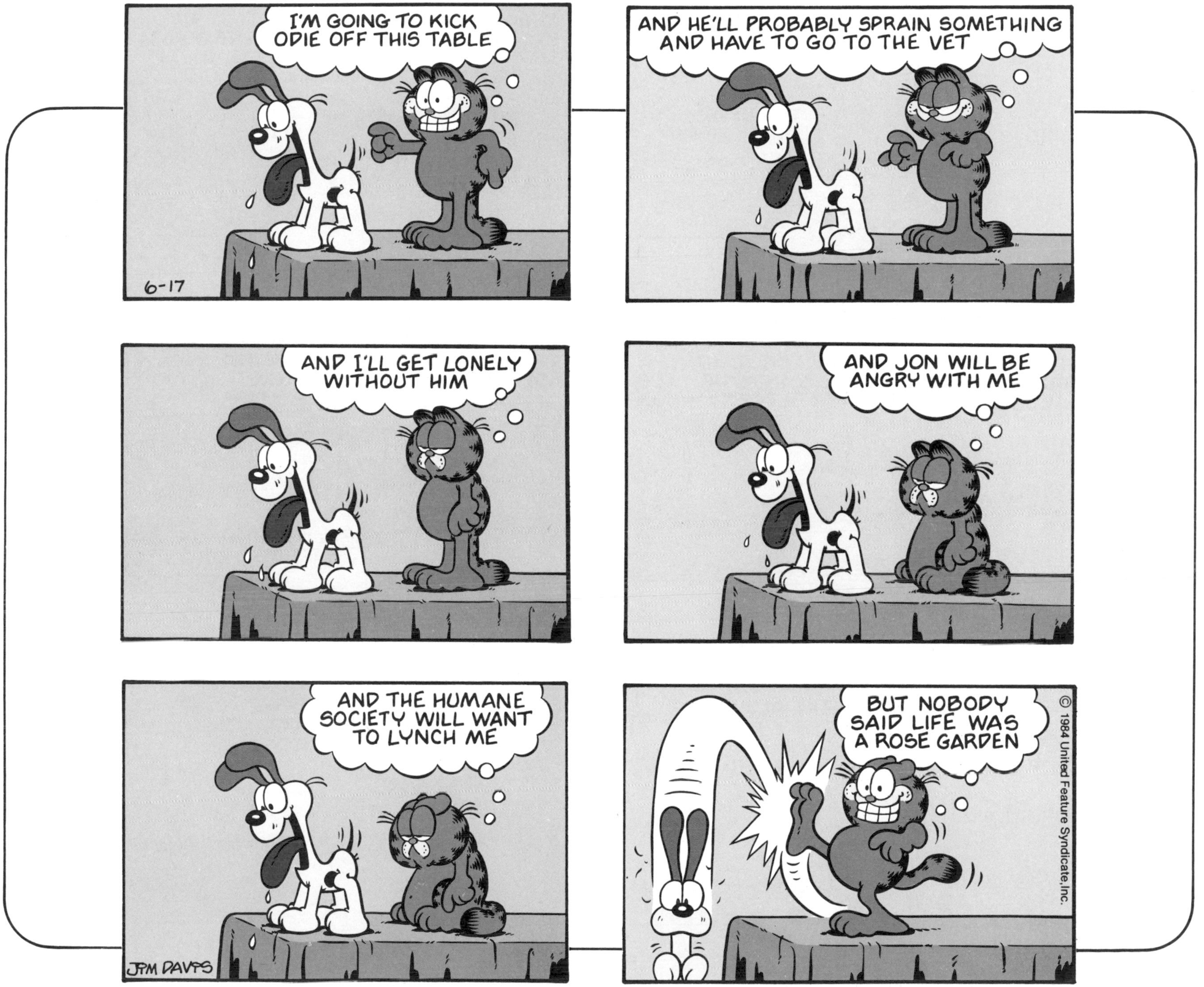
I'M GOING TO KICK ODIE OFF THIS TABLE
6-17
AND HE'LL PROBABLY SPRAIN SOMETHING AND HAVE TO GO TO THE VET
AND I'LL GET LONELY WITHOUT HIM
AND JON WILL BE ANGRY WITH ME
AND THE HUMANE SOCIETY WILL WANT TO LYNCH ME
JIM DAVIS
BUT NOBODY SAID LIFE WAS A ROSE GARDEN
© 1984 United Feature Syndicate, Inc.

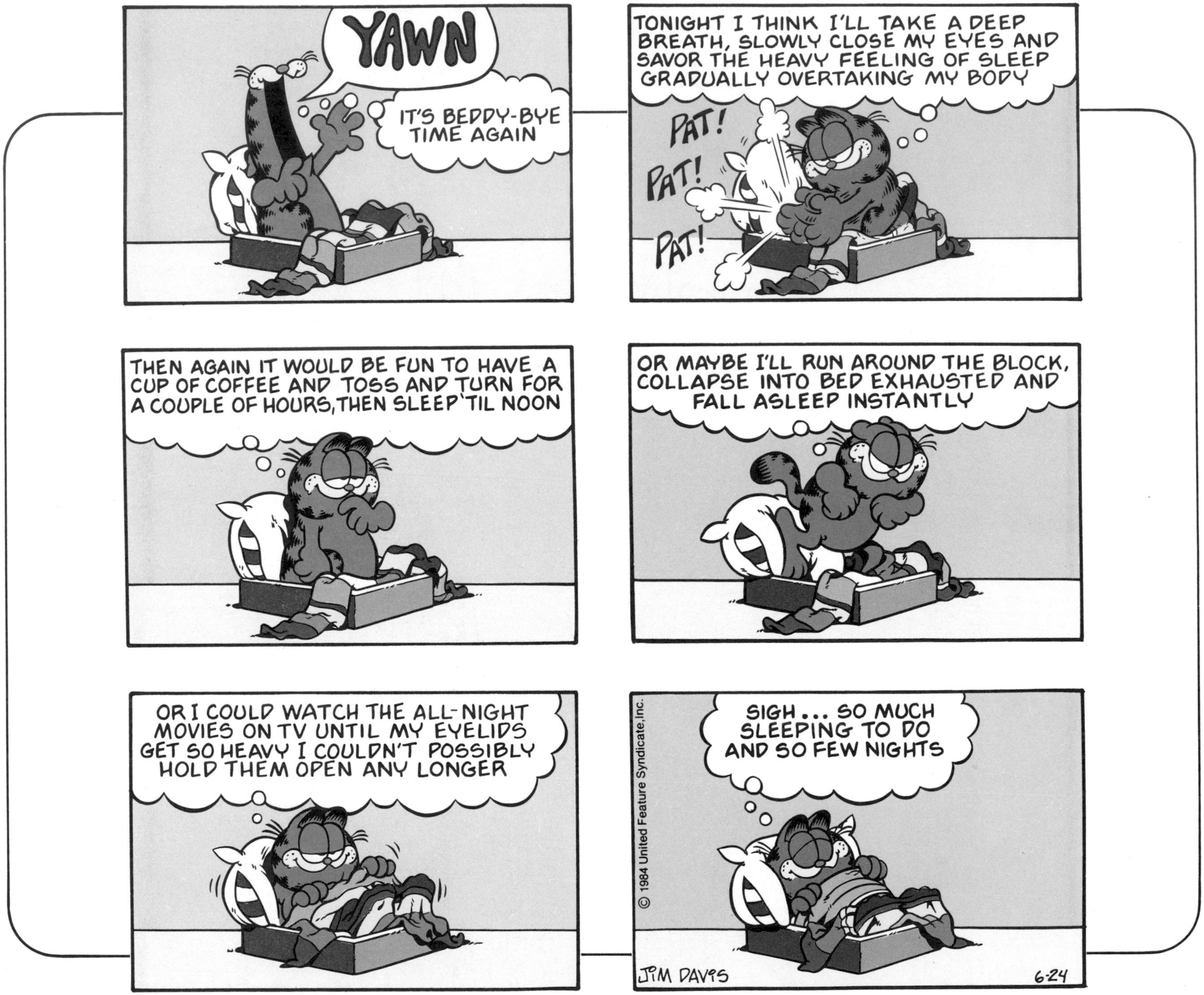
YAWN
IT'S BEDDY-BYE TIME AGAIN
TONIGHT I THINK I'LL TAKE A DEEP BREATH, SLOWLY CLOSE MY EYES AND SAVOR THE HEAVY FEELING OF SLEEP GRADUALLY OVERTAKING MY BODY
PAT! PAT! PAT!
THEN AGAIN IT WOULD BE FUN TO HAVE A CUP OF COFFEE AND TOSS AND TURN FOR A COUPLE OF HOURS, THEN SLEEP 'TIL NOON
OR MAYBE I'LL RUN AROUND THE BLOCK, COLLAPSE INTO BED EXHAUSTED AND FALL ASLEEP INSTANTLY
OR I COULD WATCH THE ALL-NIGHT MOVIES ON TV UNTIL MY EYELIDS GET SO HEAVY I COULDN'T POSSIBLY HOLD THEM OPEN ANY LONGER
SIGH... SO MUCH SLEEPING TO DO AND SO FEW NIGHTS
© 1984 United Feature Syndicate, Inc.
JIM DAVIS
6-24

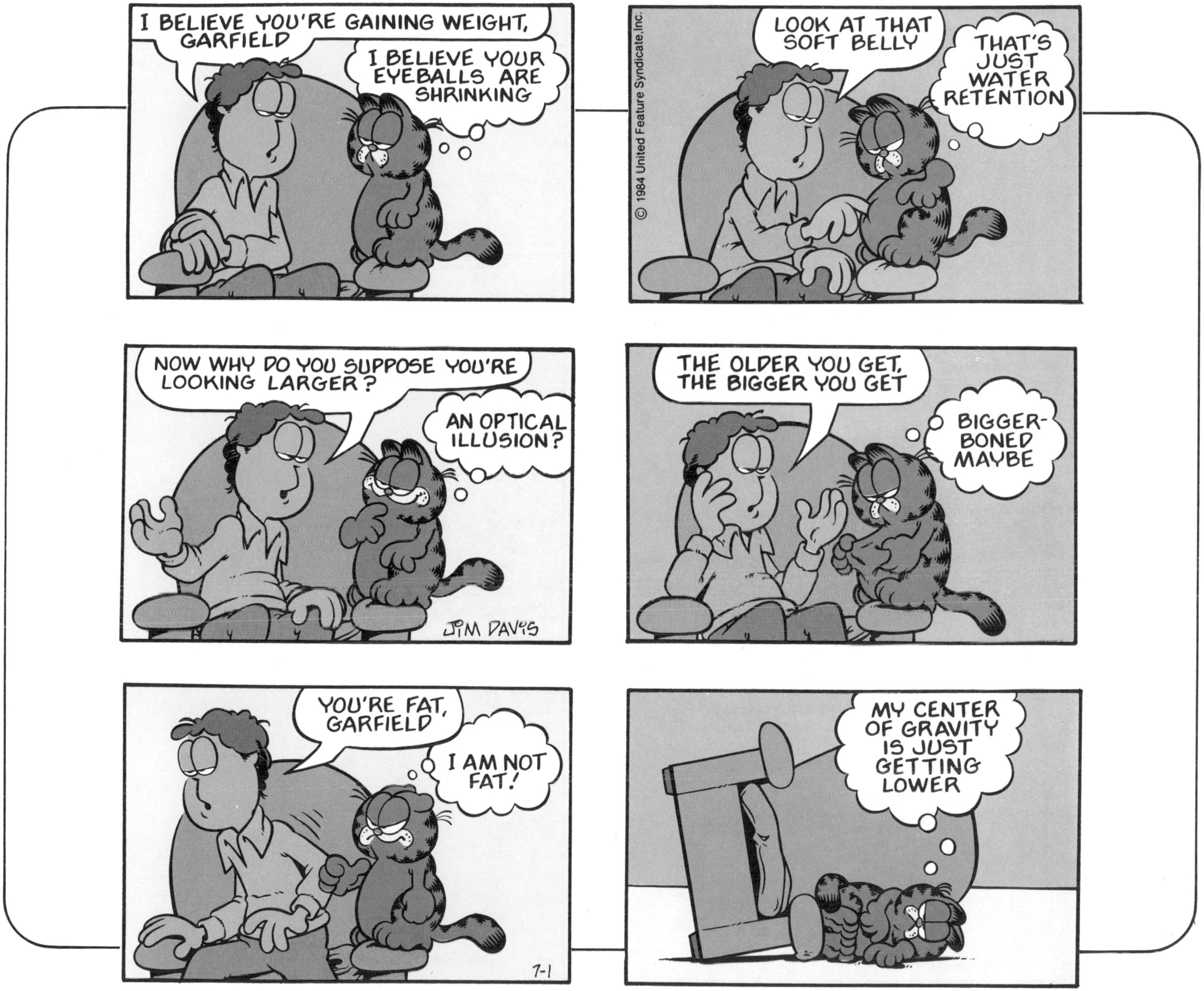
I BELIEVE YOU'RE GAINING WEIGHT, GARFIELD
I BELIEVE YOUR EYEBALLS ARE SHRINKING
© 1984 United Feature Syndicate, Inc.
LOOK AT THAT SOFT BELLY
THAT'S JUST WATER RETENTION
NOW WHY DO YOU SUPPOSE YOU'RE LOOKING LARGER?
AN OPTICAL ILLUSION?
JIM DAVIS
THE OLDER YOU GET, THE BIGGER YOU GET
BIGGER-BONED MAYBE
YOU'RE FAT, GARFIELD
I AM NOT FAT!
7-1
MY CENTER OF GRAVITY IS JUST GETTING LOWER

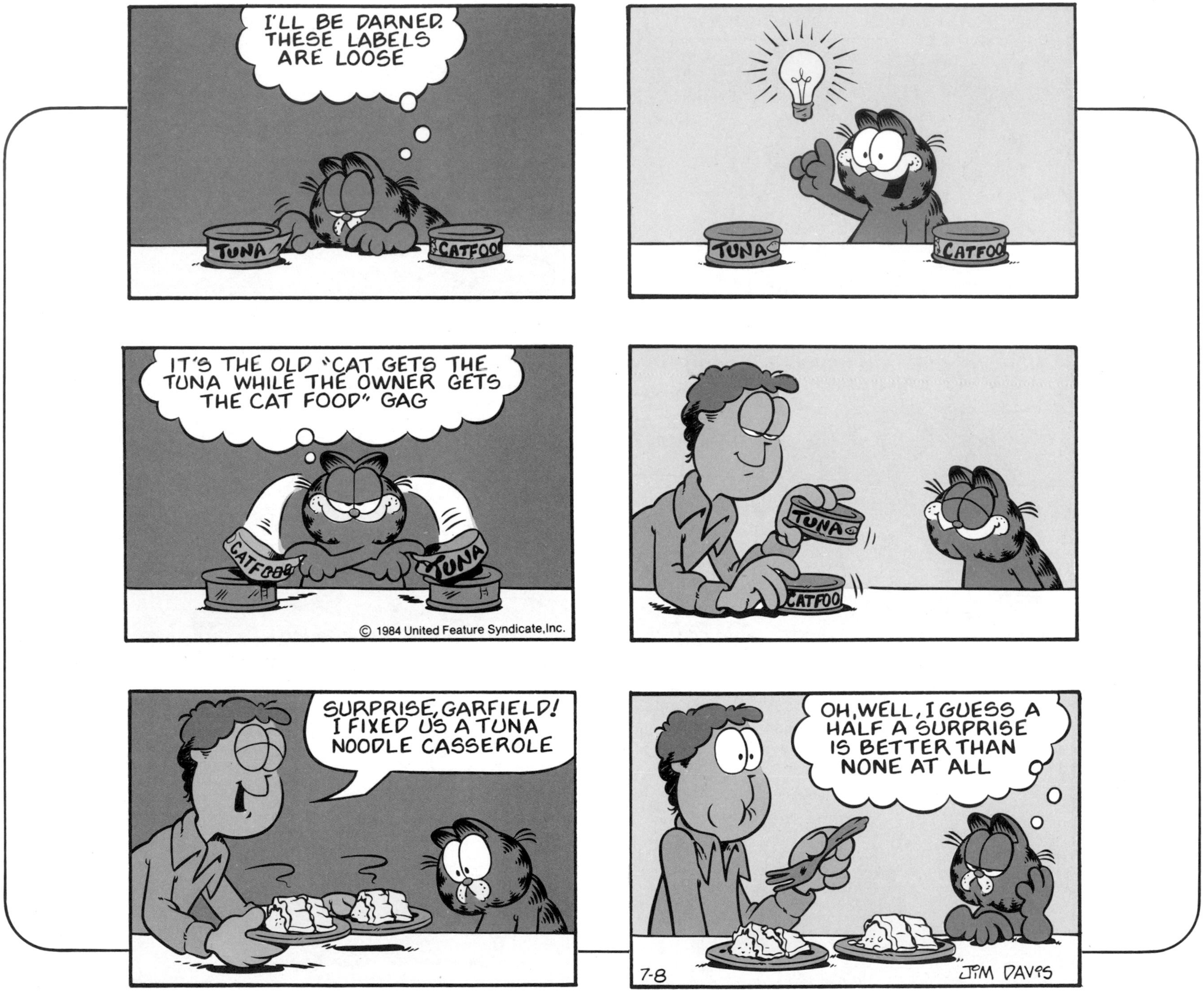
I'LL BE DARNED. THESE LABELS ARE LOOSE
TUNA
CATFOO
TUNA
CATFOO
IT'S THE OLD "CAT GETS THE TUNA WHILE THE OWNER GETS THE CAT FOOD" GAG
CATFOOD
TUNA
© 1984 United Feature Syndicate, Inc.
TUNA
CATFOO
SURPRISE, GARFIELD! I FIXED US A TUNA NOODLE CASSEROLE
OH, WELL, I GUESS A HALF A SURPRISE IS BETTER THAN NONE AT ALL
7-8
JIM DAVIS

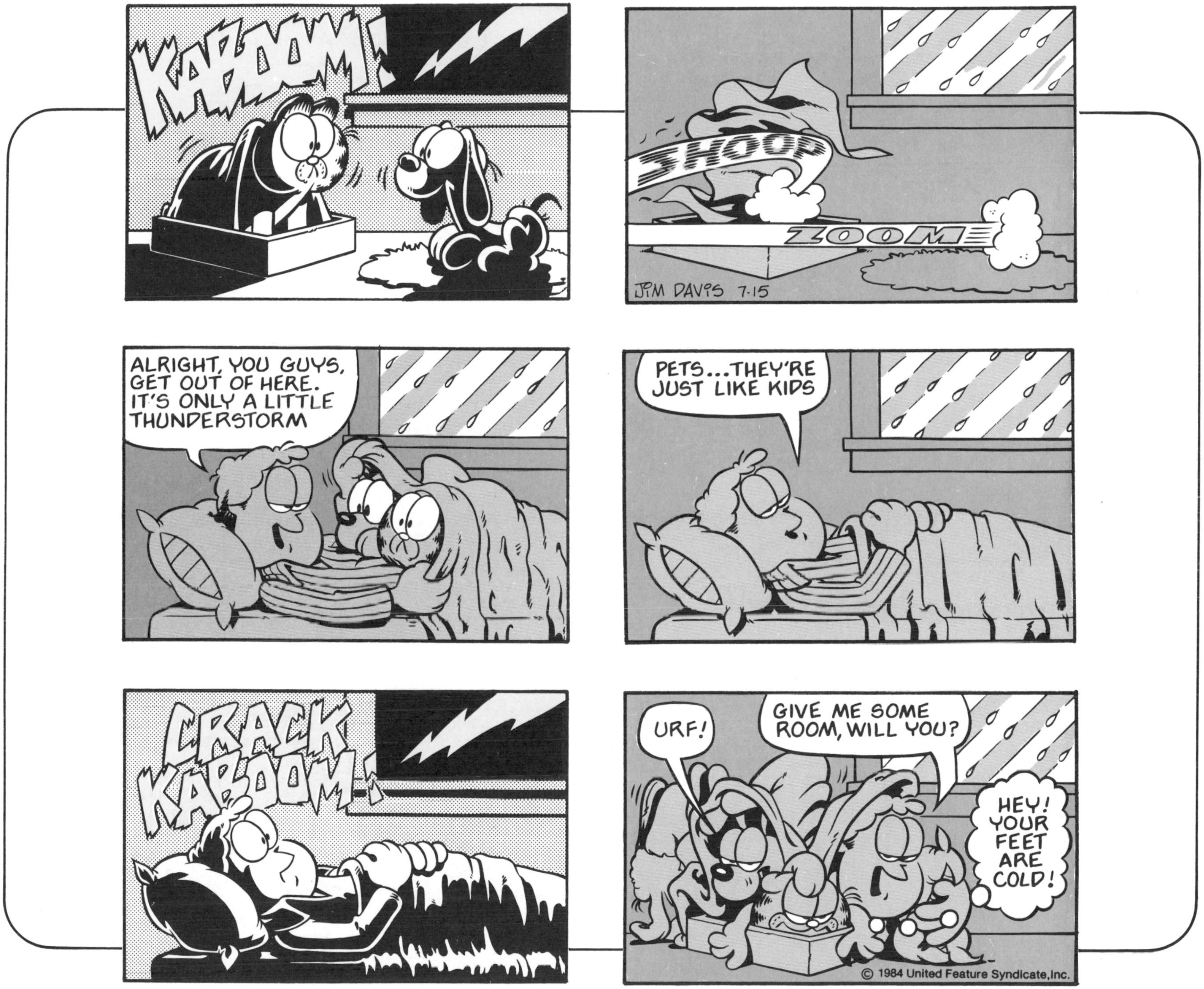
KABOOM!
SHOOP
ZOOM
JIM DAVIS 7-15
ALRIGHT, YOU GUYS, GET OUT OF HERE. IT'S ONLY A LITTLE THUNDERSTORM
PETS...THEY'RE JUST LIKE KIDS
CRACK KABOOM!
URF!
GIVE ME SOME ROOM, WILL YOU?
HEY! YOUR FEET ARE COLD!
© 1984 United Feature Syndicate, Inc.

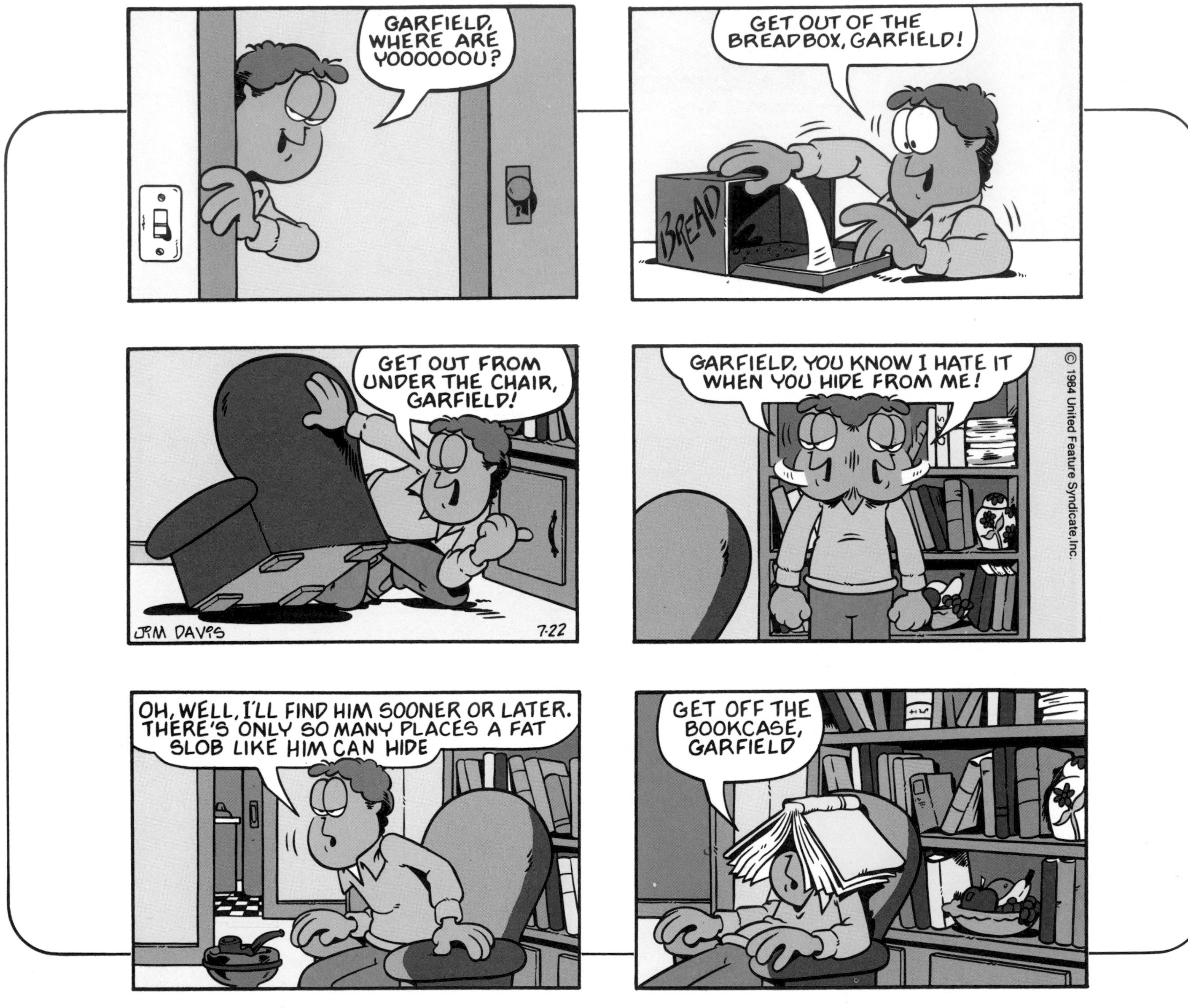
GARFIELD, WHERE ARE YOOOOOOU?
GET OUT OF THE BREADBOX, GARFIELD!
BREAD
GET OUT FROM UNDER THE CHAIR, GARFIELD!
JIM DAVIS
7-22
GARFIELD, YOU KNOW I HATE IT WHEN YOU HIDE FROM ME!
© 1984 United Feature Syndicate, Inc.
OH, WELL, I'LL FIND HIM SOONER OR LATER. THERE'S ONLY SO MANY PLACES A FAT SLOB LIKE HIM CAN HIDE
GET OFF THE BOOKCASE, GARFIELD

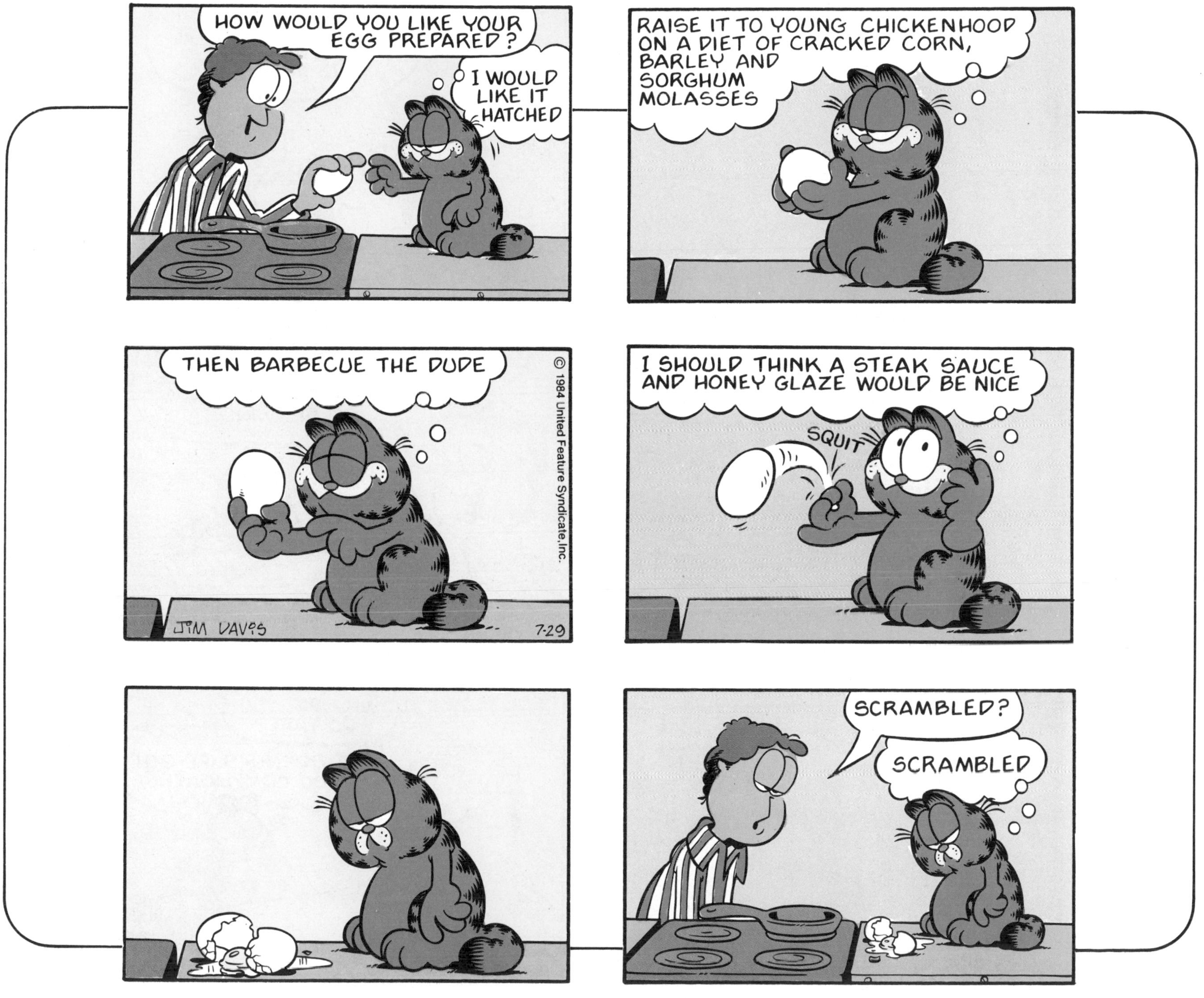
HOW WOULD YOU LIKE YOUR EGG PREPARED?
I WOULD LIKE IT HATCHED
RAISE IT TO YOUNG CHICKENHOOD ON A DIET OF CRACKED CORN, BARLEY AND SORGHUM MOLASSES
THEN BARBECUE THE DUDE
© 1984 United Feature Syndicate, Inc.
JIM DAVIS
7-29
I SHOULD THINK A STEAK SAUCE AND HONEY GLAZE WOULD BE NICE
SQUIT
SCRAMBLED?
SCRAMBLED

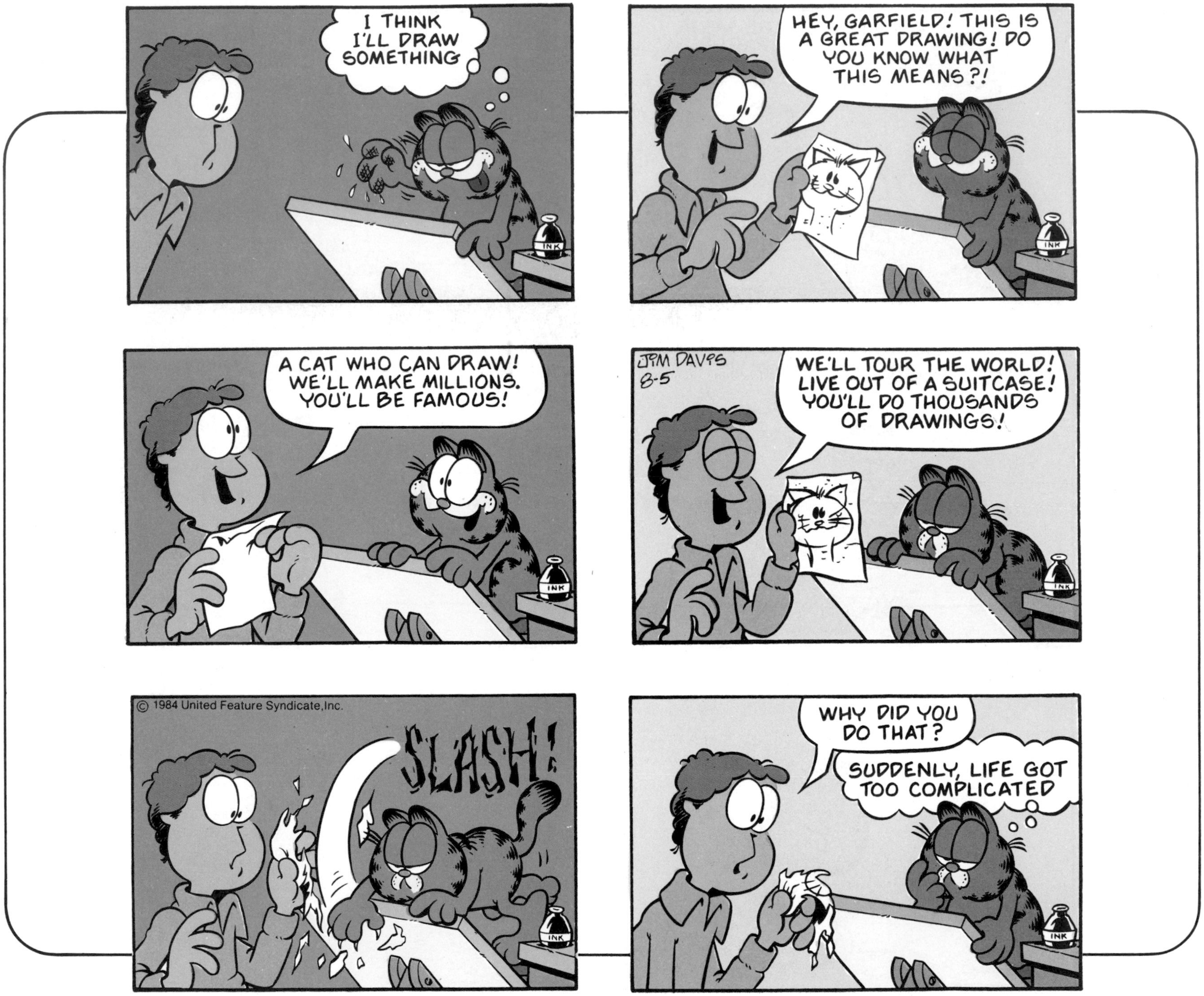
I THINK I'LL DRAW SOMETHING
HEY, GARFIELD! THIS IS A GREAT DRAWING! DO YOU KNOW WHAT THIS MEANS?!
A CAT WHO CAN DRAW! WE'LL MAKE MILLIONS. YOU'LL BE FAMOUS!
JIM DAVIS 8-5
WE'LL TOUR THE WORLD! LIVE OUT OF A SUITCASE! YOU'LL DO THOUSANDS OF DRAWINGS!
© 1984 United Feature Syndicate, Inc.
SLASH!
WHY DID YOU DO THAT?
SUDDENLY, LIFE GOT TOO COMPLICATED

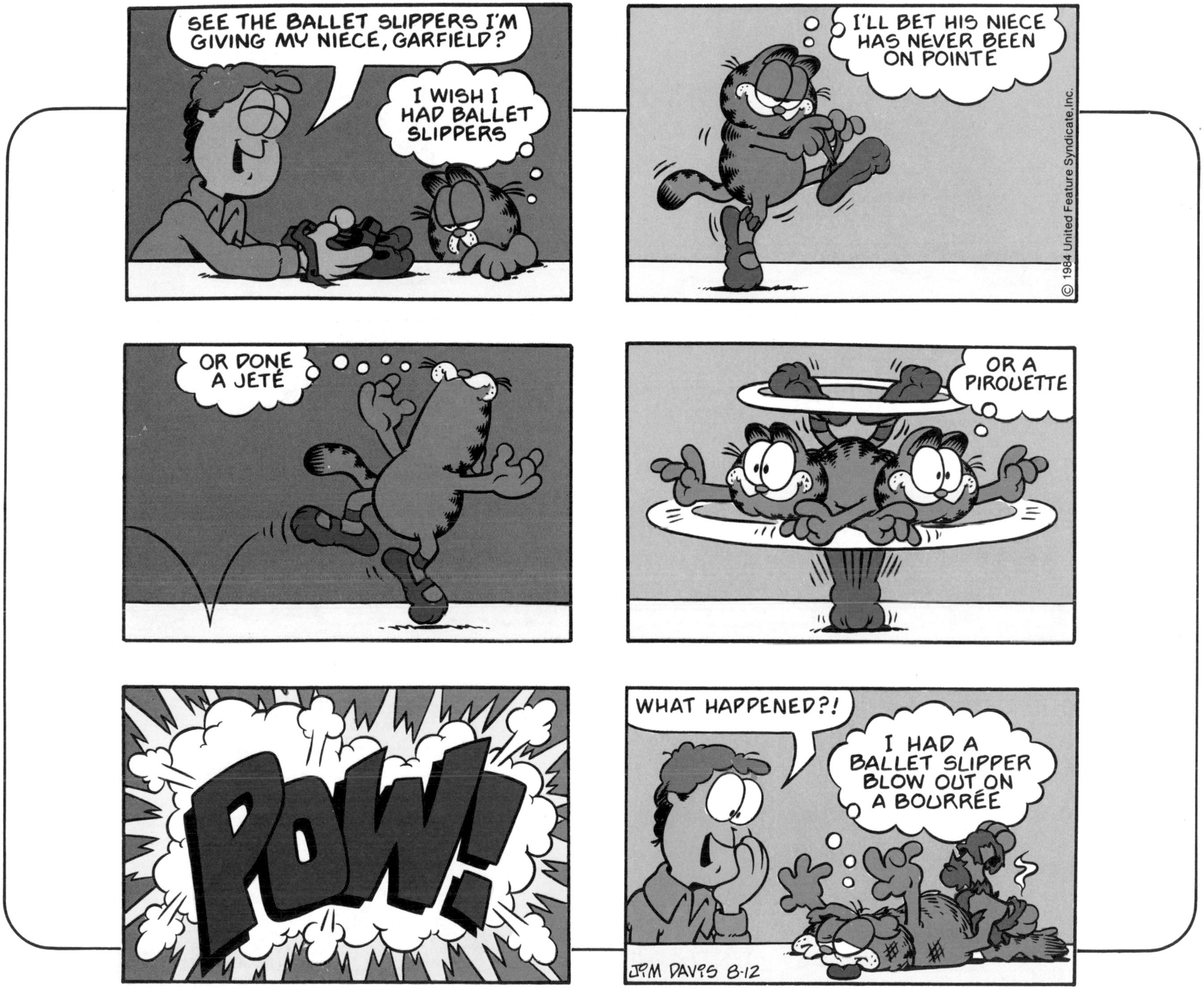
SEE THE BALLET SLIPPERS I'M GIVING MY NIECE, GARFIELD?
I WISH I HAD BALLET SLIPPERS
I'LL BET HIS NIECE HAS NEVER BEEN ON POINTE
© 1984 United Feature Syndicate, Inc.
OR DONE A JETÉ
OR A PIROUETTE
POW!
WHAT HAPPENED?!
I HAD A BALLET SLIPPER BLOW OUT ON A BOURRÉE
JIM DAVIS 8-12

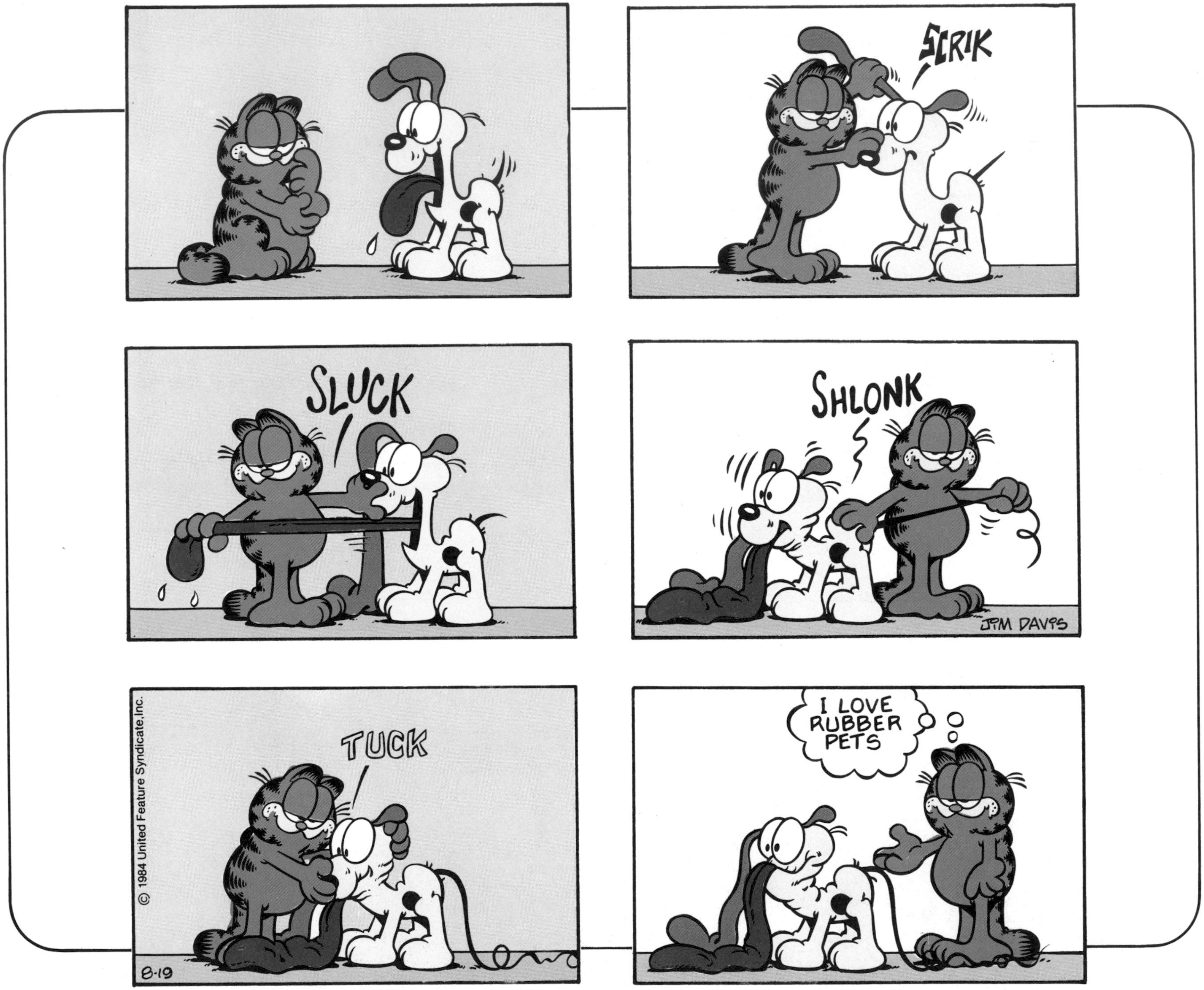
SCRIK
SLUCK
SHLONK
JIM DAVIS
© 1984 United Feature Syndicate, Inc.
TUCK
8-19
I LOVE RUBBER PETS

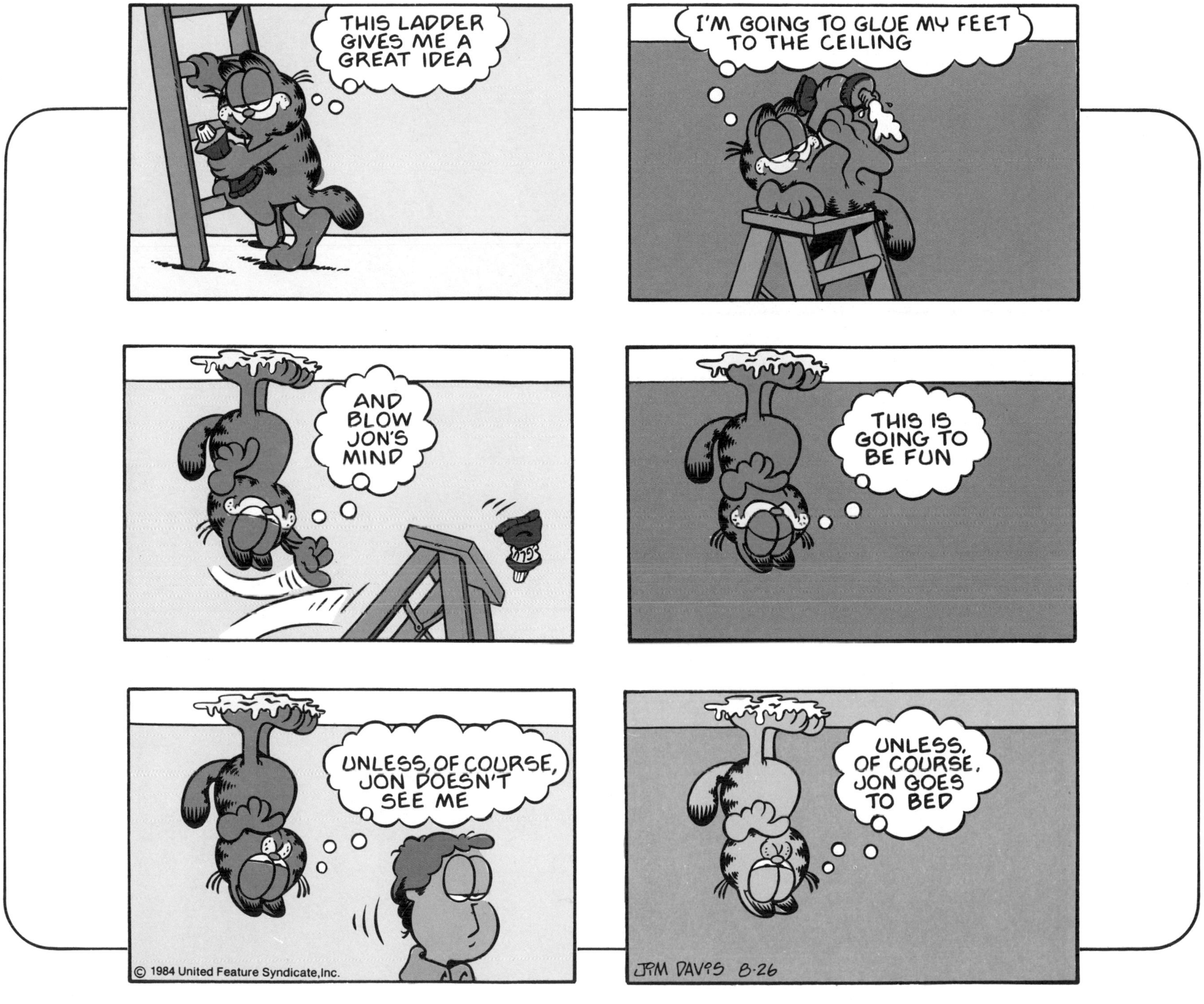
THIS LADDER GIVES ME A GREAT IDEA
I'M GOING TO GLUE MY FEET TO THE CEILING
AND BLOW JON'S MIND
THIS IS GOING TO BE FUN
UNLESS, OF COURSE, JON DOESN'T SEE ME
UNLESS, OF COURSE, JON GOES TO BED
© 1984 United Feature Syndicate, Inc.
JIM DAVIS 8·26

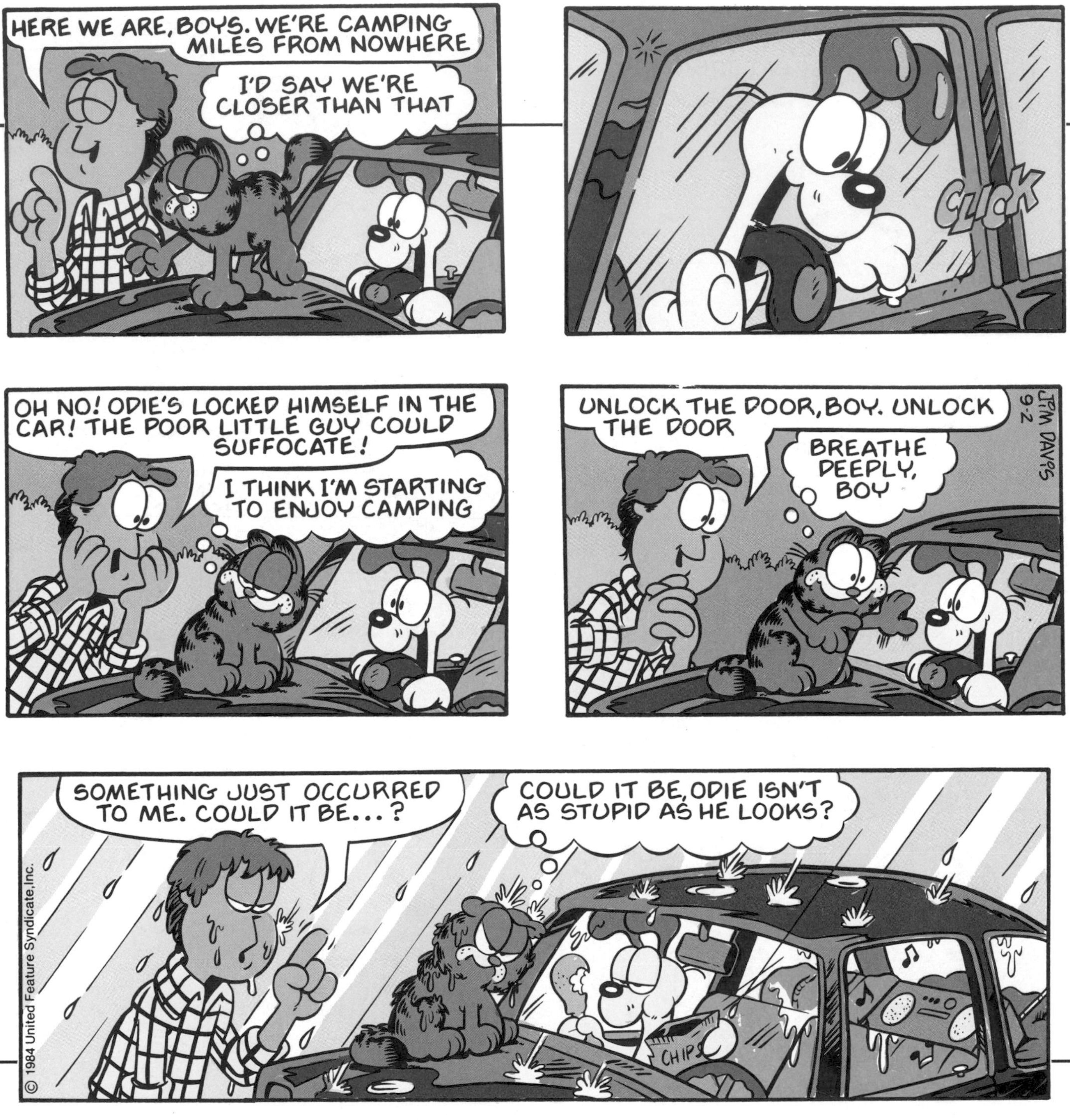
HERE WE ARE, BOYS. WE'RE CAMPING MILES FROM NOWHERE
I'D SAY WE'RE CLOSER THAN THAT
CLICK
OH NO! ODIE'S LOCKED HIMSELF IN THE CAR! THE POOR LITTLE GUY COULD SUFFOCATE!
I THINK I'M STARTING TO ENJOY CAMPING
UNLOCK THE DOOR, BOY. UNLOCK THE DOOR
BREATHE DEEPLY, BOY
JPM DAVPS 9-2
SOMETHING JUST OCCURRED TO ME. COULD IT BE...?
COULD IT BE, ODIE ISN'T AS STUPID AS HE LOOKS?
CHIPS
© 1984 United Feature Syndicate, Inc.

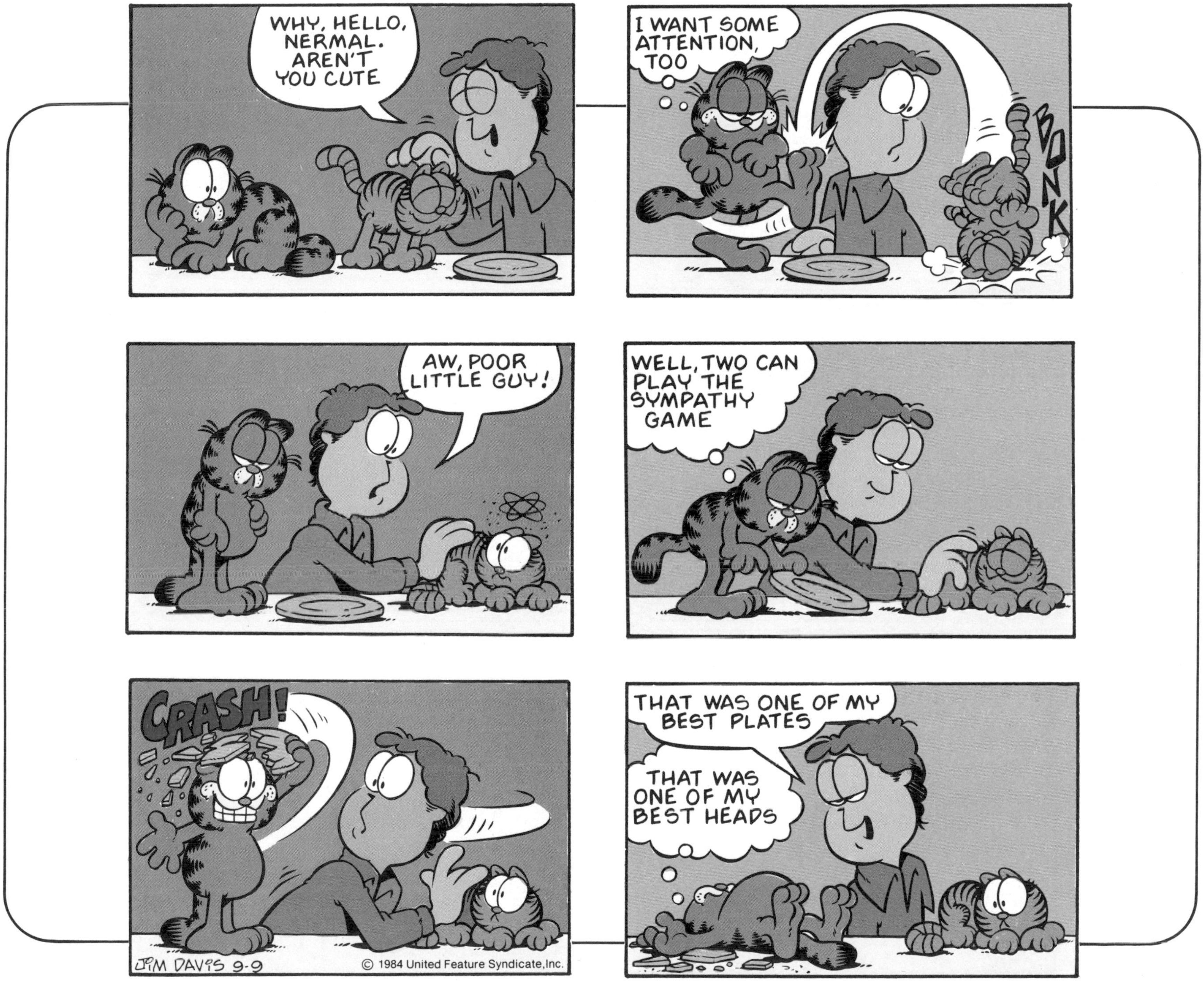
WHY, HELLO, NERMAL. AREN'T YOU CUTE
I WANT SOME ATTENTION, TOO
BONK
AW, POOR LITTLE GUY!
WELL, TWO CAN PLAY THE SYMPATHY GAME
CRASH!
JIM DAVIS 9-9
© 1984 United Feature Syndicate, Inc.
THAT WAS ONE OF MY BEST PLATES
THAT WAS ONE OF MY BEST HEADS

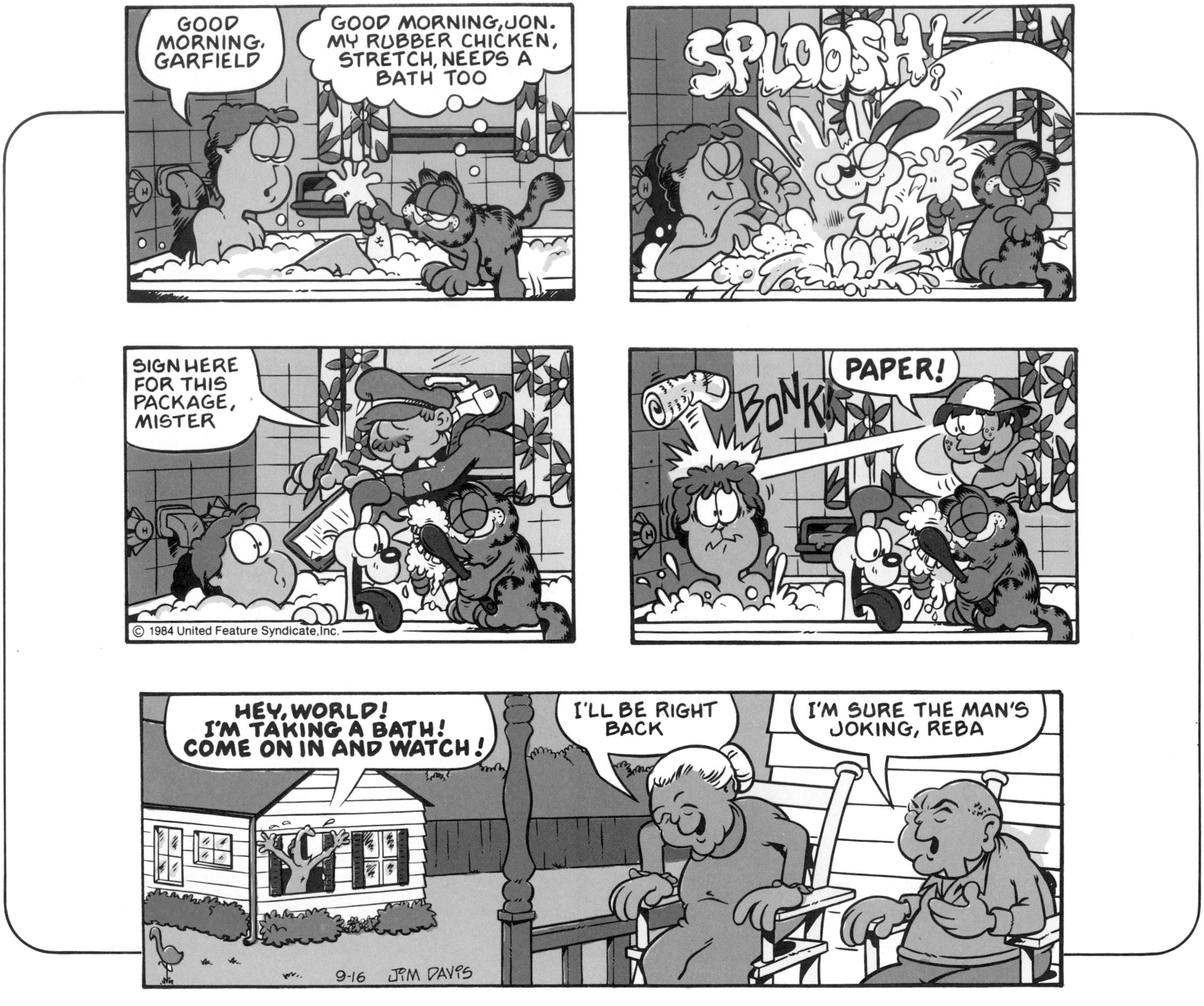
GOOD MORNING, GARFIELD
GOOD MORNING, JON. MY RUBBER CHICKEN, STRETCH, NEEDS A BATH TOO
SPLOOSH!
SIGN HERE FOR THIS PACKAGE, MISTER
© 1984 United Feature Syndicate, Inc.
BONK!
PAPER!
HEY, WORLD! I'M TAKING A BATH! COME ON IN AND WATCH!
I'LL BE RIGHT BACK
I'M SURE THE MAN'S JOKING, REBA
9-16 JIM DAVIS

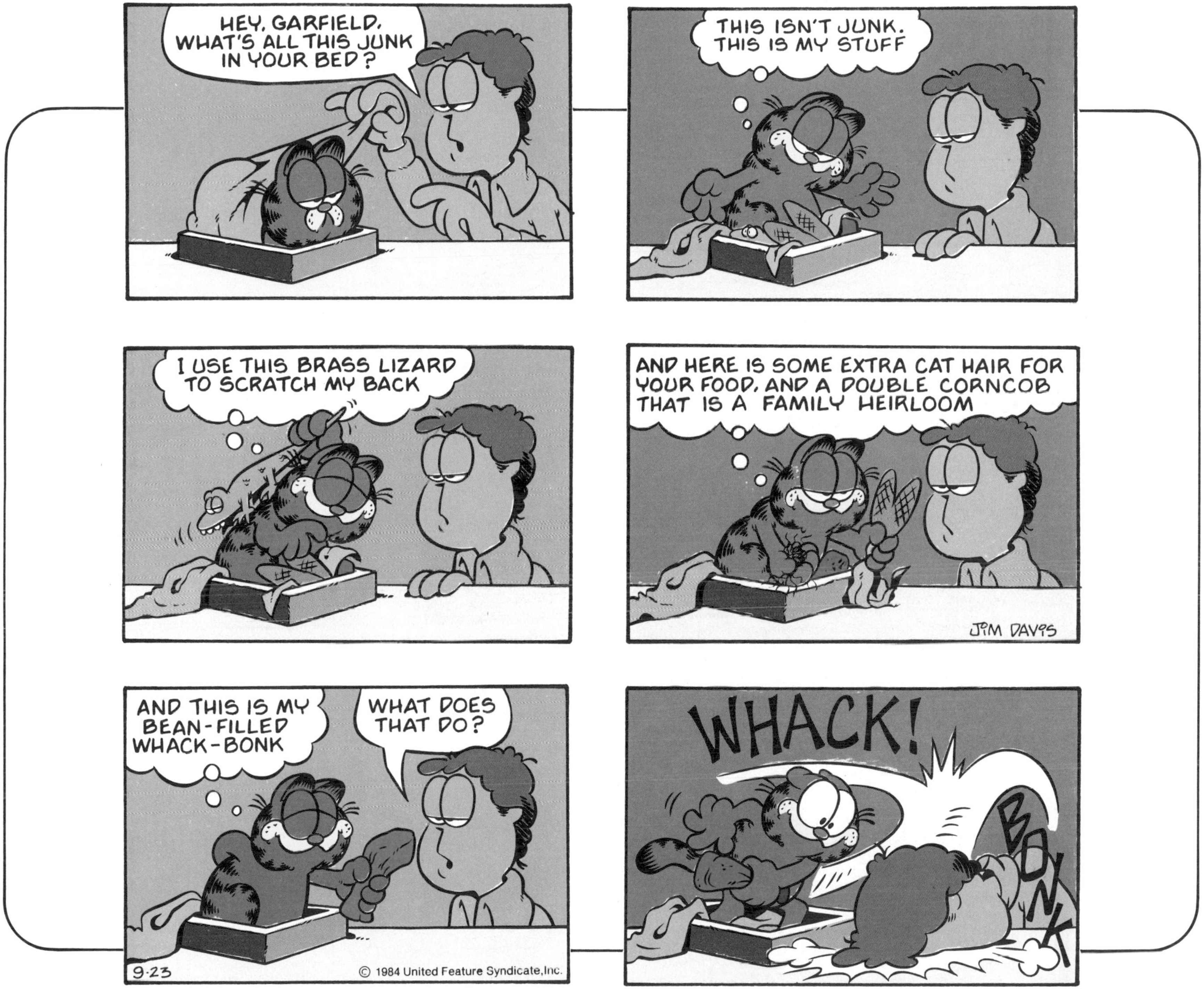
HEY, GARFIELD, WHAT'S ALL THIS JUNK IN YOUR BED?
THIS ISN'T JUNK. THIS IS MY STUFF
I USE THIS BRASS LIZARD TO SCRATCH MY BACK
AND HERE IS SOME EXTRA CAT HAIR FOR YOUR FOOD, AND A DOUBLE CORNCOB THAT IS A FAMILY HEIRLOOM
JIM DAVIS
AND THIS IS MY BEAN-FILLED WHACK-BONK
WHAT DOES THAT DO?
9-23
WHACK!
BONK

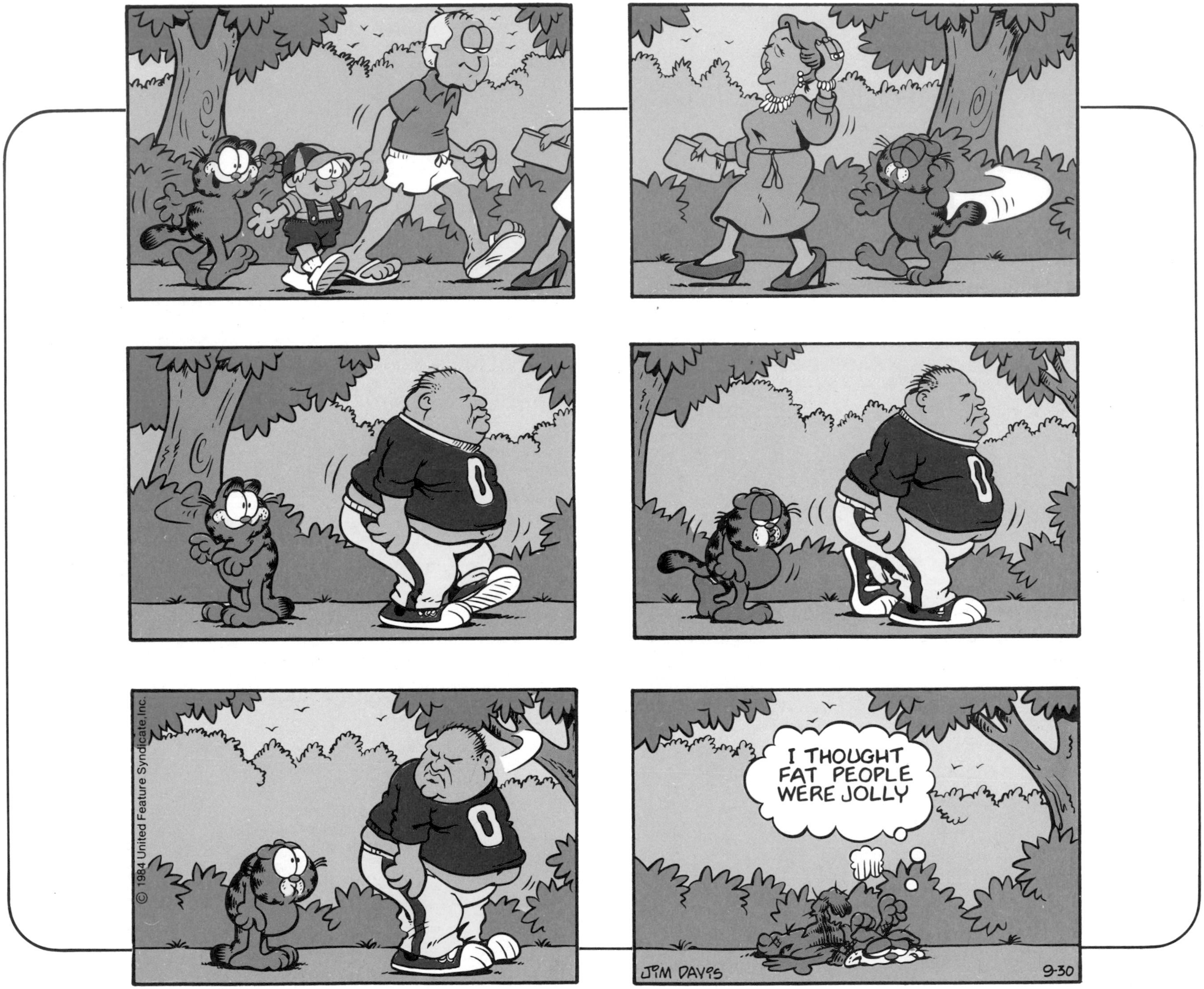
© 1984 United Feature Syndicate, Inc.
I THOUGHT FAT PEOPLE WERE JOLLY
JIM DAVIS
9-30

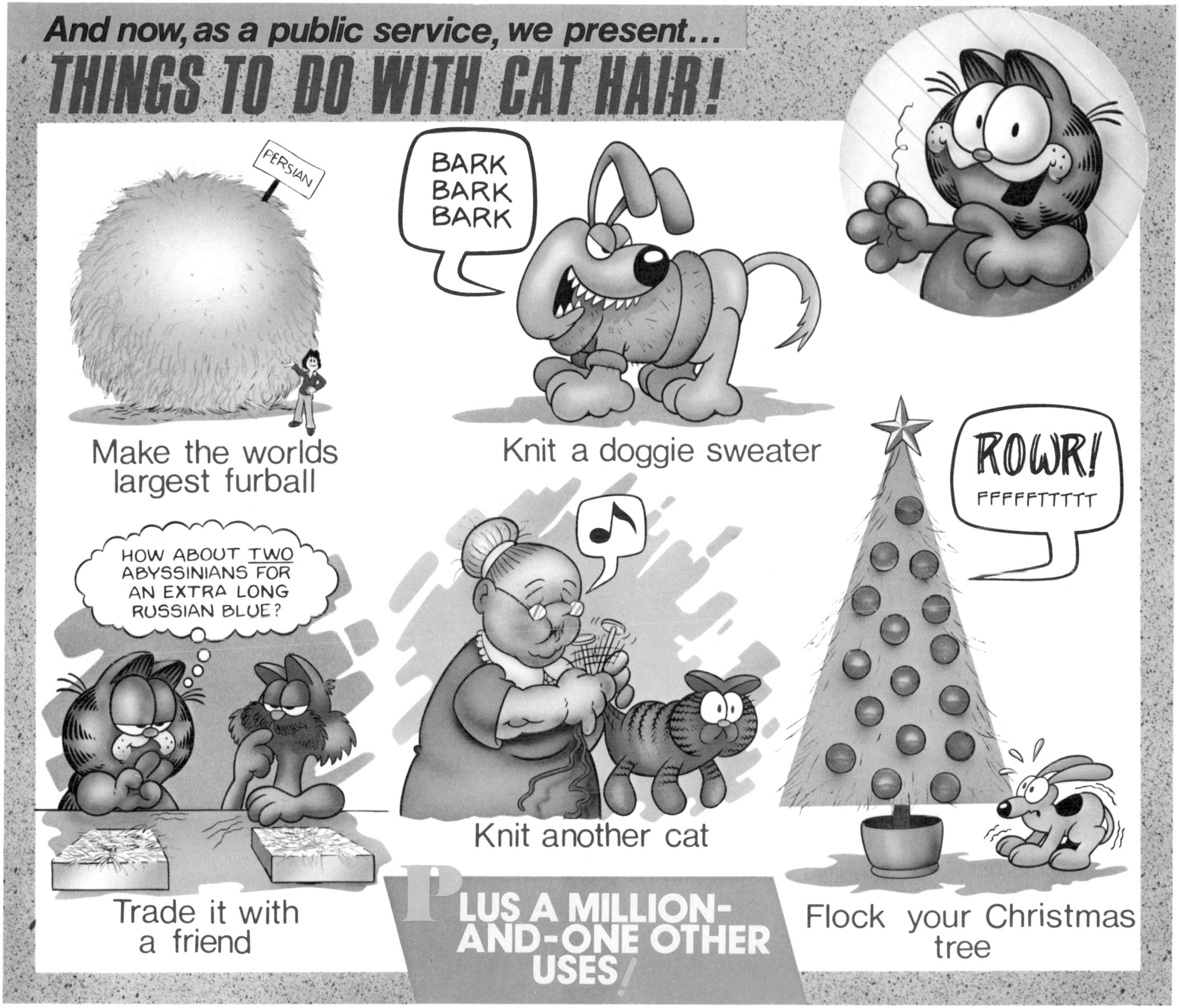
And now, as a public service, we present...
THINGS TO DO WITH CAT HAIR!
PERSIAN
Make the worlds largest furball
BARK BARK BARK
Knit a doggie sweater
HOW ABOUT TWO ABYSSINIANS FOR AN EXTRA LONG RUSSIAN BLUE?
Trade it with a friend
Knit another cat
ROWR! FFFFFTTTTT
Flock your Christmas tree
PLUS A MILLION-AND-ONE OTHER USES!